TRANSLATION AND REPETITION

Translation and Repetition: Rewriting (Un)original Literature offers a new and original perspective in translation studies by considering creative repetition from the perspective of the translator. This is done by analyzing so-called "unoriginal literature" and thus expanding the definition of translation.

In Western thought, repetition has long been regarded as something negative, as a kind of cliché, stereotype, or automatism that is the opposite of creation. On the other hand, in the eyes of many contemporary philosophers from Wittgenstein and Derrida to Deleuze and Guattari, repetition is more about difference. It involves rewriting stories initially told in other contexts so that they acquire a different perspective. In this sense, repeating is often a political act. Repetition is a creative impulse for the making of what is new. Repetition as iteration is understood in this book as an action that recognizes the creative and critical potential of copying.

The author analyzes how our time understands originality and authorship differently from past eras, and how the new philosophical ways of approaching repetition imply a new way of understanding the concept of originality and authorship. Deconstruction of these notions also implies subverting the traditional ways of approaching translation. This is vital reading for all courses on literary translation, comparative literature, and literature in translation within translation studies and literature.

Mª Carmen África Vidal Claramonte is Full Professor of Translation at the University of Salamanca, Spain. She is the author of many books, including *Translation and Contemporary Art* (Routledge, 2022) and *Translating Borrowed Tongues* (Routledge, 2023), and several co-edited volumes (among them the *Routledge Handbook of Spanish Translation Studies*, 2019, with Roberto Valdeón).

TRANSLATION AND REPETITION

Rewriting (Un)original Literature

Mª Carmen África Vidal Claramonte

LONDON AND NEW YORK

First published 2024
by Routledge
4 Park Square, Milton Park, Abingdon, Oxon OX14 4RN

and by Routledge
605 Third Avenue, New York, NY 10158

Routledge is an imprint of the Taylor & Francis Group, an informa business

© 2024 Mª Carmen África Vidal Claramonte

The right of Mª Carmen África Vidal Claramonte to be identified as author of this work has been asserted in accordance with sections 77 and 78 of the Copyright, Designs and Patents Act 1988.

All rights reserved. No part of this book may be reprinted or reproduced or utilised in any form or by any electronic, mechanical, or other means, now known or hereafter invented, including photocopying and recording, or in any information storage or retrieval system, without permission in writing from the publishers.

Trademark notice: Product or corporate names may be trademarks or registered trademarks, and are used only for identification and explanation without intent to infringe.

British Library Cataloguing-in-Publication Data
A catalogue record for this book is available from the British Library

Library of Congress Cataloging-in-Publication Data
Names: Vidal, M. Carmen Africa, author.
Title: Translation and repetition : rewriting (un)original literature / Ma. Carmen África Vidal Claramonte.
Description: Abingdon, Oxon ; New York, NY : Routledge, 2023. | Includes bibliographical references and index.
Identifiers: LCCN 2022061057 | ISBN 9781032490250 (hardback) | ISBN 9781032481289 (paperback) | ISBN 9781003391890 (ebook)
Subjects: LCSH: Literature—Translations—History and criticism. | Translating and interpreting. | Repetition (Philosophy) | Originality.
Classification: LCC PN241 .V53 2023 | DDC 418/.04—dc23/eng/20230315
LC record available at https://lccn.loc.gov/2022061057

ISBN: 978-1-032-49025-0 (hbk)
ISBN: 978-1-032-48128-9 (pbk)
ISBN: 978-1-003-39189-0 (ebk)

DOI: 10.4324/9781003391890

Typeset in Bembo
by Apex CoVantage, LLC

CONTENTS

*Ackn*owledgments   *vii*
Preface   *viii*

Introduction   1

1 On repetition   7

   1.1 On repetitions and beginnings 7
   1.2 On (creative) repetition 13

2 Repetitive (un)original literature   20

   2.1 Writing through 24
   2.2 Three original copyists 39
   2.3 (Un)creative writers 44

3 (Un)original translators   57

   3.1 Translation as transcreation: Haroldo
      and Augusto de Campos 59
      3.1.1 Transcreation 59
      3.1.2 Haroldo de Campos and Octavio Paz 70
   3.2 From transcreation to total translation:
      Jerome Rothenberg 71
   3.3 Pierre Menard and his precursors 77

4 Translating repetition: (un)creative translations 92
   4.1 Creative translation in the 21st century 92
   4.2 Toward a ludic and creative translation 106

5 Echoes, echoes 130

   References *136*
   Index *153*

ACKNOWLEDGMENTS

A book is a resonance box, an interweaving, a textile. It is a space without limits in which the reader (and the author) listens to multiple voices. A book is a deterritorialized, palimpsestic territory, with multiple layers of meanings. Therefore, a book always owes much to all those who have sung melodies in the author's ear from different perspectives. This book is indebted to many voices. To Susan Bassnett, whose ideas have been crucial to me and whose generosity I cannot describe in words. To Tong King Lee, for being a constant source of inspiration to think of translation in groundbreaking ways, for having read the very first manuscript, and for his true and selfless support. I am also extremely grateful to the AHRC Experiential Translation Network, whose members, under the leadership of Madeleine Campbell and Ricarda Vidal, are opening translation to infinite and incredibly enriching avenues. I would like to express my profound thanks to Christopher Mellinger for writing the preface and for all of his suggestions and comments. His voice is heard here before mine but is also a constant echo. My deepest thanks too to Louisa Semlyen for guiding me throughout this journey. Her professionalism, patience, and kindness have resulted in a trouble-free publication process.

PREFACE

History, adventure, erudition, romance, and tragedy echo through the streets and resonate off the warm, blonde sandstone facades of Salamanca. Cervantes ascribed to that city an enchanting allure that leaves every visitor—myself among them—longing to return. Perhaps it is living and working among these reverberating memories that partially inspired África Vidal to reflect on repetition and rewriting.

Fittingly, the opening chapter of this volume starts with Calvino's query of where a text begins. This question invites any number of starting points for reflection on repetition, from textual and metaphorical allusion to the embeddedness of a work in a broader literary landscape. One such starting point might even be reminiscent of a Proustian memory; a text may simply begin from an involuntary memory of a time and place, in which corporality and materiality blend with memory and reflection *in medias res*. But rather than a madeleine, a corporeal memory provoked by the taste of *jamón ibérico* might instead transport readers back to the memory-laden streets of Salamanca amidst the bustle of outdoor restaurants in the main square. One need only a single visit to remember the delight of the spontaneous illumination of the Plaza Mayor, a moment that is simultaneously wondrous in the crisp evening air and wholly expected by virtue of its clockwork, and thus unoriginal, arrival.

In certain circles, translation has been pejoratively and incorrectly viewed as derivative and uncreative. The idea of translations being "lesser than" or "derivative" as a repetition of a text in a new language is often the first stone cast in arguments regarding why translation ought to be subservient to what constitutes an "original" piece of writing. Vidal challenges these trodden paths by articulating how translation can instead be viewed as a generative act, particularly in the artistic and literary realm, adding layers of meaning in an inventive palimpsest as well as being a joyful and playful task in ludic translation. As she notes, hierarchical positions have been challenged in the field in order to nuance the relative situatedness of author and text, translator and translation, to describe translations as works worthy of inquiry unto themselves. Meanwhile, there is certainly plenty of support to position translation as being on par with whatever constitutes "original production".

The mythos of creative works as appearing *ex nihilo* from the mind of a singular genius is both untrue and damaging to the arts and their translation. While there is little doubt that artists innovate and create, Vidal highlights the originality and subversiveness of (un)original literature. In doing so, she draws attention to an extreme form of what Harold Bloom terms the anxiety of influence: the challenge of any writer to offer novelty. Furthermore, the volume makes a strong case for the creative originality of translation by emphasizing the iterative nature of writing and other artistic forms as a series of complex decision-making tasks, echoing Jiří Levý's characterization of translation. Other scholars have modeled this process from various perspectives, yet repetition remains a common, albeit often unstated, dimension as we reflect on the task of the translator, moving from source to target and back again.

These themes extend beyond literature to other creative art forms; music provides many such examples. Performance of a musical score is an act of translation, interpreting symbols and instructions into sound, mood, and performance. Composers can explicitly instruct performers to repeat a portion of a score at various points: the instruction *D.S. al Coda* is a command to return to a symbol (*dal segno*) for a repetition before skipping to a coda. Western classical structures such as the sonata form will present an opening motif again in a recapitulation near the end of a movement, while modern DJs resample and remix music electronically. Musical theatre will often include a reprise in the second act, and the new setting can dramatically change the meaning and impact of a show tune. All this is to say, repetition finds itself at the core of many a musical rendition that is, in and of itself, a translation.

Vidal has previously written explicitly about music in her volume *Dile que le he escrito un "blues"*. Thus, this preface can revisit David Johnston's preface to that monograph, in which he invokes a suitably musical reference to harmonics and their ability to add layers and familiarity to a musical score. These sounds and overtones float above the melodic line, adding dimension and texture to a work as musical voices come together in harmony. The melody and harmony do not necessarily coincide, but rather intertwine and modulate as musicians move through the musical score. In transposing the image to Vidal's volume, he remarks that this effect—one in which readers recognize a familiar emotion while reading a new text—cannot, in fact, be easily referred to in translation. How, then, might we describe these entangled ideas of familiarity and novelty, particularly when thinking of translation?

At hand in the present volume may well yet be Vidal's answer. The point of departure in translation finds familiar roots in literary studies, specifically those that challenge what constitutes originality to describe (un)original literature. The general premise, that ideas in literature are not necessarily novel but rather draw on intertextual allusion and inspiration from previous writing, is not always expressly stated in scholarship and instead rumbles just beneath the surface. Yet many cling to the idea of creative genius and inspiration as the source of literary or creative production, when it is only natural for writers, musicians, artists, and other artists to draw inspiration from and repeat ideas with which they resonate. This volume speaks to the question of what it means to resonate and, more specifically, the willingness to invoke and recognize this type of creative repetition, transposition, and iteration as part and parcel of translation.

As such, the challenge and question of repetition, iteration, and creativity are an exciting means by which to view translation—it is a disruptive concept that allows insights to emerge related to affective or experiential engagement with a text. This discussion provides an opportunity to challenge the stability of several concepts (i.e., authenticity, authorship, creativity) that have been central to certain circles of reflection on the topic, further questioning what constitutes the "new" and how texts are created or constructed. These constellations of concepts blur the lines of what constitutes the act of creation and the necessary creative skills of a translator, in addition to the necessary linguistic and cultural facility.

After all, a translator must always understand and navigate nuance in language; the difference between *nada* and *nothing* has the power to destroy a silly interlingual pun. One of any number of challenges known to translators, the creative resolution is often unremarked when the new text resonates with readers. Where and how these textual curiosities are addressed is a matter of a translator's style and approach, yet the individualized process still will revisit the repetitive task of creating a novel rendition.

al Coda

Even literary forms that are touted as new find familiar traces in repetition. For example, the celebrated Salmantino sage and scholar Miguel de Unamuno advanced literature structurally and thematically with his publication of the tragicomic work *Niebla*. Despite the first coined usage of its self-referential form as *nivola*, the story still emerges from a mist (or is it a fog? or a cloud?) of references. A plot built partially on a leading character falling in love with a woman on first sight recalls Dante's Beatrice, Romeo's infatuation with Juliet, or Marius glimpsing Cosette. Personal interpretations of literature differ in much the same way as translations do, just as Augusto asks his dog Orfeo the difference between thinking one is in love and being in love. Great stories are told and retold, taking on new shapes and faces with familiar undertones that remind readers of their pasts. Thus, works as disparate in time, place, and theme as Virgil's *Aeneid* and Joyce's *Ulysses* consciously echo the proto-epic of Homer's *Odyssey*, itself beginning in an oral tradition that is still being retranslated and reinterpreted (most recently by Emily Wilson). Vidal's focus on unoriginal translations, echoes, and repetitions thus draws the reader's attention to how these same phenomena are ever present in any act of translation.

Continuing to reflect on the translation of artistic forms, one can consider theatre. Aficionados do not always refer to the original script (which served as the source text that is translated to the stage), but rather center their discussions on specific productions, recordings, casts, or artists who have interpreted these works. Attending a recent performance of *The Hours*, a new opera produced by the Metropolitan Opera in New York City, I was struck by the evident intertextuality as the production reinterpreted the story's previous incarnations in film and literature, which themselves took inspiration from Virginia Woolf's novel *Mrs. Dalloway*. Woolf's novel itself draws its title character from the author's childhood friend, and the work reflects stylistic influence from Joyce's innovative stream of consciousness narration. Each repetition and adaptation translate and expand the artistic themes. Not all works lend themselves to such ready identification of their influences, yet the overtones remain nonetheless. Vidal's erudition to integrate repetition into the act of translation provides an opportunity to reflect on these fragmentary voices that linger in memory.

Repetition, reproduction, and iteration in creative expression also take on new meaning when situated in specific spaces. Consider, for instance, an art installation or a museum exhibit for which creative choices can encompass frames, location and viewing angles, lighting, and progression through the exhibit. In some museums, preparatory sketches that an artist might never have intended to be seen become objects of art in themselves, showing the creative process (much like an author's handwritten edits in a manuscript can be studied to understand creative intention, meaning, and process). Sometimes artists purposely play with repetition, such as etchings or silkscreen printings. Iterations on a theme can even be seen as the mark of creative development due to sustained engagement with a particular idea. In all cases, art is encountered in a particular time and place, whether chosen by the artist, a curator, a patron, or a customer.

Curated spaces can remind us that movement and travel are also forms of repetition, whether a daily commute, a return to a childhood home, or a trip back to a favorite vacation destination. Travelers always find themselves living in translation; even if no explicit language barrier exists, the local vernacular, jargon, customs, and knowledge will differ. People travel to Salamanca today for myriad reasons, including students from around the world who arrive to immerse themselves in a city steeped in history, artistic expression, and culture. They will surely savor the food, explore the museums, and enjoy the music of the city. As a university town, visitors and international students will be abuzz in classrooms learning the language, conjugating verbs, and translating sentences, perhaps even such a silly question as "¿Qué hace un pez aburrido?"

D.S. al Coda

Thus, authors can use structure and repetition to their advantage, sometimes to great artistic effect and other times for ludic, even silly ends. Vidal's final chapter, "Echoes, echoes", highlights the themes of sound and rhythm while evoking

Benjamin's metaphor of a person at the edge of a forest, calling out into this expansive space and being returned an echo. She ends the volume with the imagery of translation as perpetual movement, for there is no stable, Platonic original underlying the creative act of translation. (Her occasional reference to Platonism throughout the volume is particularly apt in light of Alfred North Whitehead's characterization of Western philosophy as a series of footnotes to Plato, suggesting the echoes, repetitions, variations, and translations within that discipline.)

Another Greek philosopher who understood this notion of perpetual change was Heraclitus, originator of the koan that stepping into the same river twice is an impossibility. However, despite the inevitable change that surrounds us, we all so often yearn to return to familiar places.

When I someday return to Salamanca, the city and I will be the same but different. Vidal's volume delights in the power of the creative arts and translation, exploring what it means to repeat and reverberate. And much like any translation, the city's art and literature, the taste of its gastronomic delights such as *jamón ibérico*, and its architecture and lights will all resonate with new layers of meaning, echoes, and repetitions of the past.

Christopher D. Mellinger
Charlotte, NC, December 2022

INTRODUCTION

Translating has always been an activity linked to the epistemological changes of the contexts in which it is performed. Translators are never oblivious to what is happening around them. That is why, for several decades now, translation studies has been changing the way of understanding basic concepts in our discipline, such as fidelity, equivalence, or origin. These are notions that affect not only translation but also the very way of understanding our reality and existence. In this context, repetition is a key concept, because it is directly related to others, such as authorship and originality.

In Western thought, repetition has long been regarded as a negative concept, one that should be avoided at all costs. However, in line with contemporary philosophers such as Ludwig Wittgenstein, Jacques Derrida, Gilles Deleuze and Felix Guattari, and others, this book views repetition as difference or, more specifically, as creation. Repetition is a way of situating texts in new contexts and thus bringing to light their plurality. *Translation and Repetition: Rewriting (Un)original Literature* studies repetition from a new perspective: creative repetition.

Our analysis focuses on "unoriginal" literature, which has been examined in depth by literary critics such as Marjorie Perloff, Kenneth Goldsmith, and Craig Dworkin, as well as by other authors outside the field of translation studies. Based on the reflections of these and other poets and literary critics, this book applies creative repetition to translation. From this innovative perspective, (un)original literature is itself a kind of rewriting of previous works. It is a palimpsest. A fabric. A tissue in perpetual motion that is never finished. In fact, it is always being transformed after subsequent readings and translations (both interlinguistically and intralinguistically). This is an unstable literature, constructed on the basis of a proliferation of iterations. The literature we will analyze in these pages is "unfinished works riddled with variants, whose visual and material aspect many consider crucial to their modes of meaning" (Emmerich 2017: 161). These works consequently offer a new way of understanding the concepts of originality and authorship in the world today. These notions are now perceived much differently than they were in the past. In fact, when they are deconstructed, traditional ways of addressing translation and the translation process are also subverted.

Philosophy is a fertile source of innovative perspectives on repetition, which can shed new light on originality and authorship. Chapter 1 approaches repetition from a contemporary philosophical perspective. As suggested some lines earlier, the concept of repetition is understood here not as reproduction but rather as the production, modification, and creation of something new. When something is repeated or translated, it becomes transfigured in a new context. Starting from the theories of Ludwig Wittgenstein, Gayatri Spivak, Jacques Derrida, Gilles Deleuze and Felix Guattari, and Douglas Hofstadter on beginnings and repetition, this chapter examines contemporary approaches to repetition, which view this concept not as the repetition of the same, that is, as Greek re-production, but rather as a *creative* production that advances and produces *as* it repeats.

These new modes of understanding repetition as creative are reflected in the (un)creative writings of (un)original authors in Chapter 2, which provides an overview of writers who create unsettling derivative texts through repetition. These (un)original texts, originals born from other originals, are subversive. Because they require a different mode of translating, they give rise to a singular kind of translation. In the first section, special attention is paid to Samuel Beckett's repetitions, John Cage's *writing through*, Simon Morris' *Getting Inside Jack Kerouac's Head*, and Christian Bök's *Eunoia*. Also analyzed is erasure, a technique used by Jonathan Safran Foer in *Tree of Codes* (2010), Nick Thurston in *Reading the Remove of Literature* (2006), and Derek Beaulieu in *a, A Novel* (2017), an erasure-based translative response to Warhol's *a: a novel*. The second part of this chapter also examines the works of three important contemporary writers/copyists/translators, namely, *Bartleby & Co.* and *Mac & His Problem* by Enrique Vila-Matas, *The Recognitions* by William Gaddis, and *Absent City* by Ricardo Piglia. The third section approaches other (un)creative writers such as Kenneth Goldsmith, Charles Bernstein, Nicole Brossard, and Susan Daitch or Susan Howe, among others. Thus, this chapter shows how many contemporary writers create through (creative) repetition and through these new philosophical modes of understanding repetition, which are reflected in the (un)creative writings of (un)original authors. These writers construct derivative texts that require a type of translation that is totally opposed to prescriptivist approaches. In these traditional approaches, translation merely signifies reformulating the text in another language so that it is "faithful" and thus equivalent to the original. These texts show the need to deal with the materiality of the sign, with the performative nature of these (un)original writings, and with the way they approach meaning, as "a multifaceted, context-dependent and mutable phenomenon which inevitably dissipates and alters during the translation process" (Bennett 2019: 1).

Chapters 3 and 4 explain how the new theories of translation transcend the essentialist binary oppositions between original and translation, and between primary and secondary. As shall be seen, these are ways of approaching translation that not only can be applied to this (un)original literature but also fit the requirements of the 21st century. Chapter 3 deals with four acclaimed 20th-century writers and translators: Haroldo and Augusto de Campos, Jerome Rothenberg, and Jorge Luis Borges. Rothenberg's ethnopoetics has been widely analyzed, but his translations have not, and even less so his theory of "total translation". Although these are well-known authors in translation studies, the approach in this book is new because it focuses on aspects of their translation theories that have not been studied in sufficient depth in connection with repetition, namely, the "transcreation" of Haroldo de Campos, the "porous prose" of Augusto de Campos, and Jerome Rothenberg's "total translation", applied here, for instance, to the work of Caroline Bergvall, among others. As for Borges, I focus on his "Pierre Menard", a story that perfectly defines and embodies creative repetition and that has been reused by such artists as Michel Lafon, Glenn Gould, Pierre Huyghe, or (Elaine) Sturtevant. This chapter shows how these rewriters create a theory of translation that can be applied to ethically approach the texts described in the previous chapter.

Chapter 4 expands the ideas of these 20th-century translators analyzed in the previous chapter with 21st-century views on translation, such as those by Susan Bassnett, Anne Coldiron, Kirsten Malmkjaer, Loredana Polezzi, Theo Hermans, or Lawrence Venuti.

These authors, as well as others with different perspectives, agree that translation is infinitely more complex than the mere substitution of one linguistic system for another. In the 21st century, translating consists of "the weaving together of languages, the searching out of linguistic sympathies, linguistic versatilities, linguistic multiplicity, the self-renewing concertedness of a heterogeneity, which has no telos" (Scott 2018: 30). And in this context, translation becomes a form of creativity. According to Borges, translation completes the original, multiplies its meanings, and brings to light what the text hides in its interstices. This is why translating is not repeating: "Translation is not the repetition of a text in another language, but a complicity between texts to converge on something that lies beyond them" (Scott 2018: 31).

Chapter 4 thus shows that the new ways of understanding translation as something always in motion, as something that must move in order to superimpose new meanings derived from new contexts, are very appropriate for translating the (un)original texts discussed in the previous chapters, for instance, Caroline Bergvall, Jen Bervin, and others: namely, original texts, whose creation is based on appropriations, citations, quotations, and intertexts; texts whose dynamic materiality turns the page into a nonhierarchical territory full of traces that do not move as a linear progression but invite the reader to see new interconnections in new ways; derivative texts that reveal by effacing, by presenting what is absent.

4 Introduction

Consequently, in these texts and their translations, fidelity and equivalence "are not, of course, simple terms, and have become increasingly relativized in both translation practice and translation studies" (Scott 2011: 215). During the 20th century, the definitions of fidelity and equivalence have evolved in many disciplines, and this is also true of translation. Because the meaning of these concepts has shifted, the attitude toward translators has also been transformed (Bassnett 2022b: 237–238). In line with authors such as Tong King Lee, Clive Scott, Madeleine Campbell, Ricarda Vidal, and many others, the concept of translation in this book is broad and transformative. It is thus conceived as always on the move, experiential, ludic, and creative. It is a translation that finds meaning not only in words but also in forms, sounds, silences, smells, and textures. It is an interactive and participative translation that is the result of a holistic approach that "recognizes that there are multiple possible versions of both source and target texts and this can help mitigate the biases and preconceptions a static, intralingual translation can sometimes introduce" (Campbell and Vidal 2019: xxvi).

In translation, what is important is not so much the result but the process itself (Campbell and Vidal 2019: 2), because, if reading is an active and creative process with many layers, translating is an endless semiosis that is never finished: "No text can be fixed in time, because it will always be open to new interpretations and each translation is a new version in what is a long line of earlier versions" (Bassnett 2022b: 245). To rewrite these texts, we need a translation

> which realizes language's metamorphic impulses, its solicitation towards the allophonic and the allomorphic. Translation begins in equivalence, but is itself the very process of superseding equivalence, of setting language on the move; in translation, we use words precisely in order to reinflect them towards, or away from, the languages they confront or summon up, indeed by means of the languages they confront or summon up.
>
> *(Scott 2011: 215)*

(Un)original writings bring with them a proliferation of versions of the "original" text. Here, language is always a living organism, a performance in motion that invites the reader to approach multiplicity. Translating these texts is in itself an open experience:

> In order not to become itself an unwitting instrument of closure and textual decision, translation will tend to multiply obstructions to a fluent, linear, recapitulative kind of reading and pass on its own constructivist persuasions to its readers, by various processes of linguistic provocation.
>
> *(Scott 2011: 216)*

Translation is relational becoming, creation; it is thus "necessarily experimental, unable to draw exclusively on the known, begetting knowledge, not meaning" (Scott

2018: 63). In this context, Tong King Lee's theory of *ludic translation*, which Lee applies to concrete experimental Chinese poetry, is most relevant. Ludic translation is a subversive, rhizomatic translation in which

> play can serve as a lubricant in negotiating the tensions between original and translation. It proffers a conceptual route out of irreconcilable dualities by opening up to the possibilities of creative and critical intertextualities across languages and cultures. It transcends a zero-sum (all-or-nothing) conception under which the translator is either submissive to or subversive of the original text and its author. Instead, play spotlights the liquidity of the source—target interface, from which translational identity formations are engendered.
>
> *(Lee 2022: 6)*

It is my assertion that the derivative, quotational texts studied in this book not only subvert our way of understanding authenticity, originality, and authorship but also challenge our ideas of the construction of the real and of previously established cultural values. Consequently, these texts require an ethical translation, which is unique, creative, and ludic. The study of this (un)original literature explains how new theories of translation transcend the essentialist binary oppositions between original and translation, and between primary and secondary. In order to translate these (un)original writings, which are already rewritings of previous texts, it will be essential to start from the latest translation theories that have broadened the scope of translation and that point the way to new research perspectives in the field. Translation will be seen in this book as an encompassing process, as a (original) performance, as a sensual experience that plays not only with language but also with our senses. This translation will be appropriate to rewrite texts that are canvases on which words are transformed into visual events, something that once again expands and enhances the concept of translation. Ludic and creative translation is an adventure because it invites us to experience language, to create new language(s) with all our senses.

Ludic translation is perfectly applicable to texts that defy the notion of origin. These are texts that are characterized by their indeterminacy and that allow "for radial strands of thinking" (Lee 2022: 46). Like these (un)original writings, ludic translations are never the same. In them, repetition implies both creativity and playfulness: "Each time a work is translated, even by the same translator, the outcome will inevitably be different because the extraneous circumstances impinging on each instance of translation can never be exactly the same" (Lee 2022: 46). Like other contemporary theories of translation, ludic translation is political: "Play transforms normativized identities, thereby gaining its politico-ethical force" (Lee 2022: 6). Translation is seen in terms of a heterogeneous, affective phenomenology,

> a method to democratize expression and level the ground of linguistic transaction, such that "no one is permanently on top, no one is permanently at the

> bottom", resonates with how the dyadic relation between source and target, author and translator, can be reconfigured through ludic translation. This is particularly the case with overtly performative modes of translation, where the distance from one language to another is mediated not through relations of semantic equivalence but through relations of semiotic analogy grounded in the materialities of representation.
>
> *(Lee 2022: 7)*

I apply this view of translation to (un)original literature such as *Poetamenos* by Augusto de Campos, Caroline Bergvall's *Alisoun Sings*, Christian Bök's five translations of Arthur Rimbaud's "Voyelles" in his 2009 edition of *Eunoia*, and others. In these and many other examples, translation and the previous text are experimented, experienced with all our senses.

(Un)original literature shows that experimentalism does not only mean playing with language. These writers demonstrate that texts have not only one interpretation and, therefore, not only one translation. Every reading enables a plurality of new meanings because each reading and each translation place the text into a new context. A text is always open. And so are translations. Meaning is always plural, never exhausted. As Borges will show us in Chapter 3, each translation completes the original because it develops and reveals new possibilities. The text is never stabilized by looking at its archeology. New Foucaultian genealogies are generated by creatively repeating what has already been repeated, endlessly connecting the never-ending ends with beginnings. As will be shown in Chapter 1, a beginning is never a beginning because a text, like a translation, is always a palimpsest waiting to be discovered by each new translator.

These rewritings play with language. They play with the visual, with the materiality of words, and with the page seen as a canvas. By doing so, they make the reader conscious of the deviance of meaning, of its reflection effect in writing, of pluralism, and of new cohesions that are not apparent because we have not been taught to see them as "logical". This literature needs a ludic translator who brings to light the contingency of sense by plunging into the many layers of these palimpsests, (un)original writings full of resonances, quotations, and other texts, which provide further connections, perhaps even more connections than we are supposed to discover.

1
ON REPETITION

In *If on a Winter's Night a Traveller* (1979/1981), Italo Calvino wonders where and when a story actually begins. Because his interest is in the origins of a story, the implicit question in this metafictional novel is the identity of the originator:

> But how to establish the exact moment in which a story begins? Everything has already begun before, the first line of the first page of every novel refers to something that has already happened outside the book. Or else the real story is the one that begins ten or a hundred pages further on, and everything that precedes it is only a prologue.
> *(Calvino 1979/1981: 110)*

As the story progresses, the reader observes that the fictional readers are also engaged in reading the novel. Both the actual reader and the fictional one(s) arrive at the end of the book by reading it. During this process, Calvino's Readers, one male and the other female, discover stories that they never finish and, along the way, even uncover a web of forgery. The ten stories in *If on a Winter's Night a Traveller* thus create an intricately crafted literary labyrinth with multiple beginnings and different origins (Robinson 2022).

The book that you now hold in your hands is a book about translation. And a book about translation is also a book about repetition because translating is repeating. Is translating repeating? Or is it a new beginning? Is it reading again? My initial assumption is that translating is not repetition because repetition does not exist. Repetition does not exist.

1.1 On repetitions and beginnings

This has been a hotly debated issue in various disciplines, but especially in philosophy. For example, Ludwig Wittgenstein (unlike Hegel) did not believe in repetition:

> Hegel seems to me to be always wanting to say that things which look different are really the same. Whereas my interest is in showing that things which look the same are really different.
>
> *(Wittgenstein in Drury 1981: 171)*

In fact, in §203 of his *Philosophical Investigations*, Wittgenstein (1953/1084: 82) writes that "language is a labyrinth of paths. You approach from *one* side and know your way about; you approach the same place from another side and no longer know your way about". In §215 and §216, he reinforces this statement by stating that the same is not the same:

> 215. But isn't *the same* at least the same?
> We seem to have an infallible paradigm of identity in the identity of a thing with itself. I feel like saying: "Here at any rate there can't be a variety of interpretations. If you are seeing a thing you are seeing identity too".
> Then are two things the same when they are what *one* thing is? And how am I to apply what the *one* thing shews me to the case of two things?
> 216. "A thing is identical with itself".—There is no finer example of a useless proposition.
>
> *(Wittgenstein 1953/1984: 84)*

And in *Culture and Value*, he explains,

> I still find my own way of philosophizing new, and it keeps striking me so afresh; that is why I need to repeat myself so often. It will have become second nature to a new generation, to whom the repetitions will be boring. I find them necessary.
>
> *(Wittgenstein 1977/1984: 1)*

Marjorie Perloff (2021; see also Perloff 2004a: 60–81 and Perloff 1996) reflects on Wittgenstein's question, "But isn't the same at least *the same*"? and concludes that "translation might be precisely that 'interval we experience as we recognize that even the same is not the same'" (Goldfajn 2022). It is true that Platonism distinguishes good repetition, which gives and presents the *Eidos*, from bad repetition. Nevertheless, in this book, repetition (and translation) are understood as processes in constant motion and change. In this sense, they are similar to Heraclitus' river, which no man could ever step in twice because a second later it was no longer the same river. Repeating, like translating, is not reproduction, but rather the production, modification, and creation of something new. When something is repeated or translated, it becomes transfigured in a new context:

> Repetition thus is not the repetition of the same, Greek re-production, but a creative production which pushes ahead, which produces *as* it repeats, which

produces *what* it repeats, which makes a life for itself in the midst of the difficulties of the flux.

(Caputo 1987: 3)

To repeat is thus to transform, to make anew, to translate, and to (re)create. Representation makes presence possible:

> To repeat is to produce and to alter, to make and to make anew. Repetition is a principle of irrepressible creativity and novelty; it would be impossible to repeat without making and without altering what is already made. Even to repeat "exactly the same thing" is to repeat it in a new context which gives it a new sense.
>
> *(Caputo 1987: 142)*

As a kind of productive and ever-creative repetition, translation explores the tainted or gritty surface on the reverse side of the mirror. It goes behind the mirror to question the nature of reflection. Seen in this light, translation is not iteration but iterability (Venuti 2019: 3). In (un)original literature a previous text is cited at another time, in another text and context, a countless number of times. Thus, the repeated material

> breaks with the old context and creates numerous new ones . . . whenever we endeavor to decipher or reinstitute a context as we do when we cite a text, we end up grafting onto the very context we seek to communicate, creating a new context beyond the control of the original.
>
> *(Tucker 2010: 43)*

Iterability encompasses two opposite ideas: iteration or repetition and the possibility of alteration. Iterability is not only present in literature and the arts—it is "the force behind every form of experience" (Derrida 1972/1984: 318).

Translation is original repetition, iterability, and supplementarity (Gasche 1986: 212). To write about translation also means to write about origins, about beginnings. Where and when does a text begin? Does it begin by returning to the beginning, like John Milton's *Paradise Lost*, or by referring back to other texts like *Wild Sargasso Sea*? Where is the beginning if the text begins *in media res*? Does a text begin when the author begins to think about it or when the reader starts reading it? Or does a text begin with Genette's "peritexts", images and other elements surrounding the main body of the published text (Bennett and Royle 2004: 1–8)? And where does a translation begin? Is the beginning the same for a reader who knows the original language as for one who does not?

Theo Hermans begins to speak of beginnings in his 1996 inaugural lecture at University College London:

> If it is true that in the beginning was the word, then almost from the beginning there was a problem of translation. Or rather: there is in that beginning a problem of translation; it is still here, in this beginning, in the very word which was there when I began.
>
> *(Hermans 1996: n.p.)*

There are many scholars who have focused their work on beginnings from different perspectives. George Steiner (2001: 2) begins his *Grammars of Creation* with, "We have no more beginnings". Also very significant are Edward Said's (2012) ideas in *Beginnings* and those of Michel Foucault (1974/1990) on origins in "La Vérité et les formes juridiques" ["Truth and Juridical Forms"]. In fact, the problem of beginning is one of the most important in philosophy and has been studied by philosophers as different in their views as Descartes, Hegel, Heidegger, and Wittgenstein.

Hegel cautions us against prefaces, and one of Jean Hyppolite's essays even warns us against Hegel's preface to his *Phenomenology*. In contrast, Derrida is convinced that Hegel's prefaces contain an important part of his work. And everything becomes even more complex when the preface is written by someone else, as Gayatri Spivak warns in her preface to *Grammatology*: "The preface is a necessary gesture of homage and parricide, for the book (the father) makes a claim of authority or origin which is both true and false" (Spivak 1967/1984: xi). In 1975, Borges published, with Miguel de Torre, his *Prologue with a Prologue of Prologues* (Borges 1975). Gerard Genette (1987) devotes three chapters to the prologue in *Seuils*. Origins and repetitions, once again.

The answer to Nietzsche's question, "Who speaks?" can be found in Mallarmé's compelling reply, "Language itself". Traditionally, there was no choice but to opt for an original text that could never be perfectly translated because it had to remain pristine and untouched. However, today this is no longer the case. New perceptions of translation now begin with the supposition that the Real, that Platonic original with only one possible interpretation, does not exist. What does exist is its (re)construction through language, the language spoken by each of us.

The problem of beginnings is none other than the problem of the original (London 2019). It is the problem of where to start, how to start, what it means to create an original, and whether this is even possible. To repeat is to begin again, which means that each repetition is a new beginning. Any reflection on beginnings and originals is intrinsically linked to other notions that stem from these premises. This includes the erroneous assumption that it is possible to accurately draw a border between the original or authentic and the copy or derivation, or between the primary and the secondary.

An accurate definition of beginnings opens the door to a clear formulation of the ability to define, to structure, and to classify. And, even more importantly, it reveals exactly what meaning is: "The possibility of beginning *once and for all* enables us to come to what we think of as meaning" (Gendron 2008: xiii).

This question is far from trivial, nor does it only concern linguists, writers, and translators. It is mainly a philosophical question that Hegel previously addressed in his *Enzyklopädie Zusatz*, in which he states that the idea of a beginning is an illusion because every beginning has already taken place. Gendron (2008: xiii) writes,

> If every beginning is really just *beginning again*—what happens to the notions that were derived from this now potentially incorrect assumption? How can one differentiate definitively between one thing and another without reference to where each object begins? What becomes of authenticity and authority—concepts that are based on the idea of *a first time*—if the first time has no more claim to legitimacy or originality than the second? What if the original is no more original than the copy? How do we determine truth?

All prefaces and all the beginnings of books (like this one) are a paradox because they are written at the end to explain what has previously been explained and to introduce what is inside the book. The beginning before the beginning. This genealogical project is itself an (false) origin, an original text as well as a rewriting, which invariably occurs after translation. The preface is the origin, the point at which everything begins but which happens afterward, when the writing has already occurred and then recurs in the preface. Prefaces are afterthoughts. In fact, a preface is only a simulated beginning, and perhaps so is the author's inscription of a signature (Kamuf 1988) or the title on the book cover.

Nevertheless, there has to be a beginning, however disseminated, however provisional and unstable. "There is, then, always already a preface between two hands holding open a book. And the 'prefacer', of the same or another proper name as the 'author', need not apologize for 'repeating' the text", says Spivak (1976: xiii). In her reflection on prefaces and the concept of origin, she recalls that Ferdinand de Saussure observed that "the 'same' phoneme pronounced twice or by two different people is not identical to itself. Its only identity is in its difference from all other phonemes" (Spivak 1976/1984: xi–xii). She continues,

> So do the two readings of the "same" book show an identity that can only be defined as a difference. The book is not repeatable in its "identity": each reading of the book produces a simulacrum of an "original" that is itself the mark of the shifting and unstable subject that Proust describes, using and being used by a language that is also shifting and unstable. Any preface commemorates that difference in identity by inserting itself between two readings—in our case, my reading (given of course that my language and I are shifting and unstable), my rereading, my rearranging of the text—and your reading.
>
> *(Spivak 1976/1984: xii)*

The quotation marks that Spivak adds to the words "same" and "original" are meaningful. Not only do they refer to the nonexistence of repetition, but they also define translation:

> The preface, by daring to repeat the book and reconstitute it in another register, merely enacts what is already the case: the book's repetitions are always other than the book. There is, in fact, no "book" other than these ever-different repetitions: the "book" in other words, is always already a "text", constituted by the play of identity and difference.
>
> (Spivak 1976/1984: xii)

Each act of reading is a preface, a new interpretation, a layer that adheres to the next reading. Each reading is a translation, a beginning, and a repetition. Perhaps that is why translators, on many occasions, write prefaces to their own translations (Bolduc 2018).

Repetition is related to Derrida's *sous rature* or "under erasure", a technique that began with Heidegger when he crossed out "Being" but still left the deletion in the text. However, Spivak (1976/1984: xv, xvii) underlines the difference between the deletions of Derrida and Heidegger, a difference that is important here because it is directly related to the concepts of origin and repetition, of primary and secondary. Heidegger crossed out "Being". Even though Derrida does not reject the concept of origin, he still questions it.[1] In contrast to Heidegger, he prefers *trace*, which does not refer to a previous presence or origin. This means that for Derrida, origin is only a trace, which leads to the subsequent deconstruction of the concept of author. These ideas are applied later on in this book in literary examples in which the technique of *sous rature* is used to create something new from the repetition of previous works.

Following this same line of thought, in "Freud and the Scene of Writing" (1966), an essay in *Writing and Difference*, Derrida states that "it is the very idea of a *first time* which becomes enigmatic . . . it is deferral what is at the beginning" (Derrida 1967: 2001a). In "Signature Event Context" (in Derrida 1972/1988), Derrida links iterability to otherness. Repetition implies change because, as Derrida points out, "iter" most likely comes from the Sanskrit "itara", which means "other" (Derrida 1972/1988: 7):

> Every sign, linguistic or nonlinguistic, spoken or written (in the current sense of this opposition), in a small or large unit, can be cited, put between quotation marks; in so doing it can break with every given context, engendering an infinity of new contexts in a manner which is absolutely illimitable. This does not imply that the mark is valid outside of a context, but on the contrary that there are only contexts without any center or absolute anchoring [*ancrage*]. This citationality, this duplication or duplicity, this iterability of the mark is neither an accident nor an anomaly, it is that (normal/abnormal) without which a mark could not even have a function called "normal". What would a mark be that could not be cited? Or one whose origins would not get lost along the way?
>
> (Derrida 1972/1988: 12)

Repetition alters and is related to the condition of otherness. Derridean iterability is repetition with a *différance*² and not repetition of the same. Iterability is "the capacity to be reused, which also invariably involves the capacity to be misused, misperformed, changed or twisted in some new way" (Robinson 2003: 19). According to "Plato's Pharmacy", a key essay in *Dissemination* (Derrida 1972a/1981: 67–185), repetition of the same is never identical. Derridean repetition is dynamic like the repetition of Deleuze (1968: 2001), which also embraces difference "and includes itself in the alterity of the Idea". Derridean iterability reflects

> the mutability of language in repetition, difference in the repetition of the same. It is the fact that whenever we repeat something, we change it; whenever we restate something, we reperform it . . . iterability means that one is simultaneously repeating something that went before and adapting that thing to the current speech situation, localizing it.
> *(Robinson 2003: 63, 67)*

1.2 On (creative) repetition

All these ideas are the perfect framework for this book, which argues that repetition does not exist and that repetition is a form of creation. "We always introduce novel elements into our performances. Performances are always transformations, never pure reproductions" (Robinson 2003: 64).

Like Jean Baudrillard, Umberto Eco (1985), and many others, I have always been fascinated by repetition and agree that the way that we understand repetition has important repercussions for all social orders, as reflected in literature and art. Baudrillard's three orders of simulacra remind us that the concept of repetition has changed dramatically over the course of history. Repetition ranges from the Renaissance counterfeit to the Industrial simulacrum, and from the simulacra of simulation of the post-Industrial period to the tragic destruction of repetition, which he analyzes in relation to the destruction of the Twin Towers (Baudrillard 2002/2003: 38, 39):

> First of all, why the *Twin* Towers? Why *two* towers at the World Trade Center? . . . The fact that there were two of them signifies the end of original reference. . . . Only the doubling of the sign truly puts an end to what it designates. There is a particular fascination in this reduplication.

As evidenced in the writings of Plato, Aristotle, Heraclitus, St. Augustine, Descartes, Kierkegaard, Hegel, Benjamin, Nietzsche, Freud, Eliade, Descombes, Deleuze, Guattari, Debord, Derrida, and so many others (Malmkjaer 2018; Abdulla 2001), philosophy has reflected in some depth on difference and repetition. This discussion focuses on the nature of the same and the other, of the primary and the secondary. This reflection is so important because, until 20 years ago, the original was unquestionably regarded as intrinsically more valuable than the copy. This was one of the pillars of Western thought regarding metaphysical conceptualizations of knowledge and truth, *arché* and *telos*, coherent and stable identity, meaning, authority, and authorship.

"Bienvenue dans le désert du reel"[3] is a phrase that has been used by a number of authors whose work proposes a new way to view representation and reality and, thus, the original and its translation. More specifically, in 2002, Slavoj Zizek published a book with this same title. Jean Baudrillard also uses this same phrase in "La Précession des simulacres" (*Traverses* 10, 1978, 3–37) as well as in *Pour une critique de l'économie politique du signe* (1972), in which he warns that the map never coincides with the territory, which means that the Real never coincides with its representation. In this respect, Baudrillard was clearly influenced by Jorge Luis Borges and his story about the map and the territory (which in turn inspired *Les mots et les choses* by Foucault in 1966).

In regard to this topic, an obligatory reference is Gilles Deleuze, the author who perhaps best formulated this question. In *Différence et répétition* [*Difference and Repetition*] (1968) and *Logique du sens* [*Logic of Sense*] (1969), Deleuze inverts Platonism by proposing two worlds (1969: 302), one composed of copies and another of simulacra, and he reflects on the meaning of meaning. By inverting Platonism, Deleuze rejects the traditional idea of representation and advocates simulation over reproduction. It is his belief that a simulation is not a degraded copy. On the contrary, the original and what derives from it should be internalized in the simulation without any kind of hierarchy between the two: "The mask is the true subject of repetition. . . . Difference is included in repetition" (Deleuze 1968/2001: 17). Overturning Platonism means "denying the primacy of original over copy" (Deleuze 1968/2001: 66). Deleuze thus sees language as a heterogeneous assemblage in perpetual disequilibrium. In his opinion, there are two types of repetition:

> The first repetition is repetition of the Same, explained by the identity of the concept or representation; the second includes difference, and includes itself in the alterity of the Idea, in the heterogeneity of an "a-presentation". One is negative, occurring by default in the concept; the other affirmative, occurring by excess in the Idea. One is conjectural, the other categorical. One is static, the other dynamic. One is repetition in the effect, the other in the cause. One is extensive, the other intensive. One is ordinary, the other distinctive and singular. One is horizontal, the other vertical. One is developed and explicated, the other enveloped and in need of interpretation. One is revolving, the other evolving. One involves equality, commensurability and symmetry; the other is grounded in inequality, incommensurability and dissymmetry. . . . The two repetitions are not independent. One is the singular subject, the interiority and the heart of the other, the depth of the other. . . . The repetition of dissymmetry is hidden within symmetrical ensembles or effects. . . . It is the masked, the disguised or the costumed which turns out to be the truth of the uncovered.
>
> *(Deleuze 1968/2001: 24)*

In line with these authors as well as others (e.g., Gilbert 2022; Perloff 2021, 2010; Dworkin 2020a; Emmerich 2017; Greaney 2014; Schwartz 2014; Goldsmith 2011; Boon 2010; Fitterman 2009; Home 1987), it can now be said that repeating is creating and that translation is thus a kind of creative repetition.

In Western thought, repetition has long been regarded as something negative, as a kind of cliché, stereotype, or automatism that is the opposite of creation.[4] On the other hand, in the eyes of many contemporary philosophers, repetition is more about difference, because, as shall be seen, repetition involves rewriting stories initially told in other contexts so that they acquire a different perspective. In this sense, repeating is often a political act. Repetition is "a creative impulse for the making of what is new" (Kolarov 2021: 1). Repetition as iteration "recognizes the creative and critical potential of copying. Iterating, as defined in this book, is a tendency to repeat available material as a mode of writing and art making" (Marczewska 2018: 5). It is reproduction "as production" (Gilbert 2022: 130). Therefore, repetition is understood here not as a cultural condition resulting from or fostered by our digital society but more in the sense of Jorge Luis Borges, who also starts from the idea that repetition does not exist because each repetition is born in a different context. Iteration is a space for interrogation and for cultural criticism (Marczewska 2018: 12; Dworkin 2003: 14).

In his classic *Gödel, Escher, Bach*, Douglas R. Hofstadter (1979/1999) reflects on repetition in terms of self-referentiality. This naturally leads to other concepts such as similarity, paradox, self-representation, meaning, and translation. Hofstadter simultaneously studies all of them within the context of Gödel's mathematical logic, Escher's drawings, and Bach's music. In so doing, he demonstrates that all three address the same notions in very different fields. They express continuity in the discontinuous and its alternation and simultaneity with discontinuity in the continuous. Gödel's incompleteness theorem is based on the same principle as Escher's "picture within a picture" with its architectural spaces that could be either concave or convex. (Are the inhabitants ascending or descending?) It is the famous Cretan paradox or the Möbius strip, that endless loop that can be interpreted both upside down and inside out. Especially impressive is Hofstadter's analysis of the palindrome known as Bach's *crab canon*, which is based on the concept of the copy.

> The most esoteric of "copies" is the retrograde copy—where the theme is played backwards in time. A canon which uses this trick is affectionately known as a *crab canon*, because of the peculiarities of crab locomotion. Bach included a crab canon in the *Musical Offering*, needless to say. Notice that every type of "copy" preserves all the information in the original theme, in the sense that the theme is fully recoverable from any of the copies.
>
> *(Hofstadter 1979/1999: 9)*

The most brilliant example of Bach's counterpoint can be found in the final "Contrapunctus" of *The Art of the Fugue*. In this fugue, which was the last ever written by the great composer, he creates a musical cryptogram when he ciphers his name (the BACH motif) into the last theme of the fugue by "translating" the letters into notes (B = B flat, A = A, C = C, H = B natural). Not surprisingly, Bach occasionally composed acrostics. In fact, the melody B-A-C-H, if played backwards, is exactly the same as the original (Hofstadter 1979/2013). There is also the relationship that Hofstadter establishes between Bach's delightful "Canon per Tonos", in his *Musical Offering*, and Escher's *Waterfall* (1961) and *Ascending and Descending* (1960). The crab canon in the *Musical Offering* is reminiscent of a palindrome (Hofstadter 1979/1999: 201). It also makes one think of Mozart's violin duet "Der Spiegel" ["The Mirror, Table Music for Two"], a mirror canon, that is, a canon by contrary motion, which involves two performers reading from the same score in opposite directions—one starting at the beginning and the other one at the end of the score. Repetition is played here upside down, like the reflection of two figures in the still water of a lake. Something similar happens in Mozart's *Serenade for Wind Octet* or, much later, in Anton Webern's *Symphony* Op. 21 (1928), among others. All of this is related to the question, "What is an original" (Hofstadter 1979/1999: 503–504)? It is also closely related to translation, which Hofstadter describes as "far more complex than mere dictionary look-up and word rearranging" (Hofstadter 1979/1999: 603).

Hofstadter is fascinated by what he calls "cascading translation" and "iterated translations" (1997: 337ff.). In one of his books, he observes that "each of us is a bundle of fragments of other people's souls, simply put together in a new way" (Hofstadter 2007: 252). *Le Ton beau de Marot*, which includes 88 translations (some of which are Hofstadter's own), initially appears to be a long, detailed examination of a minor French poem. However, in reality, it is about the recurring themes in his work, namely, creativity, repetition, translation, and experimentation with language.

In consonance with Derrida, as well as with many others, repetition is understood here as the place of difference rather than of sameness: "Everything begins with a reproduction" (Derrida 1967/2001: 211). Everything begins with representation. "Everything begins with citation" (Derrida 1972a/1981: 316). Repetition is "originary duplication":

> The double splits what it doubles, by adding itself to it, and the reflected or doubled is also split in itself. Because the possibility of reflective duplication must be inscribed within it, the reflected is divided by its reflection in itself. The originary duplication eliminates the possibility of establishing a last source, origin and original.
>
> *(Gasche 1986: 226)*

Each era has understood concepts such as authorship and originality differently. Ours is no exception. The way in which we perceive these notions is important, because they reflect the prism through which we view the world as well as the way that we currently access reality. This is not appropriation as mere appropriation but our way of interpreting concepts such as reality and representation.

> Quotation marks implicitly flag their contents as having an origin. . . . What has an origin is also often a construction, and, as such, it is therefore susceptible to deconstruction. . . . And yet, while an idea contained within quotation marks can be made suspect, it can also be tenaciously authoritative . . . at the very least, quotation marks indicate a contextual change.
>
> *(Richards 2015: 78, 79)*

These philosophical, sociological, literary, and artistic insights indicate that our time understands originality and authorship differently from past eras (Eco 1985). Repetition, appropriation, copy, citation, or quotation "becomes itself a mark of authenticity" (Richards 2015: 79). Authors such as Kenneth Goldsmith (2011) and Marjorie Perloff (2004a), who focus on repetition, the (un)original genius, and (un)creative writing, also reflect on the quotational method of the Arcades Project and on how Benjamin understood creativity in the age of mechanical reproduction when he spoke of the disappearance of the "aura" of the original in "The Work of Art in the Age of Mechanical Reproduction" (also Greaney 2014). In fact, there was even a time when creativity was interpreted as "an aesthetic engagement with the dynamic of repetition so characteristic of Warhol's silk screens and Burroughs's cut-outs" (Marczewska 2018: 2). Subsequently, and even more so in the Digital Age, the recycling of texts makes one think of "the creative possibility of the copy" (id.), something that has now become a reality in many literary and artistic works.

The concept of copying, and of repetition in general, has changed dramatically. The repetition of the past represents an enriching dialogue with the present, wherein the notion of "preposterous history" is very useful (Bal 1999). Repetition in any type of creative sphere or endeavor enriches the repeated with added meaning as copies multiply

> around the world, indexed, and copied again. What counts are the ways in which these common copies of a creative work can be linked, manipulated, tagged, highlighted, bookmarked, translated, enlivened by other media, and sewn together in the universal library.
>
> *(Shields 2010: paragraph 75)*

As we shall see, these texts challenge the master narratives by generating a multiplicity of unpredictable and unexpected new meanings through cutting, pasting, assembling:

> Collage . . . is characterized not by cursory quotation, or even frequent allusion, but rather variety and density. Collage consists of a plurality of quotations so

tightly packed that there are internal collisions between its constituent parts. External fragments of reference and their associated contexts and meanings become forced together in a compulsory yet distinctive marriage, where tension breeds harmony. New meanings are latent in the work due to the charged and opposing poles of its disparate contents fused together, generating a potential energy of meaning, substance, and signification. Collage is a characteristic of the work, not merely a structural rubric. Collage is not only a medium; it is an idea.

(Richards 2015: 146)

Collage creates a meaning that is neither stable nor univocal. Each repetition, each cited element

breaks the continuity of the linearity of the discourse and leads necessarily to a double reading: that of the fragment perceived in relation to its text of origin; that of the same fragment as incorporated into a new whole, a different totality.

(Ulmer 1989: 51)

Repetition has an allegorical dimension (Place and Fitterman 2009; Golston 2015). A quoted text changes meaning, as does any translated text. Examples include Heimrad Bäcker's use of quotations from *Mein Kampf* or Troy Brauntuch's appropriation of Hitler's photograph. They are always incomplete "writerly" texts that exemplify what Roland Barthes describes in "From Work to Text". Replicating, mirroring, archiving, repeating, and rewriting reflect the current way of understanding originality and creativity (Goldsmith 2011) and also translation, where

meaning is as fleeting as the moment in which it arises and as unique and unrepeatable as the momentary constellation of participants in the relationship. It is therefore not repeatable whether in the same or another language; and that insight is liberating from the point of view of translation studies. There will never be sameness of meaning; but there may be coincidence, more or less close, of passing theories, in any instance of linguistic interaction.

(Malmkjaer 2020: 56)

This is a book on translation. And a book on translation is also a book about beginning(s). Beginnings have to do with origin, as well as with translation and repetition. Translation is beginning again, once more, *Twice upon a time* (2014), to echo the title of an exhibition by Nalini Malani (Bal 2018, 2016, 2015; Butler 2020), in which she (re)tells the story of the Hindu goddess Sita, who plays with reflections and repetitions. She thus tells for the first time and many times after an ancient fairy tale rewritten in a more modern style. Translation repeats and at the same time also begins the story again. Translations turn the first time into a different time or "twice upon a time". At the beginning of his novel *Double or Nothing* (1992), Federman writes, "This is not the beginning". Each translation is and will always be a new, original, and creative beginning, a new layer, a new interpretation that adheres to the infinite readings of a text.

Notes

1 There is no longer a simple origin. For what is reflected is split in itself and not only as an addition to itself of its image. The reflection, the image, the double, splits what it doubles. The origin of speculation becomes a difference. What can look at itself is not one.
(Derrida 1967/1984: 36)

2 *Différance* is the play between presence and absence that takes place in the space between speech and writing, the condition of speech and language referring to "what in classical language would be called the origin or production of differences and the differences between the differences, the play [jeu] of differences" (Derrida 1967/1979: 130). *Différance* is connected to the relation to what is other, to alterity, to assemblage:

> The word "assemblage" seems more apt for suggesting that kind of an interlacing, a weaving, or a web, which would allow the different threads and different lines of sense or force to separate again, as well as being ready to bind others together.
> *(Derrida 1967/1979: 132)*

3 Welcome to the desert of reality.
4 I am referring not to plagiarism and the legal problems that certain authors have had for this reason (Marczewska in Cobb 2014: 157–173), but rather to the philosophical vision of repetition.

2
REPETITIVE (UN)ORIGINAL LITERATURE

Since modernism, repetition, as a creative process, has produced many fascinating literary and artistic works that have challenged the notions of originality, representation, and mimesis (Ulmer 2002; Hutcheon and O'Flynn 2006/2013; Sanders 2016; McHale 2016; Lau 2022). Examples include Eisenstein's montages, Duchamp's readymades (Paz 1978/2011; Kamien-Kazhdan 2018), Stein's "There is no such thing as repetitions, only insistence" (Stein 1998: 288), the collages of Picasso and Braque, Joyce's pastiches, Melville's Bartleby, and the cut-ups of Burroughs and Gysin (Hitchin and Ambrose 2014). Even Pound's phrase "Make it new" "is the product of later critical appropriations, and the phrase itself is a translation, a copy of a centuries old text that was probably mistranscribed from a far more ancient source" (Edmond 2016: 96):

> In the early twentieth century, many modernists grew suspicious of the idea of "originality" and the notion of the artist as a divinely-inspired creator of unique, sui generis works. "Art is theft", Pablo Picasso announced (quoted in Shields 2010), while T.S. Eliot famously declared that "immature poets imitate; mature poets steal; bad poets deface what they take and good poets make it into something better" (1975: 153). This ethos led to the development of a whole range of ground breaking practices at the heart of modernism: the creation of collages out of juxtaposed fragments, a fascination with allusion, quotation, montage, and pastiche, and a belief in the creative potential of found materials. Some crucial examples in the modernist visual arts include the cubist collages of Picasso, which featured actual pieces of fabric and newsprint pasted onto the canvas, and the work of Dada and Surrealist artists.
>
> *(Epstein 2012: 312)*

DOI: 10.4324/9781003391890-3

(See also Epstein 2016.) It is well-known that, in *The Waste Land*, T.S. Eliot used citation to the hilt, even citation "that draws on other languages" (Perloff 2010: 2). So did Ezra Pound in his *Cantos*. According to Marjorie Perloff (2010: 12), *The Waste Land* is the beginning of (un)original literature:

> In this poetic climate, *The Waste Land*, with its "zig-zag of allusion", . . . its "unoriginal" lines and borrowed "magic lantern slides", can be seen as a foundational text. Together with Pound's *Cantos*, with their amalgam of citation and found text, it looks ahead not only to the mosaic of borrowings found in Louis Zukovsky's "*A*" but also to the impacted pastiche of John Ashbery's later poems, where almost every line has an intertextual referent.

Later postmodern literature used citation, appropriation, pastiche, collage, and parody as well as other strategies (Calinescu 1987, 1991). However, the general postmodern attitude toward repetition was more explicit and brazen, totally devoid of the anguish reflected in the Poundian "I cannot make it cohere" and far from "the anxiety of influence" (Bloom 1973/1997; Heys 2015). During the second half of the 20th century, after Barthes' "The Death of the Author" was published in 1968, the use of citation questioned the authority of the original text. It was a way of subverting concepts such as authenticity or primacy in order to change the way of perceiving reality. Citation

> does not reproduce the real, but constructs an object (its lexical field includes the terms "assemble, build, join, unite, add, combine, link, construct, organize" . . .) in order to intervene in the world, not to reflect but to change reality.
> *(Ulmer 2002: 97)*

It sometimes appears without quotation marks. Oppen's last poems, for instance, use citation in italics, quoting his wife and Martin Heidegger, among others, and giving those citations a new meaning (Nicholls 2005: 26–31; see also Nicholls 2007). We shall also see that citation is absorbed by the work in which it is included, unmarked and unacknowledged, as in many poems by Susan Howe (Quartermain 2008: 182–194). It can also be erased, as in many (un)original writings that use the erasure technique or that prefer "writing through". In all of these cases, citation repeats in order to create an original, by taking to a new context what previously appeared in a different situation.

Repetition and appropriation have also pervaded the art world (Young 2008; Buskirk 2003). One has only to remember *Power of Repetition* (QG Gallery, Brussels, 2018), an exhibition that brought together artists from the early 20th century to the present. Repetition was regarded as a way of redefining concepts such as originality, authenticity, and appropriation. These artists included Olivier Mosset, Daniel Buren, and Niele Toroni, the founder of BMPT, along with Allan McCollum, Carl

Andre, George Rickey, Stanley Whitney, Ron Gorchov, Peter Joseph, Alan Charlton, and Yves Klein. Similarly, repetition in the form of plagiarism and appropriation characterizes the postmodern architecture of Charles Jencks, Paolo Portoguesi, and Ricardo Bofill.

Quotation has served as a cultural agent in music, in which quotation appears as classical, experimental, jazz, and popular idioms (Metzer 2003; Fallas 2007; ap Siôn and Redhead 2014; Richards 2015). In the music world, quotation can be found in the work of Michael Nyman or Enigma, John White's *Machines*, and Terry Riley's *Keyboard Studies*. Worth mentioning is the repetition in the minimalist music of Steve Reich and Philip Glass, as well as Hugh Shrapnel's *Cantation I*. It also surfaces in the work of many creative geniuses, from Bob Dylan to jazz and blues musicians, and even in *The Simpsons*:

> Visual, sound, and text collage—which for many centuries were relatively fugitive traditions (a cento here, a folk pastiche there)—became explosively central to a series of movements in the twentieth century: futurism, cubism, Dada, musique concrète, situationism, pop art, and appropriationism. As examples accumulate—Igor Stravinsky's music and Daniel Johnston's, Francis Bacon's paintings and Henry Darger's, the novels of the Oulipo group and of Hannah Crafts (the author who pillaged Dickens's *Bleak House* to write *The Bondwoman's Narrative*), as well as cherished texts that become troubling to their admirers after the discovery of their "plagiarized" elements, like Richard Condon's novels or Martin Luther King Jr.'s sermons—it becomes apparent that appropriation, mimicry, quotation, allusion, and sublimated collaboration consist of a *sine qua non* of the creative act, cutting across all forms and genres in the realm of cultural production . . . consider the remarkable series of "plagiarisms" that link Ovid's "Pyramus and Thisbe" with Shakespeare's *Romeo and Juliet* and Leonard Bernstein's *West Side Story*, or Shakespeare's description of Cleopatra, copied nearly verbatim from Plutarch's life of Mark Antony and also later nicked by T.S. Eliot for *The Waste Land*. If these are examples of plagiarism, then we want more plagiarism.
>
> *(Lethem 2011: 126)*[1]

Repetition is a kind of game with (re)production and (re)presentation, which, ever since the Appropriationist Movement of the 1980s, has now become quite common in the contemporary art world. In fact, it was already present in the work of Robert Rauschenberg, namely, in his *Erased of Kooning Drawing* (1953), a ghost of the original in which the scraped marks suggest a reversed process of drawing (Bush 2019; Dworkin 2013), an almost blank piece of paper in a gilded frame that is Rauschenberg's erasure of a drawing obtained from Willem de Kooning for the explicit purpose of erasing it. But repetition is mainly found in Andy Warhol, the plagiarist *par excellence*, who, in an interview in 1963, asked, "But why should I be original? Why can't I be unoriginal" (Goldsmith 2011: 140)? This is an aesthetics disenchanted with the avant-gardism based on the "allegorical" strategies that fomented citation and recycling almost to the point of exhaustion. In this context, Barthes' idea of culture as an infinite palimpsest, the death of the author established by Barthes and Foucault, the repetition and nomadology of Deleuze and Guattari, and the culture of the simulacrum announced by Baudrillard were foundational for all of these developments (Castro 2014: 67; see also Burke 1995, Bennett 2005, Andersson 2018).

The exhibition that best synthesized this idea of repetition was undoubtedly *Pictures*, curated by Douglas Crimp in New York in 1977 (with the participation of artists such as Sara Charlesworth, Jack Goldstein, Sherrie Levine, Robert Longo, and Richard Prince). In fact, it was instrumental in the movement that challenged the concept of originality. However, there are also Marcel Duchamp's decontextualized objects (Perloff 1989: 193ff.; Perloff 2002: 77–120) and Francis Picabia's mechanical drawings, which are excellent examples of this tendency, as are the works of Jeff Koons, Cindy Sherman, Arakawa, Larry Rivers, and Tom Wesselman. Of course, one of the most well-known examples is Sherrie Levine, who copies Walker Evans, Joan Miró, or Marcel Duchamp,[2] among others. In her works, "what is offered to the gaze of the other is always a purloined image, a double or fake" (Owens 1992: 215). Later, Hermann Zschiegner copies Levine's copies and thus creates a palimpsest of palimpsests, a repetition from a repetition. His *+walkerevans+sherrielevine* is made up of 26 images of Allie Mae Burroughs that are the result of a Google search with the title of the series as a parameter. The same could be said of Yasumasa Morimura, who copies *Untitled 96* by Cindy Sherman, rewrites Cézanne's *Apples and Oranges* in *Criticism and the Lover A*, or repeats Manet in his 1989 painting *Daughter of Art History Theatre*. As Mieke Bal (1999: 1) states,

> Like any form of representation, art is inevitably engaged with what came before it, and that engagement is an active reworking. Hence, the work performed by later images obliterates the older images as they were before that intervention and creates new versions of old images instead.[3]

In literature, there are many authors to cite,[4] starting with Stéphane Mallarmé, passing through Gertrude Stein and Ezra Pound, to the mid-20th century with the concrete poetry and Fluxus Movements, among others. Also significant is the importance of citation in the work of Marcel Broodthaers, especially his 1973 artist book *Je hais le mouvement qui déplace les lignes by Charles Baudelaire* [*I hate the movement that displaces lines*], which is the seventh line of Baudelaire's sonnet "La Beauté" ["Beauty"]. In this first section, I would like to start by giving an overview of literary (un)creative writings by weaving together a number of authors that exemplify this repetitive original literature. The second section will concentrate on three original copyists—Enrique Vila-Matas, William Gaddis, and Ricardo Piglia; finally, the third section describes some contemporary copyists/translators such as Kenneth Goldsmith, Nicole Brossard, and Susan Daitch or Susan Howe.

2.1 Writing through

Why has the image of the double obsessed intellectuals throughout the ages? This obsession is reflected in music (Stravinsky's *Petruschka*, Falla's *El Amor Brujo*, and Richard Strauss' *Woman without a Shadow*) as well as in literature. For example, in José Saramago's *The History of the Siege of Lisbon* (1989/1996), how does a simple proofreader like Raimundo Silva dare to change the story of the siege of Lisbon and become an author (Arrojo 2018: 108–118)? In *The Double* (2002/2004), why is the reader so curious about which man is the duplicate and which is the original? Why does Tertuliano Máximo Afonso feel so uneasy about the possibility of being the copy in Saramago's novel? Is Saramago suggesting that history can be told from different perspectives? Could it be that deep down Tertualiano Máximo Afonso is afraid that the duplicate will take on a life of its own, that the re-presentation will definitively and irremediably become reality? What is the role of Herbert Quain, a nonexistent author invented by Borges, in Saramago's *The Year of the Death of Ricardo Reis* (1984/1991), Ricardo Reis being one of the three main heteronyms (copies? multiple and fragmented personalities?) of Fernando Pessoa? In this novel, why does Saramago allow the heteronym to outlive his creator by nine months? In Saramago's novels, repetition, doubles, duplication, translation, and the interplay between representation and reality are a constant (Martins and Sabine 2021).

Why are we haunted by the repetition in the sucking stones scene from Beckett's *Molloy*, a repetition also present in *Watt* as well as in his other work? In Beckett's *Quatre poèmes*, the left-hand page seems to indicate that the poems were originally written in French, but does that make them more legitimate than their "repetition"? Are they more authentic, even when we know that it was Beckett himself who translated them into English? Where is the presentation and where is the re-presentation?

Beckett is indeed one of the great masters of repetition, and he was even more captivated by the concept because of its philosophical implications. In fact, philosophers and sociologists such as Lukács, Kristeva, Lyotard, Foucault, Barthes, and Adorno have studied repetition based on his work. According to Beckett, the beginning of a play (*Molloy*, for example) and the end of a play (*Endgame* or *For to End Yet Again*) are so important because nothing spontaneously begins or ends by itself. Instead, Beckett suggests that everything is continuously in the process of beginning or ending, and each time the beginning and the end are different (Gendron 2008: xiv).

Nothing that is repeated is exactly the same. One's foot always steps into a different river. Beckett endlessly repeats and repeats (McGrath 2018; Connor 2007). He repeats objects (stones, sticks, hats) as well as characters (Murphy, Molloy, Malone, Malose, and Molly) whose names all begin with M, as though they were archetypes, versions, or rewritings of a previous one, which they almost never are. They are not simply copies. On the contrary, as the narrator of *Malone meurt* reminds us, each is a new re-presentation *sous un certain angle*. We are dealing not with a Platonic return that highlights the origin, and thus the great narratives of Western metaphysical conceptualization and its epistemology, but rather with something entirely different.

Repetition with difference triggers a disturbance at the foundations of Western thought. Notions such as those of origins and ends, arche and telos, fixed co-ordinates and stable identities, indeed the idea that there can be such a thing as meaning or truth, are all rendered suspect by this contemporary formulation of repetition.

(Gendron 2008: xv)

The beginning of *Molloy* is a magnificent example of Beckett's obsession with repetition and denial of origin. Alone in his mother's room, not knowing how he got there or why he is writing, Molloy tries to begin and does, though somewhat incoherently. In fact, the person who picks up the written pages tells him that he has made a mistake and that he should have started differently. This in turn gives rise to a philosophical reflection on whether this is indeed the first beginning or the second:

> Is the beginning to be presented that same beginning that was said to be all wrong? Is it to be a new, revised, beginning and so not the beginning that Molloy, like an old ballocks, had begun with? Why is beginning at the beginning to be condemned in the first place? Can a beginning be posited? And if posited, is the beginning merely, or necessarily, an arbitrary construct, a convenient place to start. . . . The apparent value placed on *this* beginning need not mean that this is *the* beginning. If anything, the value placed upon it by the agency would suggest that this is not the original "ballocksed" beginning, but the second beginning.
>
> *(Stewart 2006: 97)*

On the other hand, Molloy's use of present and past verb tenses, when referring to the beginning or beginnings of his writing, does not shed light on whether the beginning is actually the beginning or whether there is always a second beginning that falsifies or deconstructs the very idea of origin. The narrator highlights the problematic nature of this concept by variously repeating the beginning, though each time in a slightly different way. Oscillating between past and present, he begins again and then starts the beginning over once more, which negates the possibility of origin because this means that it is not really a beginning at all. For all these reasons, Beckett's writings are texts, though not books, at least according to Derrida's distinction in *Of Grammatology* (1967/1984). They thus exemplify what Derrida refers to as the disappearance of the identity of the origin.

And if, to all of this, we add the differences between the beginning of the French text and that of its English translation as well the countless differences in Beckett's self-translations, which are in constant dialogue, complementing and completing each other in the Borgesian sense, everything becomes considerably more complex. The difference between the originals and Beckett's translations is nothing more than an interplay of possible differences between texts, though not between books. The words "beginning" and "end", which are among the most repeated in Beckett's work, provide us with false beginnings and endings that are neither because the work never ends. As one of the narrators in *The Unnamable* observes, from the very first page, the text "begins to end". "Ending, it began". And in *Waiting for Godot*, it is not that "nothing happens" but rather that "nothing happens . . . twice".

To punish Echo, Ovid's nymph, Hera deprived her of speech, except for the ability to repeat the last words of another. In repetition, Echo repeats herself, and Narcissus reflects himself.[5] The examples of duplication and repetition unceasingly continue one after the other in Lewis Carroll's *The Other Side of the Looking Glass* and in *Seven Nights*, in which Borges confesses that the mirror is one of his nightmares. Duplication is also present in Poe's "The Oval Portrait" and "William Wilson". It can be perceived in works by François Bouvart and Juste Pécuchet, who were Flaubert's copyists, and in that of Akaky Akákievich Bashmachkin, Gógol's amanuensis, as well as in Herman Melville's Bartleby, Wilde's *Portrait of Dorian Gray*, and Woolf's *Orlando*. Further examples include Angela Carter's *The Passion of New Eve*.

According to Carlos Fuentes, "Originality is a disease". This same issue is raised in Nabokov's *Despair*, Robbe-Grillet's *Le miroir qui revient*, and Carlos Fuentes' *Aura*. It also appears in Handke's *La repetition*, in which repeating signifies beginning again instead of turning back. In Calvino's *Invisible Cities*, there is the translator of the city of Zirma, where memory is redundant and signs are repeated so that the city can begin to exist. Still another example is Calvino's *Cosmicomics*, in which Kgwgk assiduously erases the sign of Qfwfq and changes the "original" to another one that is blatantly contrived. And, of course, there is Marana, the highly visible translator of *If on a Winter's Night a Traveler*, who is perhaps a real author. Also worth mentioning is *Numbers* by Phillipe Sollers, a novel composed of quotations from Pascal, Nicolas de Cusa, Mao, Marx, Bourbaki, and Wittgenstein, as well as of Chinese ideograms, parentheses, ellipses, diagrams, etc. None of this forms a coherent whole but rather a series of grafts that creates a crooked storyline resembling a broken mirror.

The same happens with John Cage and his "found" texts, which are repeated but framed and rewritten in a different way. These are texts that, as Borges would say, complete the original. A good example is his "62 Mesostics Re Merce Cunnigham", whose typography makes it difficult to quote and whose meaning resists exegesis. Cage creates 62 mesostics that repeat the name of his partner, while writing through previous books. Subjecting them to I-Ching change operations, Cage mixes from Cunningham's *Changes*, namely, notes on *Choreography* and 32 books chosen by Cage from Cunningham's library. Here, "Mesostic 19" contains the word "Inging", meaning indefinite repetition, but this mesostic, as well as others such as number 20, repeats words like "mix", "crossing", "sum", "cross", and "we", which advocate "communal authorship" (Spinosa 2018: 23). These are mesostics that "articulate a noisy silence" (Spinosa 2016: 23).

Cage's "writings through" insist on this idea of repetition. For example, *Roaratorio* is a "writing through" of *Finnegans Wake* or Thoreau's *Empty Words*. Cage used elaborate rules for "writing through" these predecessor texts to give rise to poems that start from other poems but that are very different, such as his "writings through" of *The Cantos* (Cage 1982; Perloff 1989: 204ff.; Perloff and Junkerman 1994; Dworkin and Goldsmith 2011: 129–135; Spinosa 2018: 14–25; Kostelanetz 2003: 149–151). It is interesting to remember here that Cage, just like Stein, said that "there is no such thing as repetition" (in Kostelanetz 2003: 226). "You can't repeat anything exactly—even yourself"! he told Daniel Charles (in Perloff 1989: 203).

Also important is Cage's use of the tape recorder (Morris 1998), which so influenced poets like Frank O'Hara and John Ashbery. The tape recorder allowed them to connect and even superimpose voices. Instead of creating a collage, they were able to fashion a completely new fabric that was no longer linear, unlike the poetry of Ginsberg or Lowell (Perloff in Mallen 2012; Perloff in Morris 1998: 129–148). Perhaps because of Cage's new approach to creativity, in 1967, Ted Berrigan published an interview with Cage that was totally invented or, rather, pieced together from the cut-up texts of famous appropriationists, such as Warhol and Burroughs among others, all of which was attributed to Cage.[6]

In this sense, *a: a novel* by Andy Warhol is a paradigmatic work produced by mechanical processes. Because it is a nearly word-for-word transcription of dozens of cassette tapes, a 24-hour tape-recorded portrait of Warhol's world, a conventional reading is impossible, which was undoubtedly Warhol's goal. Each section of the book

> has a different typographical layout as a result of the idiosyncrasies of the various typists that worked on the tapes . . . maintaining all misspellings. What *a* ends up as is approaching the idea of a literary *vérité* that is a multiauthored text, riddled with the formal subjectivity of several transcribers, radically questioning the notions of singular authorial genius.
>
> (Goldsmith 2011: 145)

Furthermore,

> Warhol's other books, *The Philosophy of Andy Warhol*, *POPism*, *America*, and *Exposures*, were written by his assistants. . . . Their voice became his public voice, whereas Warhol largely remained silent. Those famous Warholian sound bites you hear—famous for fifteen minutes, etc.—often weren't written by him.
>
> (Goldsmith 2011: 46)

According to Goldsmith (2011: 149), the artistic and literary work of Warhol is an excellent example of what Roland Barthes called "text" in "The Death of the Author": "a tissue of citations, resulting from the thousand sources of culture". Writing, says Barthes, "is the destruction of every voice, of every point of origin" (Barthes 1977: 142):

> We know that a text is not a line of words releasing a single "theological" meaning (the "message" of the Author-God) but a multi-dimensional space in which a variety of writings, none of them original, blend and clash. The text is a tissue

of quotations drawn from the innumerable centres of culture. Similar to Bouvard and Pécuchet . . . the author can only imitate a gesture that is always anterior, never original.

(Barthes 1968/1977: 146)

Warhol created replicas: "It is no coincidence that the only books in which Warhol says 'I' were written by others" (Kotz 2007: 257; see also Kostelanetz 2019).

"Writing through" is also found in Jackson Mac Low, who writes through the prose and poetry of Gertrude Stein (Spinosa 2018: 3–14).[7] It is present in the works of authors such as Kathy Acker, who writes through Dickens in *Great Expectations* (1983) and through Cervantes in *Don Quixote (which was a dream)* (1986). Other examples include Eric Zboya's *un coup de dés jamais n'abolira le hasard: translations* (2018), a computerized model, a constellation in which no one of these visual, algorithmic translations of Mallarmé is the same; *Defenestration of Prague* (1983), Susan Howe's writing through Jonathan Swift's "Journal to Stella"; or *Dark Ladies*, in which Steve McCaffery writes through Shakespeare's *Sonnets*.

Repetition, understood as the original, had already appeared in 1925 in the work of Robert Desnos, Paul Éluard, André Breton, and Tristan Tzara, who proposed the creative method of the *cadavre exquis*. This technique involved writing from what had already been written and was what Pablo Neruda and Federico García Lorca would subsequently call *poemas al alimón* and what Nicanor Parra and Vicente Huidobro would refer to as *quebrantahuesos*. Also interesting are Lewis Carroll's doublets and Vladimir Nabokov's "golf language", in which a new word is formed from another with the same number of letters, as the letters are changed one at a time. William Burroughs, echoing the collages of Tristan Tzara, used the *cut-up*: by randomly juxtaposing his own texts with texts by other authors, Burroughs takes a finished text and cuts it into pieces. He recomposes and repeats to construct a new text.

From a different perspective, Robert Duncan regards his poetry as a derivative collage. In *The H. D. Book* (1961), he writes that the great art of our time "is the collagist's art, to bring all things into new complexes of meaning". In his *Diary*, Cage (2019: 13) recalls that Duncan spoke with him about appropriation:

> Robert Duncan told me his poetry was picked up from other people. The only time he felt, he said, like using quotation marks was when the words he wrote were his.

Passages is an example of Duncan's most radical poetics because of its use of allusion, rewriting, and expansion.[8] Duncan did not believe that the author had the authority to tell the reader how to interpret the text, and thus his constant use of repetition, as reflected in borrowings and quotations, in a "communal process" often seems to border on plagiarism. In *Passages*, Duncan employs the tapestry metaphor, which portrays him more as a compiler or mixer than as an author. *Ground Work* (1971) is composed of palimpsestic poems, sediments, resonances, and reworkings of other texts, thus constructing a "multilayered intertextuality, in the 'already-thereness' of the hypertext and by extension of the language structure" (Oudart 2011: 155).

Translation is one of the strategies that Duncan uses to twist and rewrite previous originals of Nerval (underlying *Passages 32*), Baudelaire (in *Ground Work* among many others), and Mallarmé (underwriting *An Interlude of Winter Light*). Duncan uniquely uses (non)translation, while reflecting "on the foreignness of the mother tongue" (Oudart in Collis and Lyons 2012: 112). His poetry is thus constructed in layers and based on citations, citations of citations, translations, and rewritings:

> Duncan's poetics of *transfiguration* is predicated upon a double displacement: quoting a fragment incurs a textual displacement, the wrenching of words from their original co-text, and this, of course, creates a first level of opacification; translating it performs another displacement, which, if no guarantor of transparency, renders the original accessible to the reader. Both displacements could be described as acts of appropriation. In appropriation resonates the word *propre*, used by Duncan in his diary entry. It consists in making what is foreign one's own.
>
> *(Oudart in Collis and Lyons 2012: 114)*

Duncan's palimpsests are objects that are never totally completed. Always in process, they are a continuous interplay between originals and translations. Consequently, in "At the Loom (Passages 2)" (*Bending the Bow* 9–10), Duncan is a weaver who is more interested in the process of intertwining threads, combining colors, and creating patterns than in the final tapestry. And in other poems, which are appropriations of the poetry of Nerval,

> Duncan conceals the next quote in his translation of Nerval's depiction of the riches from the temple housed in the Museum of Naples. . . . This passage is in turn intertwined with a quoted fragment drawn from the description of the sun and moon casting a dim, eerie light over the ruins of the temple at dusk. . . . Finally, the poem switches back to an unmarked translation until the end . . . only departing from the original source on two occasions. By keeping the word "ensemble," which is found in English in other contexts (musical, for instance), Duncan leaves in a trace of the original, a word with a foreign taste, possibly hinting at an underlying textual ground. Secondly, he performs another transformation of the ur-text by substituting "the scientists" for "les philosophes" in the closing lines of the poem.
>
> *(Oudart 2011: 157)*

Duncan's technique is so subtle that critics have difficulty discerning which is the original and which is the repetition: "Duncan's treacherous, half-said handling of quotations and translations—which partly turns the intertextual clues into red herrings—may induce unwary critics to quote him when they are in fact unwittingly quoting Duncan quoting Nerval" (Oudart 2011: 158). His use of translation in his derivative poems, which are appropriations and repetitions of preceding ones, involves viewing it as a way of enriching the original text with additional readings as Borges did (see Chapter 3). For example, in his Passage "Et", he defamiliarizes a Renaissance translation of *The Odyssey* used by Pound:

> In translating Pound's first "song", the poet performs both appropriation and defamiliarization. In the process he creates the possibility to "make it new", for in translating this fragment, both writer and reader rediscover the inaugural magic of a new reading. In steering away from the mother tongue, the poet vivifies the infant mind. The "foreign" tongue resulting from this procedure, I would argue, is the paradigm of the Other language: for the native speaker of English and French alike . . . Duncan's process of writing is not driven by a teleological aim or an urge to "make it cohere" but, rather, one "to copy this palimpsest".
>
> *(Oudart in Collis and Lyons 2012: 115, 122)*

Duncan uses repetition in these and other poems such as *The Concert*, in which he repeats without explicitly quoting or changing a word written by Charles Olson (whom he refers to as "the Poet"). Nevertheless, this is not plagiarism, because Duncan believed that one never owns the words that one has written. His repetitions of Olson's *Projective Verse* are fairly easy to identify. On the other hand, he quotes Rudolf Bultmann twice, describing him as "the scholar", while changing only a few of the original words. All this transforms *The Concert* into a grand collage in which the repetition of texts by other authors represents a way of understanding the world (Spinosa 2018: 27–28).

In addition, Duncan's multilingualism adds to the complexity of his work.[9] This occurs in *Transmissions*, in which there are uncredited quotes in Greek from Heraclitus and Italian quotes from Dante, which are not translated perhaps because of their difficulty and/or their multiple meanings. Duncan is a clear example of a derivative writer whose work "is built around the central refusal of genius and originality as such, taking on instead the mantle of 'derivative' poet" (Collis in Collis and Lyons 2012: xi).

Raymond Queneau of the OuLiPo group[10] repeats the same event in 99 different ways in his *Exercises of Style* (1947), and he expects the reader to be able to repeat and combine the same words from only ten sonnets and, thus, create 100 million million poems, *Cent millards de poèmes* (1961). This is similar to the infinite combinations proposed by Maux Aub's *Juego de cartas* (1964), B.S. Johnson's *The Unfortunates* (1969), and Marc Saporta's *Composition N1* (1962). Currently, poets such as Kenneth Goldsmith, Leevi Lehto, Craig Dworkin, and Caroline Bergvall use repetition as a strategy to create what Perloff (2010) and Goldsmith (2011) call (un)creative, (un)original writings.

For example, *OO: Typewriter Poems* (2020) by Dani Spinosa is a collection of poems that are

> deeply citational . . . quoting "lines" from visual and concrete poems and playing fast and loose with the form of the *glosa*, where four lines from an original poem are repurposed in a new poem as the final lines of four ten-line stanzas.
>
> *(Spinosa 2020: 1)*

Glosas are Renaissance courtly forms that pay tribute to another poet by constructing lines from that poet. Because Spinosa's *glosas* pay homage to visual poets, such as John Cage, Carl Andre, Christian Bök, Bob Cobbing, Steve McCaffery, Derek Beaulieu, and Raymond Federman (among others), layout, font choice, and page design are important elements. Nonetheless, Spinosa does not merely retype their poems. The wide variety of processes that she uses are infinitely more complex and ultimately depend on poets and their poetry. Spinosa's poems are already a kind of rewriting of the poets to whom she pays homage: "I mean to show that love by re-representing these poems amongst my own words and letterforms" (Spinosa 2020: 2). In an interview with Eva Heisler (*Asymptote*), she explains:

> For the poem "Eric Schmaltz", I took four lines from Schmaltz's work in *Surfaces*, which took its lexicon from Amazon descriptions of printing and writing technology, and then I mined my own typewriter manuals for words of the exact same length to produce four ten-line stanzas where each line had the exact same number of letters. For the poem "Steve McCaffrey", I took four lines from his "Suprematist Alphabet" and took away letters to produce lines that reverse-cleaned themselves up in their stanzas. For the poem "Bob Cobbing", I typed his four lines spaced out, and then I just played around until I thought it looked like a teenage girl Bob Cobbing could have written in. For the poem "John Cage", I used a Cagean mesostic procedure to create and then manipulate the poem I found by using Cage's mesostic rules on Claudia Rankine's *Don't Let Me Be Lonely*. I figured Cage wouldn't want me to use his own name or writing.
>
> *(www.asymptotejournal.com/visual/typewriters-desire-community-dani-spinosa/)*

This kind of pre-hypertextual literature has a fragmentary structure that the Internet will doubtlessly develop to infinity (Perloff 2010; Perloff 2013), because there are multiple possibilities and no preestablished order. New technologies have greatly influenced repetition (Marczewska 2018) and have now become a key factor to understanding text and author as Barthesian concepts. To cite one example of many, there are currently several web-based versions of Queneau's poems that encourage digital literary construction.

Critics such as Goldsmith (2011, 2015a, 2015c, 2016b, 2020) and Dworkin (2020a) have analyzed how new technologies encourage the use of repetition as a creative strategy and as a "raging cultural practice" (Goldsmith in Morris 2009: xi; see also Edmond 2019). One of the most pertinent examples of this is *Twitterature. The World's Greatest Books Retold Through Twitter* (Penguin 2009), a book by Alexander Aciman and Emmet Rensin, both students at the University of Chicago, who transformed 80 literary classics into a maximum of 20 Twitter posts. This tool also generated stories based on retweets, such as the one by Teju Cole, who composed it as a *cadavre exquise*.

Repetition is also present in "flarf poetry" (Milesi 2015; Epstein 2012: 318ff.) or in the many digital repetitions of literary works, such as the retyping of Kerouac's *On the Road* (1951). From May 31, 2008, to March 2009, Simon Morris, a British artist, wrote a page a day in his blog *Getting Inside Jack Kerouac's Head*. He decided to conduct this experiment after reading Kenneth Goldsmith. In *Uncreative Writing*, Goldsmith devotes a chapter to Morris' retyping of Kerouac. There, as well as in his introduction to Morris' novel, Goldsmith mentions how art students copy the old masters and wonders if that activity could be successfully applied to literature. He recalls that Walter Benjamin, in *Reflections*, asserts that "the power of the text is different when it is read from when it is copied out" (Goldsmith in Morris 2009: viii). Goldsmith agrees that copying Kerouac is not the same as reading him and also points out that Morris added words in his retyping, because Kerouac's shorthand allows the reader to complete his sentences. Although Morris claims that he removed the additions when he proofread the text, some may have remained. This example is used by Goldsmith to demonstrate that identical repetition does not exist and that repetition can be creative, a different text. This is how Morris shows that appropriation is more than the same: it is the way to reach "a different sort of creativity in the 'author', producing different versions and additions—remixes even—of an existing text. Morris is both reader and writer in the most active sense of the word" (Goldsmith 2011: 153).

Morris (2009) eventually published his performative retyping, his (un)creative writing, with the title *Getting Inside of Kerouac's Head*. The book cover is almost an exact repetition of the design and typography of the edition of *On the Road* published by Penguin Modern Classics. Repetition was thus also present in the book cover and in the paratexts. According to the blurb on the back cover, the book follows the default logic of a blog archive because the last post is at the beginning, followed by the rest of the entries in reverse order. Thus, whereas Kerouac traveled from the East coast to the West, Morris makes the journey in the opposite direction.

This idea is also reflected in the page numbers of the novel, which begin on page 408 and end on page 109. This forces readers to take a different path than the one to which they are accustomed. They are obliged to read backward and turn the pages in reverse. The sensations experienced are thus different from those when readers turn the pages in the forward direction. In this way, Morris not only forces us to reflect on the process of reading but also highlights the relationship of the novel with the initial blog:

Getting Inside Jack Kerouac's Head is a reprint of Morris's blog devoted to retyping Kerouac's novel, one page at a time. The paperback version of the project follows the logic of blog publishing, to preserve the reversed order in which blog posts typically appear, foregrounding their commitment to the new as a characteristic feature of this publishing method. While Morris worked his way through *On the Road* a page per blog post, in a traditional, linear fashion, from the first page to the novel's closing sentence, Morris's reader is faced first with what Morris read and retyped last.

(Marczewska 2018: 38)

Published in the digital age, Morris' novel is not, nor can it ever be (as is the case with Pierre Menard), a mere repetition of Kerouac's. In fact, Morris plays with the well-known beginning of *On the Road* and with the last entry of his blog, something that clearly shows that it is impossible to repeat because the context is always different:

When you open Morris's book, the famous first line of *On the Road*, "I first met Dean not long after my wife and I split up", is nowhere to be seen. Instead, the first line is a sentence already in progress: "concert tickets, and the names Jack and Joan and Henri and Vicki, the girl, together with a series of sad jokes and some of his favorite sayings such as 'You can't teach the old maestro a new tune'." Of course, the first page of Morris's book is his final blog entry from his marathon retyping, and so, the end of the first page of Morris's book is the ending of Kerouac's scroll, "I think of Neal Cassidy". The book unfolds this way throughout, progressing backward, page by page (Morris's first page is numbered 408, his second is 407, etc.) until he reaches the start of Kerouac's original text . . . Morris eloquently sums up the project by claiming "there are more differences than similarities which makes it challenging that the same piece of writing, typed up in a different context, is an entirely new piece of writing".

(Goldsmith 2011: 156)

Eunoia (2001) by Christian Bök is also based on repetition. This text takes the lipogram to extremes because each chapter uses a single vowel, which the author repeats in each word. *Eunoia* won Canada's Griffin Poetry Prize in 2002 and, despite the difficulty of the text, sold thousands of copies. "Eunoia", which means "beautiful thinking", is the shortest English word that contains all five vowels. The work has five parts, each of which has a constraint because it only uses words containing one vowel. Given Bök's admiration for Perec, he dedicated the "W" of "Oiseau" (Bök 2001: 92–94) and "Emended Excess" (ibid.: 95–100) to him:

"Oiseau" (the French word for "bird") is the shortest word in French to contain all five vowels. *Oiseau* pays tribute to the French precedents for *Eunoia*.

"And Sometimes" itemizes every English word that contains only consonants. "Vowels" is an anagrammatic text, permuting every letter in the title. "Voile" is a homophonic translation of the sonnet "Voyelle" by Arthur Rimbaud. "W" is an elegy for the favourite letter of Georges Perec, who . . . admires one of the few consonants that can make a vowel sound. "Emended Excess" exhausts vocabulary unsuitable for use in the retelling of the Iliad.

(Bök 2001: 104–105)

Taking *La Disaparition* (1969) as a model but reversing Perec's process (Perloff 2004b: 34; Bök 2001: 105; Hofstadter 1997: 107–232), Bök repeats a vowel instead of eliminating it, thus making a rather peculiar use of the dictionary (Dworkin 2020b: 16). As Bök himself points out,

All chapters allude to the art of writing. All chapters must describe a culinary banquet, a prurient debauch, a pastoral tableau and a nautical voyage. All sentences must accent internal rhyme through the use of syntactical parallelism. The text must exhaust the lexicon for each vowel, citing at 98% of the available repertoire (although a few words do go unused, despite efforts to include them: *parallax, belvedere, gingivitis, monochord,* and *tumulus*).

(Bök 2001: 103–104)

Bök aspires not only to exhaust the lexicon for each vowel but also to closely examine the intrinsic nature of each one. As Perloff (2004b: 36–37) observes, the *A* is evocative of the exotic East as well as of law and bans. It contrasts with the *E*, which is elegiac and recurrent in polite speech. *I* is lyrical and appears in the language of wit; *O* reflects solemnity (with words such as "book", "Oxford dons", "Word", and "God"), whereas *U* is the dirty vowel (with words like "fuck" or "cunt"):

Ubu untucks Ruth's muumuu; thus Ruth must untruss Ubu's tux. Ubu fluffs Lulu's tutu. Ubu cups Lulu's dugs; Ubu rubs Lulu's buns; thus Lulu must pull Ubu's pud. Ubu sucks Ruth's cunt; Ubu cuffs Ruth's butt. Ubu stuffs Ruth's bum (such fun). Ubu pumps Lulu's plush, sun-burnt tush. Ubu humps Lulu's plump, upthrust rump. Ubu ruts. Ubu huffs; Ubu puffs. Ubu blurts; *push, push*. Ubu thrusts. Ubu bucks. Cum spurts. Ubu cums.

(Bök 2001: 79)

Not surprisingly, a text like this poses major translation problems, which have not only one solution but many. In fact, there are probably as many solutions as there are readers and translators in the different cultures in which *Eunoia* has been read/interpreted/translated. For example, the connotations that Bök attributes to each vowel do not necessarily coincide in different languages and cultures (Cisneros 2018: 52).

Translation of such a work demands that the translator must be creative and dare to adopt imaginative, rhizomatic solutions. Such solutions do not pursue a faithful translation in the prescriptivist sense of the word but rather aspire to a rewriting that maintains the author's intentionality but that allows the translator to intervene. Bök is the author of other unconventional works that would also require creative translations, such as *The Xenotext Experiment* (2008), a BioArt project in which he "translates" (his choice of verb) poetry into DNA and DNA into poetry. He also wrote *The Kazimir Effect* (2021), which was listed in the *Times Literary Supplement* as one of the Books of the Year for 2021.

Undoubtedly, there are many authors who play with language form (Stephens 2020; Terry 2019), as well as with the alphabet, and create alphabet poetry (Bassnett in Corbett and Huang 2020: 14–16). An excellent example is *Alphabetical Africa* (1974) by Walter Abish, which has now become a classic. In the first chapter, all of the words begin with *a*; in the second chapter, they all start with *a* and *b*, and so on down to *z*. From then on, Abish eliminates letters until he reaches the last chapter, which, like the first, contains only words beginning with *a*:

> Ages ago, Alex, Allen and Alva arrived at Antibes, and Alva allowing all, allowing anyone, against Alex's admonition, against Allen's angry assertion: another African amusement . . . anyhow, as all argued, an awesome African army assembled and arduously advanced against an African anthill, assiduously annihilating ant after ant, and afterward, Alex astonishingly accuses Albert as also accepting Africa's antipodal ant annexation. Albert argumentatively answers at another apartment. Answers: ants are Ameisen. Ants are Ameisen?
>
> *(Abish 1974: 1)*

Another example is Mark Dunn, the author of *Ella Minnow Pea: A Novel in Letters* (2001), which is an epistolary novel published the same year as *Eunoia*. The story is set on the fictional island of Nollop, where the pangram "The quick brown fox jumps over the lazy dog" is greatly revered. This pangram or holoalphabetic sentence is a sentence composed of all the letters of the alphabet. Perfect pangrams are those that are also a heterogram, a sentence in which none of the letters is repeated. To some extent, a pangram is the opposite of a lipogram, in which a certain letter or group of letters is intentionally omitted.

Ella Minnow Pea begins at the moment when the tiles containing the letters of the holoalphabetic inscription begin to progressively fall from the monument that commemorates the iconic sentence. In view of the divine respect for the phrase on the island, the government of Nollop prohibits both the spoken and written use of the fallen letters under penalty of law. As the letters continue to drop off, they also disappear from the narrative, which becomes increasingly lipogramatic. Finally, only five letters (*L*, *M*, *N*, *O*, and *P*) can be used by the fictitious inhabitants and by the author. This book has been translated into languages such as French (*L'Isle Lettrée* by Marie-Claude Plourde), Italian (*Lettere: Fiaba epistolare in lipogrammi progressivi* by Daniele Petruccioli), and German (*Nollops Vermächtnis* by Henning Ahrens).

Three years later, in 2004, Mark Dunn published *Ibid: A Novel* created from endnotes, because the original text had disappeared. The novel is preceded by an epistolary exchange between Mark Dunn, who is one of the characters (and who, incidentally, claims to have a twin brother), and Pat, his editor. When, in a first letter, Dunn confesses that he has not made a copy of his extensively documented novel, the editor writes to sadly inform him that that the original manuscript no longer exists because her naughty son accidentally knocked it into a bathtub and destroyed it. In this case, the nonexistence of repetition or copies is the origin of the original. The resulting novel is composed entirely of endnotes, which in most publications are regarded as secondary or marginal.

Also worth mentioning is Jonathan Safran Foer's *Tree of Codes* (2010), in which he takes the erasure technique[11] to the extreme. Erasure reminds the reader that texts are made out of other texts. Texts are palimpsests.[12] As is well-known, *Tree of Codes* is constructed from a translation of Bruno Schulz' *Street of Crocodiles*. In *Tree of Codes*, the title is carved out of the previous title, *Street of Crocodiles*. Foer progressively deletes words from Schulz' English translation, literally cutting them out. The result is a peculiar book that is the creative repetition of an earlier one, which in turn is the rewriting of another. *Tree of Codes* is a translated palimpsest that has been extensively analyzed (Szymanska 2020; Pressman 2018; Hayles 2013; Gibbons 2012). Like Derrida's *sous rature*, repetition is used here along with erasure to reconstruct "what is always already inscribed" (Spivak 1967/1984: lxxvii).

A similar strategy is applied by Nick Thurston in *Reading the Remove of Literature* (2006), which is written from the English translation of Maurice Blanchot's *L'Espace littéraire* (1955). Thurston erases it and resets his own marginalia, thus reducing it to referential notation. The absent space left by the original text remains there to remind us that the new text, Thurston's annotative writing, does not replace it. Thurston repeats, appropriates, and "erasures" Blanchot's translated text, thus transforming it into a new repeated book through the transposition of handwriting into formal typography. Eight years later, Kristen Muller wrote *Partially Removing the Remove of Literature* (No Press 2014), a palimpsest created from Thurston's palimpsest. Kristen Mueller appropriates the appropriation of Nick Thurston by partially erasing every page of his book, leaving only the nonverbal diagrammatic traces, namely, Thurston's extratextual markings (parentheses, exclamation marks, underlining, arrows, circles, and asterisks).

Of course, in this context, one must not forget Derek Beaulieu's *a, A Novel* (2017), commissioned by Jean Boîte Editions. Like Goldsmith's erasures of Gertrude Stein, Beaulieu's is an erasure-based translative response to Warhol's (1968) previously mentioned novel of the same title. In this digitally erased version, he deletes everything in the pages of Warhol's novel except the punctuation marks, typists' insertions, and onomatopoeic words. The result is totally visual and musical, reminiscent of the traffic signs and bustling street noise of New York City in the 1960s. Furthermore, Beaulieu evidences the work of all the uncredited transcribers upon whom Warhol relied to "create" "his" novel, as pointed out by Gilda Williams (Beaulieu 2017: 462). In addition, Beaulieu's *Local Color* (ntamo 2008) is a series of color blocks based on *Ghosts*, a novella by Paul Auster, and his *Flatland* (2008), also a writing through, is a visual, palimpsestic translation, whose visual patterns are based on the typography of Edwin Abbott's classic novel of the same title.

In this same line, another well-known example is Thomas Phillips' *A Humument: A Treated Victorian Novel*, a work in progress since 1966. Phillips wanted to find a second-hand book for three pennies and alter each page through painting, collage, and cut-up to create a new book resembling a pack of cards (Marczewska 2018: 71). The book that he found was W.H. Mallock's *A Human Document* (1892), a fragmented book full of letters and journals and "covered with images which obscure the content but leave a selection of words visible, words that create the text of from which came *A Humument*" (Marczewska 2018: 71). The title, *A Humument*, is a creative repetition of *A Human Document*. Phillips cuts, pastes, paints, circles, types, collages, and covers Mallock's work, so that a new repeated and erased text is born with a few words from the source text remaining on each page. As Marczewska (2018: 74) explains, the process lasted from 1966 to 2016, during which he added iterations, repetitions, alterations, and cultural adaptations, depending on the prevailing context at the time (for example, the 9/11 attack on the Twin Towers in the fifth edition of 2012), with each edition of the book providing a rewriting of the first "original" text. Today *A Humument* is a literary work and a widely exhibited visual art piece. The story is a nonlinear, iterative, fragmented narrative with many orders. The compositional technique used is reminiscent of Queneau's *Cent mille milliards de poèmes* (1961) [*A Hundred Thousand Billion Poems*], Marc Saporta's *Composition No. 1* (1962), and B.S. Johnson's *The Unfortunates* (1969), all "examples of books in a box, comprising a set of loose pages" (Marczewska 2018: 73).

There are many other examples of creations through erasure. These range from Ronald Johnson's *Radi os* (1977), a rewriting by excision of the first four books of the 1892 edition of John Milton's *Paradise Lost*, to works such as Mary Ruefle's *A Little White Shadow* (2006), which brings new meaning by painting over much of a forgotten 19th-century book, or Jen Bervin's *The Desert* (2008), an art piece in which Bervin sews with blue thread over the "erased" words of John Van Dyke's *The Desert* (1901), a text that is in fact a palimpsest because the "original" is still visible beneath the threads (see also Bervin 2012: 126–131).[13] Bervin creates *The Desert* using a method that is "literally textile". What is important here is that

> the calibrated engagement and source is visible apparent to a reader so that they can draw all of the interconnections, arguments, and arrows created in the friction and conjoined space of what Donna Haraway would call a "contact zone", where the dynamics of the authors involved, the literary and historical context, approach and process all matter. Instead of erasure, let's definitely call it "entanglement"—in the quantum and enmeshed textile senses of the word. . . . What if

"being many, seeming one" meant being more fully us? I like to think readers are "many" too—in that readers differ in what a poem means to them, but also that ant reader holds "being many" in their intersectionality.

(Bervin to Rankine 2021: 69)

In *Nets* (2004/2019), Bervin uses Shakespeare's sonnets as her material for writing anew. She feels that "erasure" is a misnomer for a work whose title suggests, Claudia Rankine (2021: 69) argues, "what cannot be contained and also what gets caught", what has been "dropped out but remains tethered". In *Nets*, Bervin plays with the font color of some words—those of the source text are faded, and from them Bervin's poem emerges:

> I stripped Shakespeare's sonnets bare to the "nets" to make the space of the poems open, porous, possible—a divergent elsewhere. When we write poems, the history of poetry is with us, preinscribed in the white of the page; when we read or write poems, we do it with or against this palimpsest.
>
> (Bervin 2004/2019: n.p.)

Travis Macdonald's *The O Mission Repo* (2008) could also be mentioned here. This is an iteration and erasure of the official 9/11 Report, which was extremely controversial because of its omissions and distortions (Marczewska 2018: 89–102). Another example is Vanessa Place's *Tragodía 1: Statement of Facts* (2010), an appropriation of witness reports by victims of sexual assault (she is a writer, an artist, and an attorney), her series of poems called "Self Portraits" taken from other's impressionistic selfies as posted on Facebook, her retyping on Twitter of *Gone with the Wind* (2011), or *ONE* (2012), a book co-written with Blake Butler and assembled by Christopher Higgs, who merged Place's and Butler's narrations by only copying and pasting their words. And additional examples include Janet Holmes' *The ms of m y kin* (2009), a repeating and erasing of Emily Dickinson, Yedda Morrison's *Darkness* (2012), constructed by erasing the first chapter of Joseph Conrad's *Heart of Darkness*, and Robert Fitterman's "The Sun Also Also Rises" (1959), which erases Hemingway, leaving only the phrases beginning with the pronoun *I* (Marczewska 2018: 74ff.; Kaufmann 2017; Horn 2015: 196ff.; Epstein 2012: 319ff.; Place and Fitterman 2009; Dworkin 2003: 128ff.; Dworkin 2013: 40ff.; McCaffery 2002: 124; Bush 2019). In his 2009 version, *My Sun Also Rises*, Fitterman translates "the erased version of the first part into my own experience of moving to downtown Manhattan in 1981. In the chapbook version, there is a 3rd book, Also Also Also Rises, The Sun, written by Nayland Blake" (Fitterman 2009: 107).

In all of these cases and many others, the end result is an enormous palimpsest in which an act of erasure "is always an act of repetition" (Marczewska 2018: 75). Writing by means of erasure is, in these examples, a collaborative repetition

> that gives rise to a third subjectivity . . . a repetition of the complete source text that assumes not only a hybrid subjectivity, but also a hybrid form, with erasure

structured as an act of textual removal and a graft at the same time, of a trace and a supplement.

(Marczewska 2018: 83)[14]

The same is true of the other novels previously mentioned that bring earlier texts into a new context. This involves, like any Borgesian translation, a reframing of old texts into new contexts, a reinterpretation, a rewriting that produces a "book-eating book" (see Ho 2016). Here "the relationship between the reinscribed text and the so-called original text is not that of patency and latency, but rather the relationship between the two palimpsests" (Spivak 1967/1984: lvxxv). And a palimpsest

> always enacts a double play of concealment and revelation, erasing one text to inscribe another and then suppressing the latter to display the first. The palimpsest obstructs to make a view possible. Appropriately, the word means both a document that has been erased as well as one on which writing appears, and it records that doubling etymologically. "Palimpsest", from the classical Latin *palimpsestus* (paper or parchment that has been written on again), derives from the Hellenistic Greek παλίμψηστος (scraped again) and παλίμψηστον (a parchment from which writing has been erased), which in turn ultimately derive from the ancient Greek πάλιν (again) plus ψηστός, from the verb "to sand". . . . Balanced between its verbal and nominative senses—between removing and delivering, erasing and communicating—"sand", like "palimpsest", encompasses both the emission of a message and its omission.
>
> (Dworkin 2013: 43–44)

2.2 Three original copyists

Viewed in this light, repetition has to do with Deleuze and Guattari's concept of rhizome and Foucault's archive. Repetition is a platypus, an animal that, according to Borges, is composed of pieces of other animals. It is thus a kind of "ircocervo", a game described by Umberto Eco in his *Second Minimal Diary*, which involves the creation of a "new" author from two others that are already known.

At this point, I would like to refer to three writers who use repetition, copies, and copyists to create original writings. An important reference is Bartleby, Melville's mysterious and cryptic copyist, whom Enrique Vila-Matas (2000/2005) repeats, copies, and takes as a starting point in his *Bartleby & Co*.[15] The novel begins as a diary and then goes on to become a book of footnotes, commenting on an invisible text. *Mac & His Problem* (2017/2019) is a novel about copying and about the pleasure of repetition, about words written on words written on top of more words. *Esta bruma insensata* (2019) [*This Senseless Haze*], a title taken from Queneau, is about Simon Schneider, a "previous translator" or *hokusai*, as he calls himself. Simon collects other people's words. He provides "distant authors" (including Thomas Pynchon) with quotations. Vila-Matas assumes the role of copyist/translator because he doubts the existence of the original. His wish is to go unnoticed and to hide behind his text, which he does not consider a close territory with a single and ultimate meaning. He writes in order to stop writing so that the story can finally leave its mark. Writing allows him to express what he most needs to say, but it also permits him to gradually discover where his words are leading him. For Mac, for Simon, and for Vila-Matas, authorship is

> a slippery notion. . . . Writers repeat when they write, readers repeat when they read, and even when Mac is doing neither of these things, "the mere act of breathing, of course, meant I was repeating myself . . . voices and stories and phrases are endlessly reflected—repeated and modified, quoted and archived".
>
> *(McDermott 2019: 22)*

Borges, Vila-Matas, and Deleuze all know that writers are repeaters and that their most cherished illusion is to falsify. In this regard, Vila-Matas repeats by modifying the text. He copies the copy of a copy of a copy. He is a repeater who never stops altering words and phrases. Paradoxically, his originality relies on the fact that his writing "is marked by a dazzling array of quotation, plagiarism, frames, self-plagiarism, digressions and meta-digressions" (Thirlwell 2020: n.p.). Many of his novels are magnificent reflections on the translation process, on repetition as creation, and on the potential capacity of any origin to gradually unfold and expand into new universes. Like his Walter, the translator is a ventriloquist with an infinite number of voices that, in Borgesian style, progressively complete the original.

It is in the fissures where the secret signs or contradictions dwell. They are what finally transforms a literary work into a masterpiece. Like Vila-Matas, translators are also aware that the original is a Chinese box, always full of stories and references to other authors, because literature, in the same way as its translation, is never a definitive place. It can always accommodate a new turn of the screw. Literature is Vila-Matas' *Dublinesque*, a palimpsest.

Still another copyist/translator is the one in William Gaddis' *The Recognitions* (1955), a novel abounding in forgery, falsification, and plagiarism. In fact, it is "perhaps the first American novel to deal at length with the quandaries of assessing originality in a cultural environment predicated on an abundance of copies, representations and simulacra" (Benesch 2007: 30). Like Benjamin's vase, its fragments can never be put back together again in quite the same way, though one never stops trying. Gaddis' novel is full of historical, pseudo-historical, or counterfeit figures (Moore 1982). Two central themes are originality and creativity:

> Layers of citations simultaneously frame his analysis and deliberately call into question its originality. As if to mock his own literary ambitions, Gaddis freely admits that his work is not original but is a copy of a work whose author is a fake. His novel, in other words, is a copy of a copy whose origin is unknown.
>
> *(Taylor 2013: 16)*

Wyatt, the main character, makes us feel as though we are always on the verge of remembering something that is just outside our grasp such as crossed-out meanings (in the sense of Derrida's *sous rature*), which are there yet not there, because recognition is repetition. Like Andy Warhol, Gaddis repeats and translates each cultural reference, each echo, and each origin. Nevertheless, according to Lacan, repetition is not mere duplication but an action that allows us to bring the past to the present and to relive it: "Chapter upon chapter, association upon association, allusion upon allusion, the work unravels and becomes hypertextual—click on any name, word, term, idea, or image, and you are led to another node in a seemingly infinite textual web" (Taylor 2013: 18).

That is why the novel plays with the concepts of original and copy, as when the protagonist's father buys the original of *The Seven Deadly Sins*, a painting by Hieronymous Bosch, but when he goes through customs he declares it as a copy. Years later, Wyatt makes a copy of the painting and substitutes it for the "original", which he sells to a collector, but he realizes that in fact "it was only a copy after all that his father had bought and that he had copied" (Johnston 1990: 10). Then he discovers that the trick that he had intended to play on his father, namely, to exchange the copy for the original, was also played on him. So, as it turns out, the painting was, in fact, the original, although "in [a] final reversal, Wyatt discovers the painting he has taken to be the 'original' was indeed only a copy" (Johnston 1990: 10): "And it was false all the time! He spoke with more effort than he had yet made to control his voice.—Copying a copy? is that where I started" (Gaddis 1955/1993: 381)?

The Recognitions shows the reversal of the Platonic paradigm within "a situation in which 'originals' no longer automatically assume primacy over copies, or a model over its image" (Johnston 2004: 136). Unlike Saramago's duplicated man, Wyatt, who eventually becomes his own fictional character, is finally convinced that only a falsification can achieve true perfection. In fact, Wyatt not only copies great masters

> but also fabricates, under their name, works they have never painted. Using genuine canvass and other material of the period he fakes their style to make an original, and he thus falsifies precisely what Benjamin calls the "historical testimony" of art. What makes those forgeries interesting is that they are unoriginal originals.
> *(Gutbrodt 2003: 14)*

Thus, Wyatt "copies" the 15th-century Flemish painter Hans Memling, a Baudrillardian simulacrum because

> Wyatt's painting is neither an imitation nor an original but a simulation of a Memling or a simulacrum. It is not an imitation or copy because there is (was) no original, but it is not an original either since it was not painted by Memling himself.
> *(Johnston 1990: 11)*

Gaddis' text offers us a multidimensional Barthesian space in which a series of writings intermingle and collide. These writings, which are not original either, are quotations taken from numerous sources. Wyatt is a painter of translations who offers us writable texts while copying the great masters, whose original form he has no wish to retain.

Another fascinating example of this game of mirrors between reality and fiction, between translation and original, is the work of Ricardo Piglia. His complex and intricate novels abound in parody, quotations, and translations, all of which embrace what is foreign, different, and not "original", where fiction intersects with nonfiction. Little wonder that Piglia, the copyist, is fascinated by the episode in *Ulysses* in which Stephen Dedalus and his friends meet in a library to discuss *Hamlet* and end up proposing a series of deviant, eccentric, and even delirious readings of the play. He is also fascinated by translators, who for him are a disturbing type of writer, because they work with the texts of others in the precarious and shifting limit between one language and another, that fissure populated by a legion of misalignments, mismatches, and imbalances. For Piglia, to switch languages is one of his secret desires, which he believes can be achieved without leaving one's own language.

For this reason, in *Artificial Respiration* (1981/1994), Piglia translates the well-known phrase from *Ulysses*, "History is a nightmare from which I am trying to wake up", as "La historia es el único lugar donde consigo aliviarme de esta pesadilla de la que trato de despertar".[16] This phrase encompasses what translation means to him. It is a process that creates a complex connection between two languages in which one language is interwoven into the other and vice versa. Each language needs the other not only because of the way they differ but also because of how they differ. As Borges would say, they complement and complete each other. The game of mirrors, repetition, and translation is a parallelism that is always different yet the same.

Nevertheless, it is in *The Absent City* (1992/2000) where Piglia best develops his idea that all communication is translated. The novel is actually many possible novels, with a multitude of centers that broadcast many voices. The real protagonist, however, is a machine that recovers the collective memory that the State is trying to erase. *The Absent City* consists of stories and characters that are duplicated. Its main goal is not only to re-produce Elena de Obieta but also to translate stories and challenge the lies of the State. Repetition is a constant in Piglia's work, such as "Homage to Roberto Artl", *Artificial Respiration*, and "Prisión perpetua", but here it becomes a way of rejecting imposed readings and challenging a single enforced interpretation.

For this reason, Sergio Waisman, the English translator of *Assumed Name* and *The Absent City*, states that while translating these novels, he realized that these texts were themselves translations. Despite the fact that they overflowed with quotations, references, allusions, and characters taken from other writers, their originality was undeniable. Like Borges and Arlt, whom he greatly admires, Piglia shows us that translation can be an act of resistance. Thus, as in Borges' work, the game with Arlt's unpublished (and false) manuscript in *Assumed Name* (1975) deconstructs the concepts of original, authorship, reality, identity, ownership, and fiction. This is achieved through the search for a manuscript that does not exist, which is then included in a narrator's book and apocryphally attributed to the wrong author.

For Piglia, representation, the game of mirrors, and the dissolution of the Real are a modus operandi. It is hardly surprising that Roque, one of the characters in *Artificial Respiration*, is a translator and that, in *The Absent City*, Macedonio is trying to produce a replica not of a man but rather of a machine for reproducing replicas, for translating, and for transforming stories. This machine produces narratives from the memory of the author as well as from the memories of others. At the same time, however, the government is trying to control such narratives, first by putting the machine in a museum (where the order of the past is preserved above all else) and then by trying to disconnect it. Nevertheless, its efforts to silence the machine fail because the stories are copied and thus are able to circulate as reproductions, images, and simulacra.

Translation and "bad" translation challenge hegemonic discourse and its attempt to dictate and impose an official history of Argentina. This is because the machine is composed of apocryphal stories, texts pasted on walls, diagrams, and recordings, which create a fragmented plot, an irreverent mixture of references from Joyce to Faulkner, passing through Artl and Macedonio Fernández. This blurs the ideas of authorship and of original text in this translation machine, which was given the task of translating Poe's "William Wilson" one afternoon. The resulting text was a deconstructed origin because the machine transforms the stories, uses what there is, and transforms what seems to be lost into something quite different.

The initial story of the machine, which should be an original, is already the product of skewed translations because the machine takes fragments that seem lost and transforms them into something else. In Piglia's work, translation is a metaphor for the reconstruction of collective memory, and mistranslation makes it possible to recreate this memory when faced with an official discourse that seeks to interrupt the process. The novel has an evidently Beckettian and Joycean conclusion. It is clearly Molly Bloom's monologue and her insistence on moving forward, even when it is not possible:

> Estoy llena de historias, no puedo parar, las patrullas controlan la ciudad y los locales de la Nueve de Julio . . . estoy en la arena, cerca de la bahía, en el filo del agua puedo aún recordar las viejas voces perdidas, estoy sola al sol, nadie se acerca, nadie viene, pero voy a seguir, enfrente está el desierto, el sol calcina las piedras, me arrastro a veces, pero voy a seguir, hasta el borde del agua, sí.
>
> *(Piglia 1992: 178)*

In this sense, Waisman's translation of Piglia is striking because he consciously manipulates the fragment but at the same time maintains the "original", which is in itself a translation. Waisman is able to seamlessly translate the context of the Río de la Plata, the Avenida Nueve de Julio, and the desert, which in Argentinian literature is the symbol of barbarity. Nevertheless, he consciously adds an "I will" at the end of the most famous monologue in 20th-century literature, which was also famously translated by Borges into Argentinian Spanish. Waisman's translation is the following:

> I am full of stories, I cannot stop, the patrol cars control the city and the locals below Av. Nueve de Julio have been abandoned . . . I am on the sand, near the bay, I can still remember the old voices where the water laps ashore, I am alone in the sun, no one comes near me, no one comes, but I will go on, the desert is before me, the stones calcined by the sun, sometimes I have to drag myself, but I will go on, to the edge of the water, I will, yes.
>
> *(Piglia 1992/2000: 244)*

In *The Absent City*, there are many more citations, whose presence is in their absence, from *The 1001 Nights* to *Finnegans Wake*, the quintessential Babel novel. *The Absent City* is populated by exiles from all over the world and is surrounded by a river that could be the Plata, the Liffey, or any river in the world. In that place, *Finnegans Wake* is the only written text that is regarded as a sacred book. And the fact is that the islanders speak a fluid language whose rules and semantics are constantly changing from one utterance to the next. What is spoken never remains the same, and the lexicon and morphology change so rapidly that the speaker transmits his messages by translating them. In these circumstances, the mother tongue and the language of identity are the language of difference, a language in a state of permanent translation.

These three original copyists, Vila-Matas, Gaddis, and Piglia, experiment with repetition and copying. They create "writerly" texts in the sense of Roland Barthes, which are based on Derridean iterations. Their texts champion copying, as well as the simultaneous and even contradictory views of Michel Foucault in *The Order of Things* and the rhizome, composed of "plateaus", by Deleuze and Guattari.

2.3 (Un)creative writers

Even though the "Seven Numbers Poems" (1971) by Neil Mills, the "Pure Poems" (2001) by Shigeru Matsui, "Lift Off" (1979) by Charles Bernstein, and the mimeographic poems of Bob Cobbing or his *Three Sequences: Volume 50 (Xerolage)* are quite different, they are all based on repetition, borrowing, and pastiche. These poets are a few of the many whom Kenneth Goldsmith calls "uncreative writers". Paradoxically, uncreative writers are not uncreative at all; they are actually creators in the sense of Roland Barthes. As Gertrude Stein insisted, repetition does not exist because every time a word is repeated, it is different or new (Kostelanetz 1990: 10). For this reason, the rose poem in circular form is different in the same way that each repeated word is different: "a rose is a rose is a rose" (see Perloff 2021a). "Words, words, words",

Shakespeare said. Furthermore, the subsequent repetitions of Stein's poem are also new creations, like Marcel Duchamp's famous alias "Rrose Selavy", which is related to Stein. Carl Andre later rewrote the poem, highlighting its plasticity:

> "My plastic poem about the rose," Andre tells Hollis Frampton, "will not be primed in a blooming, petalled pattern":
>
> roseroseroseroserose
> roseroseroseroserose
> roseroseroseroserose
> roseroseroseroserose
> roseroseroseroserose
> roseroseroseroserose
> roseroseroseroserose
> roseroseroseroserose
>
> "I have typed the alphabet in consecutive and contiguous squares. I think you have seen the result. Painterly areas of various and contrasting values are generated. Miss Stein wrote: 'A rose is a rose, etc.' and Miss Stein is not to be put down lightly. The word 'rose' has a very different plastic appearance from the word 'violet'. The difference is, I think, worth exploiting".
>
> *(Andre quoted by Isaak in Kostelanetz 1990: 35).*

As observed by Perloff when referring to Duchamp and Stein, based on the philosophy of Wittgenstein, the same is not the same:

> "But isn't the same at least *the same*?" The answer, for Wittgenstein, as for Duchamp, is always no: however minuscule the difference between one word or phrase or statement and another, the "difference". And as Gertrude Stein puts it in *Tender Buttons*, "is spreading". And as Stein shows us in her endlessly complex iterative prose, the slightest repetition or shift in context changes the valence and meaning of any word or word group. A rose is a rose is a rose. And by the third enunciation, it is already something else.
>
> *(Perloff 2021a: 3)*

Indeed, many literary and artistic works focus on repetition because it provides intriguing insights into identity and existence. This is illustrated by Heinz Gappmayr in his visual poem "ser", where the repetition of the word "ser" ["being"] is not really repetition.

In addition to Marjorie Perloff, Craig Dworkin, and Kenneth Goldsmith, other authors such as Hillis Miller (1982) have analyzed how repetition can be creative and thus generate meaning in the novel. Some scholars have done this in poetry (Mazur 2005), and others have addressed "autotextuality", or self-repetition, which is the dialogue between the works of the same author (Kolarov 2021), in which repetition is interpreted as difference. Re-presenting the "same" story in another context and by another person creates another new story. To repeat is to create. This is what Kenneth Goldsmith (2011: 9) discovered when he taught creative writing:

> The suppression of self-expression is impossible. Even when we do something as seemingly "uncreative" as retyping a few pages, we express ourselves in a variety of ways. The act of choosing and reframing tells us as much about ourselves as our story about our mother's cancer operation. It's just that we've never been taught to value such choices. After a semester of forcibly suppressing a student's "creativity" by making them plagiarize and transcribe, she will approach me with a sad face at the end of the semester, telling me how disappointed she was because, in fact, what we had accomplished was not uncreative at all; by not being "creative", she produced the most creative body of work writing in her life. By taking an opposite approach to creativity—the most trite, overused, and ill-defined concept in a writer's training—she had emerged renewed and rejuvenated, on fire and in love again with writing.

Goldsmith practices his uncreative writing not only in his classes but also in his work. For example, in *Day* (2003) and *The Day* (2009), he transcribes an entire issue of *The New York Times*, repeating it word for word. The first issue that he rewrote was published on an ordinary Friday (1/11/2000). In contrast, the second issue came out on an extraordinary Tuesday (9/11/2001). In *Weather* (2005), Goldsmith recycles a year of radio weather broadcasts.[17] In all cases, the way that he plays with the typography, his defamiliarization of everyday words, and his omissions make these transcriptions subversive, "although nothing . . . is invented or added or even altered" (Perloff 2005: 8; Perloff 2010: 146–165; see also Fitterman 2009: 15). These are examples of what Charles Bernstein refers to as "conceptual poetry",[18] a 21st-century "transnational literary movement known for appropriating large amounts of found text and then transcribing, reprinting, remediating, or otherwise reproducing them in new formats. Goldsmith's *Day* (2003) and *The Weather* (2005) are among the best-known examples" (Reed 2019: 200).

Weather (2005) is the first book of Goldsmith's *Trilogy*. The second book, *Traffic* (2007), is a collection of New York City traffic reports over a 24-hour period (Perloff 2010: 146–165). The third, *Sports* (2008), is the transcription of the radio broadcast of a baseball game between the New York Yankees and the Boston Red Sox (Horn 2015: 114–195). To transcribe reports of the weather, traffic, or a baseball game is to create an original repetition or iteration in the Derridean sense of the term (Marczewska 2018: 132); it is to write what Goldsmith describes as conceptual pieces of "uncreative writing".

In these works, the original texts, though transcribed, are "undeniably deconstructed and defamiliarized" (Marczewska 2018: 139). In *Seven American Deaths*

(2013), but also earlier in his *No. 111.2.7.93–10.20.96* (1997), Goldsmith constructed by assembling sentences that were collected by the author between the two dates in the title. As Perloff (2010: 150–151) explains, the sentences were arranged alphabetically according to the number of syllables, beginning with one-syllable entries in Chapter 1 ("A, a, aar, aas, aer, aer, agh, ah, air "); two-syllable entries in Chapter 2 ("A door, à la, a pear, a peer, a rear, a ware"); and ending with Chapter VMMCCMMVIII, "the 7,228-syllable 'Rocking-Horse Winner'" (Perloff 2010: 150). Taking Perloff's "unoriginal genius" as his starting point, Goldsmith asks, both in his fiction and in his essays, what it means to create in the digital age, and the answer inevitably reminds us of Borges' "Pierre Menard":

> Even when we do something as seemingly "uncreative" as retyping a few pages, we express ourselves in a variety of ways. The act of choosing and reframing tells us as much about ourselves as our story. . . . It's just that we've never been taught to value such choices. . . . Mimesis and replication doesn't eradicate authorship, rather they simply place new demands on authors who must take these new conditions into account as part and parcel of the landscape when conceiving a work of art: if you don't want it copied, don't put it online.
>
> *(Goldsmith 2011: 9, 10)*

Capital. New York, Capital of the 20th Century (Goldsmith 2015b) is a rewriting of Walter Benjamin's *The Arcades Project* and is an assemblage composed entirely of quotations drawn from countless sources, from literary and academic texts to newspaper articles, official documents, emails, and many others. In *Theory* (2015), he states, "If you're not making art with the intention of having it copied, you're not really making art for the 21st century" (Goldsmith 2015a: n.p.). Goldsmith's "original" work, titled *Against Translation* (2016: n.p.) and published in eight languages, understands the act of translation as "approximation of discourse that produces a new discourse", as a constant displacement in the age of globalization, and as a posttranslation that is as original or even more so than the original.

From this perspective, repetition is an eternal beginning. To repeat is to begin again. To repeat is not to repeat. The story of the sirens of Ulysses is retold in an original way in the rewriting of the same story by Joyce, Kafka, and Brecht. This also occurs in the story of that body told in the space of a June 16th that Kenneth Goldsmith recounts in *Fidget* (2000), another "Bloomsday", the same yet different. His every body movement is dictated into a tape recorder and transcribed hour by hour, from 10 am to 10 pm. This is a catalogue of mechanical movements with shifting reference points, as we read in the back cover. In this novel, the last chapter is a verbal visual experiment, a Beckettian move that runs the first chapter backward, mirrors it, and then reverses every letter, as Goldsmith says (in Perloff's essay at the end of the novel: 2000/2012: 92). It is a repetition from the beginning to the end, and vice versa, since the words are written in reverse order:

.swercskroc mlaP. htuom fo tuo sedils eugnoT. hteet hguorht gnissap, htuom fo roiretni sretne eugnoT. gniliec morf yawa woble stsurht tsiwt esiwkcolcretnuoC. sdneb mrA. daeh fo kcab morf yawa wollip sehsurb mra thgir thgiartS. spord daeH. wollawS. tcartnoC. dnirG. xaler swaJ. wollawS. pil fo cra gniwollof tfel ot htuom fo edis thgir morf gnivom pil reppu ssorca snur eugnoT Eyelids close.

(Goldsmith 2000/2012: 87)

It was translated into Spanish by Carlos Bueno Vera as follows:

.laripse ne eveum es amlap aL. acob al ed roiretni le anodnaba augnel aL. setnied sol ertne odnasap acob al ne artne augnel aL. ohcet led olodnájela odoc le noc joler led sajuga sal ed oirartnoc oditnes le en ariG. albod es ozarb lE. azebac la ed sátred ed adahomla la atrapa otcer ohcered ozarb lE. eac azebac aL. agarT. eartnoc eS. anihceR. ajaler es alubídnam aL. agarT. oibal led ocra le odneiugis acob al ed adreiuqzi a ahcered ed esrazalpsed la roirepus oibal le azurc augnel aL Párpados cerrados.

(Goldsmith 2000/2014: 132)

As Barthes and Foucault both argue, it is a question not of vindicating the death of the author but rather of understanding repetition as a new way of creating (or perhaps not so new, as repetition was already flourishing at the beginning of the twentieth century):

Mimesis and replication doesn't eradicate authorship, rather they simply place new demands on authors who must take these new conditions into account as part and parcel of the landscape when conceiving of a work of art.

(Goldsmith 2011: 10)

We are witnessing a literature in which the pipe is not really a pipe, but the re-representation of a pipe. This is not a novel, according to David Markson's well-known book of the same title. In *This is Not a Novel*, the reader encounters the "Author", who is tired of inventing stories and characters that conform to the traditional structure of a novel. Even so, the Author wants to continue to seduce the reader, and so he creates an experimental novel (which, covertly, has a conventional beginning, middle, and end). This novel amalgamates aphorisms, diary entries, anecdotes, and quotations taken from novelists and artists and upon which the Writer reflects. This Author quotes Michelangelo, Baudelaire, Schopenhauer, Dickens, Flaubert, Acker, and Beethoven, who speak of their own work, as well as that of others, and then die. Citations have a new meaning here because they are recreated and incorporated into a new context.

Also memorable is Eric Doeringer's *60 Years Later: Coming Through the Rye* (2012), a project that appropriates another work of appropriation that in turn appropriates Richard Prince's well-known appropriation of Salinger's *The Catcher in the Rye*:

Evoking Prince's 2011 project and referencing the *Salinger* v. *Colting* case, Doeringer's is a reprint of Colting's novel. It is an unauthorized appropriation of an unauthorized sequel. But, as Doeringer's copyright page reads, this is "an unauthorized sequel to Richard Prince's appropriation of *The Catcher in the Rye*. Any similarity to the book is coincidental and not intended by the artist. c Eric Doeringer". Doeringer's work might look like Colting's volume, it might be a copy of Colting's text, but it is, Doeringer claims, an appropriation of Prince's piece.

(Marczewska 2018: 56)

All of these texts are Borgesian repetitions, forking paths in which the translator has to ask himself how, and to what extent, he can solve the mystery of meaning, which is transformed and completed each time the "same" word or text is incorporated into a different context. Like Borges, we would like to imagine all the possible permutations of texts, all the while knowing that every path eventually forks. As in Ts'ui Pen's work, we choose all alternatives at once, eliminating none, even if they contradict each other. Novels such as John Fowles' *The French Lieutenant's Woman*, Robert Coover's *Pricksongs and Descants* (especially "The Magic Poker" and "The Babysitter"), and Raymond Federman's *Double or Nothing* create different futures and diverse time frames, which in turn proliferate and diverge.

Still another example is *How to Write* (2010) by the previously mentioned Derek Beaulieu. Here writing is constant borrowing and cutting-and-pasting. The author starts from Lautréamont's well-known quote: "Plagiarism is necessary. It is implied in the idea of progress. It clasps the author's sentence tightly, uses his expressions, eliminates a false idea, replaces it with the right idea". *How to Write* deconstructs the concepts of origin and authorship. This gives way to a dialogue between a multitude of authors and to a veritable cacophony in which the authors are not the origin of their words, but rather borrow them from other authors. The texts that emerge are by Lawrence Sterne and Agatha Christie, among many others. Beaulieu thus exemplifies Picasso's saying, "Good artists copy. Great artists steal".

These new ways of envisaging the original are reminiscent of the work of Charles Bernstein, co-founder with Bruce Anders of the group L=A=N=G=U=A=G=E Poets, who once said, "I love originality so much I keep copying it" (in Perloff 2010: 1). For example, his "I and The" is a clear example that "even our most conventional, habitual, and seemingly natural speech and writing always plagiarizes, consciously or not, from unacknowledged sources" (Dworkin and Goldsmith 2011: 88; see also Edmond 2012: 164–192). Bernstein is particularly interesting because of his "original" works that are actually translations created by his playing with visual language. His *Shadowtime*, which he wrote with Brian Ferneyhough, is another good example of this new multimodal and translated "originality". It is a libretto for an opera, which can be read independently, about the final days and work of Walter Benjamin. Bernstein manages "to give a complex biographic account of Walter Benjamin through the repetitive structures of every simple language games in his poetic opera *Shadowtime*" (Bergvall in Thurston 2011: 80; see also Bergvall in Allegrezza 2012: 8). What Bernstein does is to use Benjamin's own words and insert them into his text. For example, in a short section where he quotes Benjamin's essay "Hashisch in Marseilles", he selects about ten sentences and translates them, rephrasing them with a considerable amount of onomatopoeia in order to make the text sound like a rewritten fantasy. Bernstein thus provides a translation based on words that are not understood, a continuous citation, and a game of anagrams (such as poem 8 titled "Anagrammatics" or the fragment "dew and die") that confuse the original with the translation, and the visual with the verbal. In this way, his rewriting is transformed into an extremely complex translation:

> The unintelligibility of the words is a basic condition of most of the opera . . . But they are still words and the words are bound to the meaning of each scene . . . the opera presents a marked translation of the words, just as the text presents a marked translation of motifs in Benjamin.
> *(Bernstein in Perloff 2005: 87; see also Perloff 2021a)*

Also intriguing is Nicole Brossard's novel *Mauve Desert* (1990), which was translated into English by Susanne de Lotbinière-Harwood. This novel is both a single novel and three separate novels in one. In this three-part novel, the third and last part is a rewriting/translation of the first one. It is signed by a certain Maude Laures, whose self-portrait merits a chapter in the second part of the novel. In addition, Nicole Brossard appears on the book cover as the author, but on the inside pages, the author's name changes to Laure Angstelle.

In *Mauve Desert*, Brossard tells the story of two women in an Arizona desert, their encounter with a man, and a murder. However, the novel becomes considerably more interesting when, in the second part, the author introduces a female translator, "who, having discovered the first story in a bookstore, keeps a notebook on translation tracking her responses to the original". The third and final part, titled *Mauve, the Horizon*, is a "translation", which actually is "a rewriting of the first section simulating its translation into another language" (Gentzler 1993: 197). This simulated translation is quite literal. On the other hand, in the second part of the novel, the author encourages the English translator, Lotbinière-Harwood, to be transgressive, to intervene in the original, and to multiply its meanings and thus become an author. The second book of *Mauve Desert* is titled "A Book to Translate". It is a reflection on the writing process of Laure Angstelle and the translation process of Maude Laures. Because the "real" writer is Nicole Brossard and the "real" translator is Lotbinière-Harwood, in the end we have a game of mirrors or a set of Russian nesting dolls, which obscures identities and makes it difficult to know who is who.

This repetitive novel transcends *either/or* dualistic thought to explore the interstitial space that embraces difference. In both *Mauve Desert* and *Picture Theory* (1991), Brossard frames translation as "a metaphor for writing that frees, transforms, and multiplies rather than possesses, controls, and defines" (Gentzler 1992: 197). Translation here is not mere repetition but a pretext to reflect on difference and to question the unity of language. Through repetition, Nicole Brossard reflects not only on writing and translation but also on language and meaning. The third part of the novel is a translation of the first part, which may or may not have been written by Laura Angstelle. However, who is the translator? Is it Maude Laures, Brossard, or Lotbinière-Harwood? The only thing that is certain is that the translation is both the same as the original as well as different from it. It is its re-presentation from the perspective of *différance*:

> "When two words are identical, you must not take undue offence or think you have been wronged in terms of choice. Simplicity is a fine patience of meaning". Maude Laures sometimes felt the need to repeat a few recommendations out loud to herself. It even happened that she would interrupt her work and, arms flailing, indulge in long oratorical jousts in the middle of her room. Words flew high, words flew low, she caught them, cast them out, recast them. Her game was a beauty, taste buds aflame. The dictionary, well too bad! Lingua of fire, long-spoken.
>
> *(Brossard 1987/1990: 156)*

Also important is the fact that the artist Adriene Jenik subsequently published *Mauve Desert: A CD-ROM Translation*, a multimedia creation that imaginatively reworks Brossard's text by rendering it hypertextual. Her work is a rewriting in four languages (English, French, Spanish, and multimedia) from a heteroglossic perspective, because it includes Jenik's correspondence with Brossard during the development of the project. This brings to mind Walter Benjamin, who believed that a real translation should give voice to the *intentio* of the original. Such a translation should also be transparent, not covering the original or blocking its true light, but allowing it to shine through in all of its beauty.

Still another example is Susan Daitch's novel *L.C.* based on Lucienne Crozier's diary, an original text written in French that the reader never gets to see except through the translation and retranslation of two other authors/translators, whose ideologies or ways of representing the world influence their translations. All of this renders the text more heteroglossic than unique. In an interview, Daitch stated that she wished to reflect on what happens when a text changes hands and on how translation alters the final result. Susan Daitch repeats, translates, and creates, in *L.C.*, Lucienne Crozier, Dr. Willa Rehnfield, and her assistant Jane Amme. In her introduction, the translator says,

> Unfortunately, it's not possible to reproduce the physical quality of the original journal: the newspaper clippings glued in at intervals, pasted letters, changes in handwriting when she was writing under pressure, drawings in the margins. A diary of many uses, occasionally Lucienne wrote letters out in her diary first, later copying over this first draft and sending the revised version.
>
> *(Daitch 2002: 5)*

The lives of those who rewrite the so-called original influence the translations that reach the reader. This is evident both in the translator's prologue and in the epilogue of the other rewriter, which Daitch incorporates into the novel. As the text passes from the hands of one person to those of another, the diary changes meaning and is rewritten and reinterpreted, just as it will be in the hands of the reader, who in turn will rewrite the diaries and the novel:

> Translating a work never intended for publication, written by an unknown woman, the translator is compelled to make decisions which, naturally, never entered the writer's mind. The voice of the translator, therefore, is destined to appear in the literal and metaphorical margins of the text.
>
> *(Daitch 2002: 8)*

Susan Daitch was initially a painter, and so her first texts were visually conceived. In fact, this was the case of *L.C.*, as she explained in an interview with Larry McCaffery. *L.C.* is a novel in which Daitch explores what happens when a text changes hands, how meaning is altered, and how translation modifies a fragment or a series of narratives. Moreover, by taking the diary as a starting point, she is using a subjective form that forces us to ask ourselves who is telling the story and whether that person is reliable: "What happens to texts, for both readers and translators, when the original goes through this transformation into another language" (McCaffery 1993: 64)?

Perloff (2005: 99–122) describes this process of constant translation and citation in Susan Howe's *The Midnight* (2003), a text with five sections, three written in poetry and two in prose (significantly titled *Scare Quotes I* and *II*; see Montgomery 2010: 17–26). It comprises earlier books by Howe (*Bed Hangings, Bed Hangings II*, and *Kidnapped*) together with new poetry and prose. The work is constructed from family photographs, book flaps, reproductions of paintings, maps, catalogues, and facsimiles, and other texts/objects. It is full of interstices that are formed

> by juxtaposing different texts and photographs of paratexts from her Uncle John's library. Thus the book becomes a bibliography. Insofar as it also reflects upon its own evolution, it may also be considered to be an autobibliography, a reflexive discourse which comments on its own textuality, intertexts, subtexts, pretexts, and contexts.
>
> *(Barbour 2011: 137)*

The Midnight is a "poem concerned with dismantling the semiotics of the book [that] opens and offers itself as a reactive web of interstices in the manner of lace, a two-sided work of edges" (Barbour 2011: 134). It is an accumulation of citations (from W.B. Yeats, Emily Dickinson, Lewis Carroll, Lady Macbeth, Thomas Sheridan, and Michael Drayton, among many others) and found texts (Perloff 2009) and a mix of genres that again deconstruct the traditional primary/secondary binary opposition. *The Midnight* is a text "fascinated by the assimilation of other texts, by the ways in which we internalize and inhabit the books we read" (Martin 2006: 760). *Kidnapped* (2002) also plays with repetition and traces:

> *Kidnapped* . . . involves the reader in a play with the "enchanted aura" of inherited books, which is the poem's chief concern. Howe supplies not only a photo of the all-important interleaf from her uncle's copy of *The Master of Ballantrae* by Robert Louis Stevenson (as she does in *The Midnight*), but a loose leaf of tissue itself so that we too can experience its "Mist-like transience", hear its "quick rustling". Likewise, halfway through the book, a yellow card marker is left, as if by a previous reader. On closer examination it turns out to be identical to the one photographed on that page, apparently written on in the same dashing hand. Characteristically, Howe leaves us to ponder which has a closer relationship to the "real" object: the photo of the original card or the reproduced copy of it.
>
> *(Martin 2006: 760–761)*

Also relevant are her *Poems Found in a Pioneer Museum* (2009), published in a small case containing 35 unbound pages; she notes, "I copied these poems, almost verbatim, from typed identification cards placed beside items in display cases at Salt Lake City's Pioneer Memorial Museum" (no page). Her collage poems in *Frolic Architecture*, contained in *That This* (2011), form a fragmented linguistic and visual collage full of references to other books (Del Toro García 2017: 144–148), *The Quarry* (2016; see Perloff 2021a for an excellent analysis), another work by Howe full of citations, allusions, and borrowings, and *Concordance* (2020), among others. Howe writes "palimtexts" (Davidson 1989: 78); she highlights "the material fact" of the trace

> to emphasize the intertextual—and inter-discursive—quality of . . . writing as well as its materiality . . . a writing-in-process that may make use of any number of textual sources. Its name implies the palimtext retains vestiges of prior writings out of which it emerges".

These are only a few examples that indicate that today, in the digital age, writing is citational and intertextual.[19] In his classic essay titled "The Work of Art in the Age of Its Technological Reproduction", Walter Benjamin states that to pry an object from its shell, to destroy its aura, is the mark of a perception whose sense of the universal equality of things has increased to such a degree that it extracts it even from a unique object by means of mechanical reproduction. The aura, at least in modern times, refers to that mysterious light that surrounds and envelops all things, to that awesome energy that seems to emanate from within an original work of art, creating its own figures and projecting onto the observer a veritable array of responses.

For Benjamin, it is identity, that universal sense of things, that destroys the aura by removing the object from the context that created it. Identity is thus defined in terms of the axioms of Euclidean geometry. The recognitions erode identity, destroy the aura, and lead us to imagine a language, which is equivalent to imagining a way of life. John Barth denied that the newness of any artistic work had to do with originality in his well-known essay "The Literature of Exhaustion" (1967). Instead,

> it is the critical use of tradition, the creative rewriting of existing artistic concepts and inherited forms and techniques (which are now perceived as having "used up" the possibility of renewing themselves from within the tradition) that confer uniqueness upon the individual artist.
>
> *(Benesch 2007: 30)*

And in "The Literature of Replenishment" (1979), he spoke of the potential of re-inventing without going back to the essentialist concept of originality.

To translate these novels we would have to agree with Wittgenstein in *Philosophical Investigations* and Derrida in *Grammatology*, both of whom reject the idea that words refer to metaphysical absolutes, to universals, and stress that they are part of a shared grammar of conventions and iterations. Reverberations are metaphors of reality, and the task of the translator is to re-know, not to define but rather to re-present. A translator must reflect or cause to resonate that historical moment in which, as Borges observes, narratives are the irresponsible game of a man who is too timid to write stories and who diverts himself by falsifying and distorting (without any aesthetic justification) the stories of others.

One sign always hides another, and thus it is both the interpreter and the interpreted who create a veritable labyrinth of textuality. And perhaps translation is the perfect locus for this, given that only in the rereading of a text is it possible to become aware of the multiplicity of texts. Reading is a rereading, a re-presentation from the beginning. And it is reading that unveils not only the secret meaning of words but also (and even more importantly) the multiple dimensions of a text. Words are never exhausted in their static and lifeless dictionary meanings, but rather they carry within them the echoes of their history. The text is thus a sponge but, as Derrida warns, a sponge that not only cleanses but also absorbs impurities. The text, both the original and its translation, thus becomes a web of impurities, meanings, crevices, and folds. It is intertextual: the text aspires to infinitely expand and multiply itself. And thus, if one text is many different texts as well as many different voices, its translation will be all these things and more.

Notes

1 It is interesting to note that in 2007, Lethem published

> a widely-read piece in *Harper's* called "An Ecstasy of Influence: A Plagiarism Mosaic", a lively tribute to the joys of appropriation and sampling, their rich history, and their vital importance to contemporary culture. Only when readers turned to the end of the essay did they learn that virtually every single word of Lethem's essay had been, appropriately enough, lifted from a wide range of other sources and stitched seamlessly together.
>
> *(Epstein 2012: 311)*

2 Duchamp's urinal has been copied into (un)original originals by Levine, David Hammons, or Robert Gober:

> In each of these cases the artist has performed an act of recontextualization, taking a familiar object and transforming it by changing where it is found or how it is made. In the process, each artist has accomplished the paradoxical feat of claiming authorship over the urinal. However, as any student of twentieth-century art knows, this particular bathroom fixture comes ready-made with yet another proper name attached. Marcel Duchamp's thorough assimilation into museum collections and art-historical discourse has insured that any use of such objects as a bicycle wheel, snow shovel, and especially a urinal will be read as a reference to Duchamp, not just a use of the object itself. Levine's remake presents the most pointed reference to Duchamp's peculiar hold over authorship. Her title, *Fountain (after Marcel Duchamp)*, acknowledges the unmistakable reference of the work.
>
> *(Buskirk 2003: 62–63)*

3 In *Answers/Questions* (1992) and in *I ask questions* (2000), Ken Aptekar superimposes texts on images of El Greco, Manet, Boucher, Raphael, and Rembrandt, among others. In *I'm in Madrid* (1999), which is superimposed on a repainting of *The Nobleman with His Hand on His Chest* by El Greco, a storyteller intervenes in the painting's narrative with his own narration. By superimposing his words on the images of other painters, Aptekar recounts modern stories. His paintings have a thick, superimposed glass that is a kind of boundary but also a layer difficult to ignore, in which the observer is reflected: a mirror in which the spectator who gazes is also gazed at. Through his glass-covered, written-over, repainted images, Aptekar rewrites masterpiece paintings and "dematerializes authenticity's authority" (Self 2001: 12; see also Bal 1999). Also worth mentioning is Glenn Ligon, whose works cite important authors of the 20th century, such as James Baldwin, Zora Neale Hurston, Jean Genet, and Gertrude Stein, among others. For example, *Untitled (I am an invisible man)* (1991) is based on a quote from Ralph Ellison's novel. Also relevant is Sharon Hayes, whose work reflects the performativity of language and reuses recent political texts, such Reagan's speeches or the communiqués sent by Patricia Hearst, who became a member of the Symbionese Liberation Army after being kidnapped by them. These are texts that Hayes recreates and re-presents. Described as an act of "oral translation", they invite us to rethink, rewrite, and complete not only the historical moment when they were created but also our own present.

4 These (un)creative texts may not be so innovative as they initially seem. It is only necessary to remember the blank pages, digressions, stories within stories, the dots, and the pages in black in Sterne's *Tristram Shandy* (1759–1767), based on a Quixote whose adventures take place in the world of ideas.

5 For a feminist and postcolonial perspective on Echo and Narcissus, see Spivak 1993 and Place in Andersson (2018: 63–62). See also Lahiri (2022).

6 Ted Berrigan, "An interview with John Cage," *Electronic Poetry Center*, http://epc.buffalo.edu/authors/berrigan/cage. See also Marczewska (2018: 2).

7 For an excellent analysis of Mac Low's "reading through" compositions, see Kotz (2007: 120–134).

8 "Passages 31–37 1-30" is contained in *Bending the Bow* (1968) and "Passages 31–37" in *Ground Work* (1984), along with three other unnumbered "Passages". Duncan finally stopped numbering them to avoid the idea of linear coherence. *Ground Work II* (1987) includes another 13 "Passages".

9 Dani Spinosa provides a detailed analysis in https://genericpronoun.com/2013/10/15/when-the-words-he-wrote-were-his/ and in Spinosa (2018: 28–30).

10 For an excellent study of the OuLiPo group, see Duncan (2019).

11 Erasure is a technique closely related to the repetition used by many authors and is reminiscent of Heidegger's crossed-out *Being* and Derrida's *trace* (see Chapter 1). For example, Shakespeare's sonnets have been erased, rewritten, written through, and repeated in many

interesting ways by Gregory Betts, Philip Terry, Richard Kostelanetz, Jen Bervin, Gary Barwin, Steve McCaffery, Harryette Mullen, and others (see Kostelanetz 2020: 175–176; for a history of erasure poetics, see Macdonald 2009; Silliman 2010).

12 The act of erasing a page conjures up similar experiments in the visual arts, such as Robert Rauschenberg's already mentioned *Erased de Kooning Drawing* (1953). This is reminiscent of the Dada gesture, typical of the avant-gardes, of André Breton erasing Francis Picabia in 1920, of Marcel Broodthaers blacking out the words of Mallarme's *Un coup de des*, or of Man Ray's blacked-out page in his sound-poem "Lautgedicht".

13 For a comment on the figure of sand as an instrument of erasure, see Dworkin (2013: 43–44).

14 It is interesting to mention that Marczewska (2018: 85) argues that Johnson's erasure of Milton represents "a negative poetics of loss", whereas Holmes, Ruefle, Morrison, and Bervin "engage in a poetic play of *différance*":

> Instead of perpetuating the set of values advocated in the sources, as Johnson does, these contemporary writers simultaneously preserve and deconstruct it, to find those moments in the reappropriated discourse that enable them to transgress the system of values exemplified by it, to transpose and translate them into the value of their own and their own time. The writing generated as a result opens the fixity of the source to the possibilities of new meaning.

15 Bartleby & Co. is also a publisher of fine limited editions. For instance, "it has often reproduced original typography of a classic (e.g., John Milton's *Paradise Lost*, Dante's *Divine Comedy*, Herman Melville's *Bartleby, the Scrivener*) along with contemporary texts in more current designs" (Kostelanetz 2020: 16).

16 History is the only place where I get relief from this nightmare from which I am trying to awaken [literal back translation].

17 For a comment on the similarities and differences between Goldsmith's *Weather* and Vito Acconci's "Act 3, Scene 4", see Perloff (2008).

18 For a discussion on conceptual writing and poetry, see Perloff (2013), Goldsmith (2012), and Reed (2019).

19 We could also mention, for instance, Barbara Wilson's amusingly ironic story titled "Mi novelista" (though the story is written in English). The protagonist is a translator, significantly named Cassandra, who aspires to be an author, not just a translator. Because she believes that her name does not have sufficient cachet to get her novel published, she invents a writer and then writes—"translates"—the imaginary writer's work, which up until then had not existed. Things become even more complicated when the supposed author of this supposed original appears out of nowhere and confronts the translator, who in reality is the creator of a novel that is nothing more than an infinite game of false origins.

3
(UN)ORIGINAL TRANSLATORS

No text has only one translation, and this is particularly the case for experimental writings. Carroll's "muddles" and Artaud's "anarchy", not to mention the material quality of the words in Stephen Mallarmé's *Un coup de dés jamais n'abolira le hasard*, in which the page becomes a canvas and the spaces between the words are as significant as the letters themselves, are very complex from the translator's perspective. Also a challenge is translating the eye-tickling repetition in Gertrude Stein's columns, John Cage's mesostics, and Robert Duncan's already mentioned derivative poetry (e.g., "Orders: Passages 24"). Still another example can be found in Borges' "The Lottery in Babylon" in *Fictions*, in which all activities are dictated by random chance in the form of an all-encompassing lottery without winners or losers, and in which nothing can be determined or calculated in advance. Other examples include Ronald Sukenick's "post-realist" world, Raymond Federman's "surfiction", and Alaisdair Gray's *Unlikely Stories Mostly*, texts that are all written in a fluid language that is in constant movement.

The Unfortunates by B.S. Johnson is sold in a box with 27 unbound sections, which, as mentioned before, readers can arrange as they please. The author of *Albert Angelo* even dares to literally pierce the pages of the book. The holes in the pages and the blank spaces are strategies reminiscent of the silences in Cage's *4'33"*. Polyhedric novels such as *House of Leaves* by Mark Z. Danielewski have a unique format with various textual levels and an infinite number of footnotes that include other footnotes that refer to books, films, and nonexistent academic articles. Novels such as *1982 Janine* by Alasdair Gray possess an unusual layout that features double-column printed pages combined with the innovative use of different typefaces and experimental typography. And there are also the visual poems of the sculptor Carl Andre, such as *One Hundred Sonnets (I . . . Flower)* (1963/1969), which are based on repetition (Kotz 2007: 146)[1]:

58 (Un)original translators

youyouyouyouyouyouyouyouyouyou
youyouyouyouyouyouyouyouyouyou
youyouyouyouyouyouyouyouyouyou
youyouyouyouyouyouyouyouyouyou
youyouyouyouyouyouyouyouyouyou
youyouyouyouyouyouyouyouyouyou
youyouyouyouyouyouyouyouyouyou
youyouyouyouyouyouyouyouyouyou

Loulou, Flaubert's parrot, was created from a borrowed parrot. In *Gustave Flaubert, un Coeur Simple* (1990), Sherrie Levine reproduces the excerpts that Flaubert devotes to Loulou and also includes the silhouette of a parrot on each page. Not surprisingly, the parrot is the animal most associated with repetition. Even Loulou, the parrot's name, is repetitive. In *Gustave Flaubert, un Coeur Simple*, Levine chooses a typeface and layout for the original text and cover and adds her name as the author of the book: Sherrie Levine, *Gustave Flaubert, un Coeur Simple*. She also includes Flaubert in her acknowledgments. This is Levine's palimpsest, a story about a story by Flaubert, the artist's feminist appropriation of a classic, "asserting a female perspective on the male-dominated history of art and literature" (Gilbert 2022: 194):

> She forces a rereading of the original, or a kind of doubled reading. The same text is read word for word, and yet what is read is a different text overlaid with new contexts, frames, and perspectives that is marked by the vibration between the male and female gaze, as well as between the original and the replica.
>
> *(Gilbert 2022: 195)*

In 2004, Levine even created 12 bronze parrots, modeled from one that she found in a flea market. These 12 parrots are allegedly the reincarnation of the bird in Flaubert's novel, which was eventually stuffed.

In *Flaubert's Parrot* (1984), Julian Barnes raises the question of the original by pointing out that there are at least two stuffed specimens in different museums, each claiming to be Loulou. Nevertheless, he does not say with any certainty which is the original. Not surprisingly, Barnes read and appreciated Borges.[2] The Museum chose the parrot that most resembled Flaubert's description, so perhaps the first parrot chosen was the true parrot, but not necessarily. As "a writer of the imagination", Flaubert

> would alter a fact for the sake of a cadence. . . . Just because he borrowed a parrot, why should he describe it as it was? . . . And perhaps [the stuffed parrots] change colour with time. . . . So you mean either of them could be the real one? Or, quite possibly, neither?
>
> *(Barnes 1984: 188)*

In uncreative writings, the text is full of false bottoms, repetitions, and mirror games. Translation here cannot simply be a mirror reflection and nothing else. It bears a greater resemblance to the cracked looking glass of the servant girl mentioned by Stephen Daedalus in the opening pages of *Ulysses* or to the looking glass in *Alice in Wonderland*, which reflects a reverse image of everything. The translator enters the mirror and explores what is on the other side.

In this type of repetitive literature, the exact equivalent or faithful representation of reality is only an illusion, perhaps the greatest illusion, as philosophy has shown us. This was also the opinion of Borges, who affirmed that an original is always unfaithful to the translation and that the translation always completes the original. This chapter discusses several translators whose approach to translation is a perfect fit for this kind of unoriginal, repetitive, and (un)creative literature because, in their view, translation is creation rather than repetition.

3.1 Translation as transcreation: Haroldo and Augusto de Campos

3.1.1 Transcreation

The concept of translation as "transcreation" began with Haroldo de Campos, who, along with his brother Augusto and Décio Pignatari, founded Noigandres (taken from Pound's *Canto* XX), one of the earliest artist collectives in the concrete poetry movement.[3] Haroldo de Campos, whose genius has been acknowledged by great literary figures such as Umberto Eco, Jacques Derrida, Guillermo Cabrera Infante, and Octavio Paz (Bessa and Cisneros 2007: xiii), is a key author in Latin American literature as well as in translation studies.

Based on his own translations (as well as those of others) of the poetry of e.e. cummings, *Ecclesiastes*, Homer, Dante, Mallarmé, Japanese haikus, Octavio Paz, and James Joyce, Haroldo de Campos states that translation "is always recreation or parallel creation, the opposite of a literal translation" (Vieira 1999: 105). De Campos' idea of translation as transcreation is explained in his 1963 essay titled "A tradução como criação e como crítica" ["Translation as Creation and Criticism"], which highlights the importance of Pound and Benjamin. In fact, he perceives Pound as "the ultimate translator-critic" (de Campos 1963/1992: 35), who significantly influenced concrete poetry as well as his own conception of translation:

> The Brazilian concrete poets also launched a program of literary translation mostly based on their model and mentor Ezra Pound, from whom they derived the title of their first little magazine, *Noigandres*, and the name of their group. This translation program involved locating examples of a similar poetics in the past (from the medieval troubadours to the avant-gardes of the interwar period, passing through key figures like Mallarmé) and translating them in a way that

made them relevant for modern poetics. Their practice of translation became, thus, a "laboratory" for writing and at the same time was the source of their theoretical reflections on translation.

(Cisneros 2012: 17)

Concrete poetry is especially difficult to translate—Odile Cisneros' translation of *Galaxias* is very good. According to Haroldo de Campos, the more complex a text is, the more seductive it becomes and the greater one's desire to recreate it. In many of the texts that he translated, de Campos was obliged not only to rewrite the language and content but also to transform the sign itself. This includes the visuals on the page, the "optical data", interlinear relations, and typographical spacing. All of these elements are highlighted when he analyzes his brother Augusto's translation of *the leaf* by e.e. cummings:

> We may say, then, that every translation of a creative text will always be a "re-creation", a parallel and autonomous, although reciprocal, translation—"transcreation". The more intricate the text is, the more seducing it is to "re-create" it. Of course in a translation of this type, not only the signified but also the sign itself is translated, that is, the sign's tangible self, its very materiality (sonorous properties, graphical-visual properties, all of that which forms, for Charles Morris, the *iconicity* of the aesthetic sign, when an iconic sign is understood as that which is "in some degree similar to its denotation").
>
> *(De Campos in Bessa and Cisneros 2007: 315)*

The concept of originality is directly challenged here. The original is a rewriting, an array of texts, and each utterance has a subtext. The new technologies now facilitate "ex-centric" translations such as those of the de Campos brothers. In *Panorama do "Finnegans Wake"* (O'Neill 2013), in which they translate passages written by Joyce, translation is a political action. The illustrations in the book are examples of pure concrete poetry at its finest. Not surprisingly, "*Panorama* is less a translation *of* Joyce than it is a found text, a transposition on its own life" (Perloff 2010: 70).

It is no coincidence that, in *Galaxias* (1984), Haroldo de Campos defines the text as a corpus of words with a wide spectrum of possibilities and potential. A text is regarded as a continuous stream of signs without punctuation marks or capital letters, which flows uninterruptedly across the page. It is a galactic expansion that plays with the verbal and the visual, based on hyperrepetitions in which a series of syllables, words, and phrases are permuted and interchanged with a verbal-visual structure reminiscent of James Joyce or Gertrude Stein. Concrete poetry highlights

> the material qualities of the signifier, something that, inevitably, will vary from language to language. Taking a step back, this means posing the question if concrete poetry is at all translatable. The answer clearly depends on what we understand by translation.
>
> *(Cisneros 2012: 18)*

Indeed, the secret lies in viewing and understanding translation from a different perspective. Repetitive, uncreative, plagiaristic literature, which plays with concepts such as authorship and originality, demands an approach to translation that is based on recreation. This is not a simple process of reproduction, but rather a creative, nourishing repetition, which is an artistic creation (Guldin 2008: 113). As observed by de Campos in his 1963 essay, the result is two texts in two languages that maintain an isomorphic relationship with each other. This is reflected in the translations by the Noigandre group of Dante, Mallarmé, Pound, Joyce, Mayakóvski, and many others.

In these translations, the traditional idea of appropriation and plagiarism vanishes, and "the simple duality of 'original' and 'translation' and the related hierarchy of 'home country' and 'colony' is questioned, introducing the idea of a possible reversibility" (Guldin 2008: 119). Despite certain differences between Haroldo de Campos and his brother (Médici Nóbrega and Milton 2009: 264–265), both regard the translator as a creator and support the independence of the translation because it is a new text:

> From the beginning of his theoretical activity, Haroldo rejected the biased view that translations are inferior products, as the translator now, far from being the author's servant or mouthpiece, or a reproducer of meanings, becomes a recreator and a critic, choosing texts that deserve to be translated, and successfully recreating them.
>
> *(Médici Nóbrega and Milton 2009: 260)*

In their cannibalistic theory of translation, this independence led to the more political vision of empowering the translator. Following Derrida, the de Campos brothers view translation as transgression, transtextualization, and cannibalization. In this regard, cannibalization is understood not as mutilation, but rather as a symbolic act of love, an act that absorbs the virtues of a body through the transfusion of blood. From this perspective, translation becomes "an empowering act, a nourishing act, an act of affirmative play [that] comes very close to the Benjamin/Derrida position, which sees translation as a life-force that ensures a literary text's survival" (Gentzler 1993: 196). Moreover, translation as transtextualization or transcreation "demythicizes the ideology of fidelity" (Vieira 1999: 110). According to Haroldo de Campos, to translate means to transcreate, and to transcreate "is not to try to reproduce the original's form . . . but to appropriate the translator's contemporary's best poetry, to use the local existing tradition" (in Vieira 1994: 70). This does not mean swallowing the original, but multiplying it:

> Translation as cannibalization, on the other hand, does not conjure away the "original", but devours it in order to create a cultural attitude nourished by foreign influences and enriched by autochthonous input which helps to dismantle the traditional asymmetrical power relations between the cultures involved.
>
> *(Wolf 2003: 126–127)*

Haroldo de Campos' 1979 translation of Goethe's *Faust* is a clear example of this as the title of the translation is not *Faust* but rather *Deus e o Diabo no Fausto de Goethe* [*God and the Devil in Goethe's Faust*]. According to Vieira (1999: 106), this title highlights the relation between Goethe and his Faust:

> The intertext in the very title suggests that the receiving culture will interweave and transform the original one, which is confirmed later, as we shall see, throughout the exposition of de Campos' translational project. Anyway, from the very title we can say that translation is no longer a one-way flow from the source to the target culture, but a two-way transcultural enterprise. The cover iconography further asserts the autonomy of the translator/recreator while problematizing the question of authorship in translation; the visibility of de Campos' signature on the cover contrasts with Goethe's less conspicuous signature which only appears on the third page. It is also worth highlighting that, at the end of the book, the section "Works by the Author" actually lists de Campos' work, which suggests the articulation of a space conventionally deemed marginal or even irrelevant as compared to the original author's centrality—that is, stresses the translator's own production.
>
> *(Vieira 1999: 106–107)*

In the eyes of Haroldo de Campos, translation is thus

> a transmutation process, an act of vampirization . . . a transfusion of blood that endows the receiver with new life . . . a rejection of the power hierarchy which privileged the source text and relegated the translator to a secondary role.
>
> *(Bassnett 1993: 155)*

Translation depends on text type as well as on the semantic meaning of the linguistic signs. Even more importantly, it also depends on the physicality of these signs, their location on the page, and their sounds and visual images. By "avoiding traditional notions of faithful/free, the de Campos brothers' theory of translation does away with a sense of loss to participate in a positive act of affirmation, of pleasure, and of joy" (Gentzler 1993: 197). One example could be the idea of "mirror-forms" in Augusto de Campos' development of a concrete poetics, as reflected in his *Viva Vaia* (1972) or in his palindromic poem *Rever* (1964) (Bessa 2009: 224–225). It is also present in the repetition that characterizes his poems "Sem um numero" (1957), "Dias dias dias" (1953), "Caracol" (1960), and "Luxo" (1965) (see Nancy Perloff 2021; see also Hilder 2016).

These poems are evidence that translation is not repetition but rather re-creation (Clüver 2020: 73). For example, "A rosa doente", a Portuguese translation by Augusto de Campos (1978) of Blake's "The Sick Rose" (1794), is undoubtedly a transcreation because it transforms the original into a concrete poem by means of an organic translation imbued with great dynamicity. The Portuguese words are arranged on the page as though the paper were a canvas. They are shaped to form the petals of a flower, into the heart of which the text eventually disappears. This translation is arguably "organic" or "extraneous" if we continue to use Holmes' terms, though here such a distinction is pointless:

> What we can say is that De Campos' translation reflects a reading of Blake that demonstrates his sensitivity to the text and his desire to experiment in terms that would not have been accessible to Blake two centuries earlier.
> (Bassnett and Lefevere 1998: 63)

This transcreation of Blake's poem generates an alliteration with the sonorous fricative phoneme /v/ "that does not exist in the original poem, [and] makes the letters diminish as a spiral is formed. This spiral is, at the same time, the movement of the worm entering a flower and the flower itself" (Hernández 2010: 153). In regard to Augusto de Campos' iconographic version of Blake, Else Vieira also agrees that he has created a new text:

> As a translator, [Augusto de Campos] transforms the text, breaking with the untouchability of the original—his translation does not represent, but *re*-presents the original. Still, further, de Campos does not silence Blake's voice, he does not translate Blake into Portuguese only, but also into Portuguese *literature*, into his own concrete poetry. Vieira's argument is that de Campos has created a new poem in a new context, one that is not so much a translation as a new piece of Brazilian literature created in the spirit of the anthropophagic function of discourse which both the de Campos brothers, Haroldo and Augusto were promoting.
> (Bassnett 2020: 17)

On the other hand, Haroldo de Campos conceived translation as transtextualization, "whereby a translation becomes an autonomous creation, albeit retaining its debt to an original" (id.). Translation is thus interpretation, and hence

> the rewriting *and* creation of a new "original" in another language. Recognizing the indeterminacy of literary texts on the one hand, and the impossibility of "faithful" translation on the other, liberates the translator from the servitude to the source from which the translation derives and undermines the old Romantic concept of authorship and at the same time revises simplistic notions of intentionality.
> (Bassnett 2014: 153)

Texts such as *Galáxias* by de Campos require a (trans)creative, playful, rhizomatic translation, because they are texts in which language is always shifting and in constant movement. *Galáxias*, whose original (Joycean) title was "prose in progress", strongly emphasizes sound. It also plays with the space on the printed page and is striking because of its lack of punctuation, as well as its many references and citations from Pound or *The Thousand and One Nights*. A book is never complete: "um libro ensaia o libro/todo libro é un libro de ensaio de ensayos do libro" (de Campos 1984/2004: n.p.). And this is true because de Campos' concept of transcreation signifies that no translation is a mere copy, but rather the opportunity to recreate a text. In this sense, translation is

> a blood transfusion, where the emphasis is on the health and nourishment of the translator. This is a far cry from the notion of faithfulness to an original, of the translator as servant of the source text. Translation, according to de Campos, is a dialogue, the translator is an all-powerful reader and a free agent as a writer.
> *(Bassnett and Trivedi 1999: 5)*

Transcreation is a type of rhizomatic translation because, in a rhizome, any point is connectable to any other in the same way as any voice can be linked to any other. In all of these cases, the goal is a deterritorialized, nonbinary, decentered, multiple translation that "ceaselessly establishes connections" (Deleuze and Guattari 1987/2005: 7). By inverting Platonism, Deleuze and Guattari reject the traditional idea of representation, sameness, and reproduction. Copies are not inferior to originals. Unlike tracings, the rhizome resembles a map to be designed and constructed. It is always dismountable, connectable, alterable, and modifiable with multiple entrances and exits, as well as myriad escape routes:

> The rhizome is altogether different, a *map and not a tracing*. Make a map, not a tracing . . . The map does not reproduce an unconscious closed in upon itself; it constructs the unconscious. It fosters connections between fields. . . . It is itself a part of the rhizome. The map is open and connectable in all its dimensions; it is detachable, reversible, susceptible to constant modification. It can be torn, reversed, adapted to any kind of mounting, reworked by an individual, group or social formation. It can be . . . constructed as a political action or as a mediation. . . . A map has multiple entryways, as opposed to the tracing, which always come back "to the same".
> *(Deleuze and Guattari 1987/2005: 12)*

What needs to be put back on maps are the tracings and not vice versa. Unlike the centered (even polycentered) systems of hierarchical communication and preestablished unions, the rhizome is a noncentered, nonhierarchical, and nonsignifying system. Rhizomatic translation is the following:

> A mixture, a schizophrenic mélange, a Harlequin costume in which very different functions of language and distinct centers of power are played out, blurring what can be said and what can't be said.
> *(Deleuze and Guattari 1975/1986: 19)*

Transcreation is thus not "molar" but "molecular" (Deleuze and Guattari 1987/2005) because it is concerned not with territoriality, but rather with representation through fluxes, connections, and disjunctions. Translation as transcreation is capable of multiplying, forking, and branching like rhizomes.

Transcreative translation could also be applied to the rewriting of John Cage's work. In her analysis of Cage's mesostics, Dani Spinosa specifically proposes approaching them as though they were a rhizome network, totally different from the downward-growing underground roots that anchor trees to the earth and the rootedness of arborescent thinking, and far removed from any binarism, dualism, or linearity. From a rhizomatic perspective, Cagean repetition can only be understood as movement.

> We must then understand the repetition in this poem as attempting to reconcile the stasis of the poem with the movement and process Cage wishes to capture. In re-encountering these concepts throughout the sequence, repeating their koan-like nature as though meditating constantly on this tension, Cage's reader is forced to reconcile this relationship between the repeated and the unique, the moving and the static, what is written in ink and what Cage's work endeavours to place in flux.
>
> *(Spinosa 2016: 34)*

The "Mesostic 31" includes the word "movegram", which is crucial to an understanding of the use of repetition:

> With "movegram", Cage's work highlights the crux of the tension between movement and stasis, between the unique and the repeated: the problem that language, in its attempts to organize, categorize, and communicate, works to make the moving static, to make the unique repeatable, to regularize and make same the different.
>
> *(Spinosa 2016: 34)*

Transcreative translation can also be applied to *Via: 48 Dante Variations* by Caroline Bergvall (2000, 2003). This poetic work is a perfect candidate for rhizomatic translation and transcreation, which demand "absolute freedom of the translator to refashion the original in any way" (Bassnett 2014: 54). Bergvall is a conceptual writer (Dworkin and Goldsmith 2011: 81), a poet and artist who uses repetition and translation as forms of creation. Her works are never static but are a constant *becoming*, in the sense of Deleuze (1969). Within this context, *becoming* is a derivation that is not derivative, the point at which two very different entities connect by means of a network of infinite relations. In *Via*, she "is acting as a sort of translator by simply recasting preexisting texts into a new poem that is entirely her own" (Goldsmith 2011: 194).

Thus, when we translate, it is with the knowledge that we are rewriting palimpsests because *Via* is a performance poem, a sound recording and a written text composed of translations and of rewritings, namely, the 19th- and 20th-century English versions catalogued archived in the British Library. Nonetheless, these translations of the first tercet of Dante's *Inferno* (from the mid-19th century to the present) are in alphabetical rather than chronological order, from "Along" to "When"; each is followed by an indication of its source, the last name of the translator, and the year of publication. The translations are ordered

> according to the first word of the translation, so that neither the translator's name nor the date of the text is prioritized. . . . Bringing these and forty-five other versions together into an archive of citations, Bergvall highlights the multiple responses to a single tercet, revealing differences within apparent continuity. She also underscores the intertextual dialogue or "colloquy" of these many translating voices, a dialogue foreshadowed by other twentieth-century print Dante collections. . . . Here, the effect is magnified by the Web-based technology allowing auditors to listen and mentally respond, and to do so whether at home, in the office, or walking down a street ("via"). In the wake of these insistent variations, the sense of a single meaning in Dante's "original", as well as its hierarchical priority, quickly recedes. Rather, its polysemous nature comes to the fore through the dramatic conversation of texts it has generated.
>
> (Bermann 2014: 286)

Repetition and variation of such words and phrases as "dark", "midway", "I found myself", and others create

> a stable backdrop against which variations from the norm stand out with unusual vividness. . . . Alphabetization creates a reassuring predictable pattern that is counterbalanced by the thoroughly randomized series of dates: 1998, 1893, 1995, 1854, 1915, 1884, and so forth. . . . "Via" begins again and again. It occupies a continuous present that could be extended indefinitely by adding more and more translations. It is a showcase, too, for Steinian insistence, that is, her belief that repetition brings to light small but crucial distinctions, the sort of tiny variations that, as Bergvall illustrates, render every translation of Dante a unique text that puts a slightly different spin on the original. Finally, Stein would have appreciated the title's bilingual pun. It conflates a spatial reference—in Italian, "via" can mean "road", as in Via Appia or Via Dolorosa—with a self-reflexive gesture—"via" in English meaning "by means of". An act of composition, an immersion in one's medium of communication, creates a "path" for oneself and others to follow.
>
> (Reed 2007: n.p.)

With these texts in which repetition predominates and authorship is dissolved, translation consecrates the original. Furthermore, Bergvall translates the original texts with her female voice contrasting with a male literary tradition. In this way, it simultaneously legitimizes and nullifies the "originality" of the text by announcing its dependence on a derived form. The original thus needs the translation. As long as it can be translated, it is not definitive. According to Bergvall (2005: 65), *Via* is about "making a copy explicitly as an act of copy". Therefore, when one is translating this type of text, it is important to approach the translation as though it were a transcreation within the theoretical context of Haroldo de Campos, for whom translation "is a form of patricide, a deliberate refusal to repeat that which has already been presented as the original" (Bassnett and Trivedi 1999: 15).[4]

In Oswald de Andrade's *The Anthropophagic Manifesto* (1922), creative translation is a cannibalistic practice, a poetics of translation that is far removed from any binary essentialism. Instead, its main goal is to create translations that unsettle "the primacy of origin" and advance "the role of the receiver as a giver in its own right, further pluralizing (in)fidelity" (Vieira 1999: 95). Originality in works such as *Via* is questioned because "the original is itself a translation, an incomplete process of translating a signifying chain into a univocal signified, and this process is both displayed and further complicated when it is translated by another signifying chain in a different language" (Venuti 1992: 7). It is interesting to remember Bergvall's definition of translation:

> A field which allows for the text in the original language to force up an activity of writing and exchange in the translation language. By which I mean one which almost certainly diffuses and stretches the arrival language. Making strange language which reveals the "other" text, the "foreign" language across the familiarity of the arrival language. Sets up the two languages in conflictual or dialogic relationality.
>
> *(Bergvall 2000: 51)*

Dworkin and Goldsmith (2011: 81) see Bergvall's reframings as "a strong and effective way of conceptual writing". Also useful for translating Bergvall's work is de Campos' concept of "plagiatropy" or plagiarism by translation. Etymologically speaking, "plagiotropy" can be regarded as "oblique" or "transversal" plagiarism. However, unlike plagiarism, which simply takes over the words or ideas of others, plagiotropy implies the dialectical movement of transformation that feeds the history of literature:

> A palimpsest attained by adding new intertextual strata on top of an already multilayered text . . . the single layers of this palimpsest are not to be understood as fixed stratifications, accumulated over time, but as constantly shifting and interacting planes.
>
> *(Guldin 2008: 118)*

From a semiotic perspective, plagiotropy is related to Peirce and Eco, to Bakhtin's dialogism and polyphony, and to Kristeva's intertextuality (Vieira 1999: 107). Understood in this way, translation is a juxtaposition of elements or "untranslation", the term used by Augusto de Campos to describe his free visual translations or new texts "whose connection with the original is mediated by the asymmetry of languages at all levels or description" (Portela 2003: 310). His untranslations are *intraduçaos* [intraductions] or *prosa porosa* [porous prose] (Gómez 2018: 371–384; Cleary 2021: 6), in which he incorporates a significant amount of sensory information (images and sound) that was not in the original. In this way, his *intraduçaos* "transform the original poem into a sort of physical object, and reveal elements not present in the original text. . . . Thus the 'intraductions' of Augusto de Campos are visual poems, which finally become 'translation art'" (Hernández 2010: 153; author's translation). Untranslations are never definitive or closed texts:

> With this, the simple dualisms of foreign and familiar, outer and inner, original and translation, central and peripheral culture, homeland and colony, are definitively overcome and inscribed within the text itself in the form of a dynamic creative principle that subverts any idea of conclusive meaning.
> *(Guldin 2008: 118)*

Therefore, transcreative translation is not copying, reproduction, or repetition. Regarding his translation of *Faust*, de Campos writes that translation "virtualizes the notion of mimesis not as a theory of copy . . . but as the production of difference in sameness" (Haroldo de Campos in Vieira 1999: 110).

In all of these texts, as well as those mentioned in the previous chapter, the original is already a translation and its translation is a transcreation as defined by de Campos. To translate is to establish a dialogue with many voices, not only with the voices of the original but also with other voices, both local and universal. It is what de Campos refers to as "transtextualization". "Translation as transtextualization or transcreation demythicizes the ideology or fidelity" (Vieira 1999: 110).

Repetition is thus never mere reproduction. The original is a text of texts, which are heterogeneous, plural, and derived. Hence, no translation is ever definitive, because one text refers to another, and that text in turn points to still another. The text is not a single unit; it is a multidimensional object with many different facets. That is why a text never has only one reading, but rather generates a veritable explosion of different interpretations. The unity and identity of a language and the determinable form of its boundaries are thus challenged. By using repetition as a creative strategy, the translations of the de Campos brothers deconstruct the traditional concepts of original, authorship, translation, primary, and secondary.

Although Gentzler's (2017: 70; 2008: 77–107) explanation of de Campos's transcreations applies the concept to other texts, he very aptly points out the following:

> The emphasis of *antropofagia* on the creative and transformative nature of translation, or, in Haroldo de Campos's creative neologisms, "*transcriação*", "*transluminação*", "*transfusão*", and . . . have challenged definitions of static texts and forced

scholars to rethink the very definition of translation. The translation/rewriting approach for the *antropofagistas* is not a domesticating or foreignizing one, but *both*: importing ideas and expressions via translation *plus* rewriting those ideas and texts in the vein of the receiving culture.

This is precisely the approach taken by the Finnish translator of Charles Bernstein's "Besotted Desquamation". Because the poem is based on the repetition of letters, it is difficult to translate because the words in each of its 27 sections all share the same initial:

> When I sat down to translate the poem into Finnish, I was disappointed, confused even, to find that the words my dictionary suggested for replacement seemed to begin with just about any letter. . . . I began . . . to have doubts as to the very fundamentals of the profession of translation. I mean, how can we imagine to translate anything, when we cannot even get the first letters right? Eventually, I think I did find a problem to the solution. What I did was to put the original away—for good, I never looked at it again. . . . I then proceeded, not to translate, not even to rewrite, but to write the poem, exactly the way Charles had done before me . . . don't think of translation as having anything to do with interlingual communication, and I'm all for inverting the currently dominant paradigm in which the languages are seen as something primary, translation as a secondary, ensuing "problem".
>
> *(Lehto 2009: 49, 51)*

Viewed in this light, translation as transcreation is as important as the original. "In the beginning was translation" (ibid.: 51). "Translation, not languages per se, forms the basis of cultures" (id.). The language used by these uncreative writers is impure, which threatens the integrity of the linguistic system and of translation—"plus d'une langue", writes Derrida in his *Memories for Paul de Man*, more than one language and at the same time only one language because language in itself is inherently multiple and various. In this context, "a translation is never quite 'faithful', always somewhat 'free', it never establishes an identity, always a lack and a supplement, and it can never be a transparent representation" (Venuti 1992: 8).

The sign here is not equal to the sum of the signifier and signified. It can only be understood in relation to the other elements, which thus become a part of it. Every sign is the imprint of another and thus can only exist as a "trace", "mark", or "trail" of something that quickly fades and is forever blurred. The authorship of texts is always transitory, inasmuch as the origin is merely a trace (Spivak 1967/1984: xviii). In any type of text, the translator has to make decisions, though in the texts under discussion, these decisions are perhaps riskier and require greater creativity. For this reason, translations of books such as Perec's *La Disparition* are undoubtedly transcreations in the sense of Haroldo de Campos:

> The act of translating can sometimes outweigh the translation itself. Think *La Disparition* into English, still *sans* the letter "e". Adair's role as translator of *A Void* is, in my opinion, an act of authorship equal to Perec's.
>
> *(Goldsmith 2015a: n.p.)*

3.1.2 Haroldo de Campos and Octavio Paz

Haroldo de Campos had an interesting relationship with Octavio Paz. Despite certain differences (Cisneros 2020), de Campos' translation as transcreation resembles Paz' translation as creation. Both were firmly convinced that to translate is to create. Every reading, writes Paz (1971/2012: 152), is a translation and every criticism is, or starts out as, an interpretation. Paz begins his well-known essay on translation by stating that learning how to speak is learning how to translate. Translation reveals the differences between languages and between cultures. According to Paz, each text is the translation of another text, because no text is entirely original. Every text is the translation of other verbal and nonverbal signs:

> Thanks to translation, we become aware that that our neighbors do not speak and think as we do. On the one hand, the world is presented to us as a collection of similarities; on the other, as a growing heap of texts, each slightly different from the one that came before it: translations of translations of translations. Each text is unique, yet at the same time it is the translation of another text. No text can be completely original because language itself, in its very essence, is already a translation—first from the nonverbal world, and then, because each sign and each phrase is a translation of another sign, another phrase. However, the inverse of this reasoning is also entirely valid. All texts are originals because each translation has its own distinctive character. Up to a point, each translation is a creation and thus constitutes a unique text.
>
> *(Paz 1971/2012: 154)*

Haroldo de Campos would doubtlessly agree with this, as he would with another statement by Octavio Paz in *Translation: Literature and Letters*, in which Paz observes that each translation is to some extent an invention and is thus a unique text. In his view, translation is "an exercise in which what is decisive . . . is the translator's initiative" (Paz 1971/2012: 157). Each reading is a translation, and thus, for both authors, translation is a dynamic process in constant movement. To translate is to create, not to repeat or to reproduce. Paz (1971/2012: 160) even goes so far as to affirm that poetic translation results in the "reproduction of the original poem in another poem that is less a copy than a transmutation". When Paz affirmed that translation is creation, de Campos doubtlessly nodded his head in agreement.

> The translator is not constructing an unalterable text from mobile characters; instead, he is dismantling the elements of the text, freeing the signs into circulation,

then returning them to language. In its first phase, the translator's activity is no different from that of a reader or critic: each reading is a translation and each criticism is, or begins as, an interpretation.

(Paz 1971/2012: 159)

As is well-known, Haroldo de Campos translated "Blanco" by Octavio Paz. In fact, it was the only time that de Campos ever translated from Spanish to English. Octavio Paz wrote "Blanco" in 1966 when he was ambassador to India. First published in 1967 in Mexico (Joaquín Mortiz), "Blanco" is an unconventional poem in which Mallarmé's "Un Coup de Dès" (1898) engages in a dialogue with the 18th-century Indo-Tibetan Tantric Buddhist philosophy of Hevajra Tantra.

As Paz himself writes, its three columns can be read in various ways. One can read all three columns at once or read each one separately. As the text unfolds, it is also possible to read different combinations of the three columns. The poem was originally published in a box containing a single accordion fold-out page in two colors and three typefaces. In this work, Octavio Paz wished to convert time into space. His goal was to transcend the conventional sequentiality of poetic discourse and transform the text into a space in which words and their meanings simultaneously coexist. In this sense, it is hardly surprising that Haroldo de Campos decided to translate "Blanco". The fact that it was so innovative and totally divorced from traditional literary forms was an attraction in itself, which was further enhanced by its relation to Mallarmé's aesthetics (Perloff 2012; Da Silva 2006).

In 1986, Haroldo de Campos translated the poem in *Transblanco* (Rio de Janeiro, Editora Guanabara). His translation is a striking example of transcreation. In addition to this translation of Paz' poem, *Transblanco* includes the correspondence between the two poets from 1968 to 1981, as well as essays by different literary critics and writers:

> *Transblanco* has become a model of what poetic pluri-dialogues can achieve through translation understood as "transcreation", as Haroldo de Campos called it. . . . The choice of the prefix—"trans"—in Campos's book title has a double function: first, it refers to transversal cultural interactions and existences; and second (albeit inexorably linked to the first), it refers to the transformations that take place in the course of these relationships and processes. The "trans" aspect is often sidelined when it comes to discussions of originality and authorship, when in the case of Pa and Campos exemplifies this type of exchange that operates trans-linguistically, transculturally, and trans-continentally.
>
> *(Librandi et al. 2020: 2)*

3.2 From transcreation to total translation: Jerome Rothenberg

Jerome Rothenberg, who coined the term "ethnopoetics" in 1960, transcreates Octavio Paz' "Blanco" by applying de Campos' transcreation and his own theory of "othering" or "total translation". In a recent volume in honor of Haroldo de

Campos (1929–2003) and Octavio Paz (1914–1998)—both key figures in the direction taken by poetry and translation in Latin America during the second half of the 20th century—Rothenberg (2020: 113–121) pays homage to them by writing transcreative variations similar to his own translations (or transcreations) of Federico Garcia Lorca:

> My strategy here was to turn, as Haroldo had before me, to the original "Blanco", so as to further the earlier act of transcreation with a transcreative work of my own. I looked in doing so to a form of othering that I had begun to practice two decades before—in a series of poems, "The Lorca Variations", derived from the vocabulary of my own translations of García Lorca's early *Suites*. In those I systematically used all of Lorca's nouns (in my English translation) as nuclei from which to compose new poems. Moving from poem to poem I arranged the translated nouns in four or five columns and proceeded to link the words in something like reverse order . . . both Lorca and not Lorca, both mine and not mine.
>
> *(Rothenberg 2020: 119)*

"The Lorca Variations XV" (Rothenberg 2020: 119–120) is, as Rothenberg states, a creative translation, because the poem is both Lorca's and Rothenberg's. The same goes for his homage to Haroldo de Campos, in which he rewrites or transcreates a transcreation: he rewrites poems written in 2013 about de Campos ("15 Antiphonals for Haroldo") in which, at the request of the editor Francesco Conz, each contributor was asked to write their poems by hand on a photograph of de Campos:

> I took phrases and lines from English translations of Haroldo's poetry and responded to them with loosely rhymed soundings of my own. I then handwrote the poems pair by pair onto a black left margin on each of the photographs.
>
> *(Rothenberg 2020: 120)*

Starting from that previous transcreation, Rothenberg transcreates again by playing with the typography (de Campos' words appear in italics and Rothenberg's in Roman type): "For me at least, the resultant work has the feel of translation/transcreation" (Rothenberg 2020: 120). In both, appropriation is a positive concept and has a sense of community. This is perhaps most evident in his translations of American Indian poetry. His concept of "total translation" and "othering" stems from the translation of that oral poetry. Rothenberg is unfamiliar with most of the languages that he translates. Because he cannot speak Navajo or Seneca, he relies on songmen and friends of his, who help him with his translations:

> In the Summer of 1968 I began to work simultaneously with two sources of Indian poetry. Settling down a mile from the Cold Spring settlement of the

Allegany (Seneca) Reservation at Steamburg, New York, I was near enough to friends who were traditional songmen to work with them on the translation of sacred & secular song-poems. At the same time David McAllester was sending me recordings, transcriptions, literal translations & his own freer reworkings of a series of seventeen "Horse Songs" that had been the property of Frank Mitchell, a Navajo singer from Chinle, Arizona (born: 1881, died: 1967). Particularly with the Senecas (where I didn't know in the first instance what, if anything, I was going to get) my first concern was with the translation process itself.

(Rothenberg 1962/1981: 76)

For Rothenberg, what is important is not the translation itself but rather the translation process. According to Rothenberg (1962/1981: 80–81), translation is collaboration and it should be used to talk about the other: "I translate, then, as a way of reporting what I've sensed or seen of another's situation". What is essential is to be able to rewrite everything that an oral poetry performance conveys. This includes not only the meaning of the words but also the meaning of all elements that are not strictly words and that have no literal translation:

As with most Indian poetry, the voice carried many sounds that weren't, strictly speaking, "words". These tended to disappear or be attenuated in translation, as if they weren't really there. But they *were* there & were at least as important as the words themselves. In both Navajo & Seneca many songs consisted of nothing but those "meaningless" vocables (not free "scat" either but fixed sounds recurring from performance to performance). Most other songs had both meaningful & non-meaningful elements, & such songs (McAllester told me for the Navajo) were often spoken of, *qua* title, by their meaningless burdens. Similar meaningless sounds, Dell Hymes had pointed out for some Kwakiutl songs, might in fact be keys to the songs' structures: "something usually disregarded, the refrain or so-called 'nonsense syllables' . . . in fact of fundamental importance . . . both structural clue & microcosm."

So there were all these indications that the exploration of "pure sound" wasn't beside the point of those poetries but at or near their heart: all of this coincidental too with concern for the sound--poem among a number of modern poets. Accepting its meaning—fulness here, I more easily accepted it there. I also realized (with the Navajo especially) that there were more than simple refrains involved: that we, as translators & poets, had been taking a rich *oral* poetry & translating it to be read primarily for meaning, thus denuding it to say the least.

(Rothenberg 1962/1981: 77)

Even though in this type of language such characteristics are especially important, they can be applied to any type of communication, because not everything is transmitted through words.⁵ We communicate through each of our five senses. Meaning is conveyed in our voice tone, accent, speech rhythm, intonation, body movements, and many other channels. That is why Rothenberg (1962/1981: 74) considers that "the translations themselves may create new forms & shapes-of-poems with their own energies & interest". This is precisely what he means by total translation:

> Let me try, then, to respond to *all* the sounds I'm made aware of, to let that awareness touch off responses or events in the English. I don't want to set English words to Indian music, but to respond poem-for-poem in the attempt to work out a "total translation"—not only of the words but of all sounds connected with the poem, including finally the music itself.
>
> *(Rothenberg 1962/1981: 78)*

Rothenberg's translations, which communicate through all our senses, remind me of "experiential translation" (Campbell and Vidal 2019) and of what Clive Scott (2010: 157) calls "eco-writings", an "eco-poetics" (Scott 2018: 61–84) that tries to exploit the flexibility of words by adopting "*affective* forms of intonation, or by vocally sculpting the word (by elongation, segmentation, varying loudness) to marry language to natural phenomena". This involves

> the translation of the non-onomatopoeic into the onomatopoeic, or the projection of the non-onomatopoeic as onomatopoeic. Ideophones, onomatopoeia, far from being confined to purely acoustic phenomena have a natural tendency to synesthetize themselves. In short, we need to develop an onomatopoeia of the other senses. This may involve not only manipulation of words in their accepted forms, but the creation of new diacritical marks to achieve maximal sensory vividness.
>
> *(Scott 2010: 157)*

In ethnopoetry, repetition is regarded as positive, transformative, and creative. That is why Rothenberg (1962/1981: 83–84) emphasizes that it is not always necessary to translate repetition with words; it can be achieved more creatively. For example, visual repetition produces creative translations that are able to "bring across (i.e. 'translate') the feeling of the Seneca word". This involves translating the emotions, feelings, and sensations expressed in the words of the other. Instead of striving for equivalence, Rothenberg seeks to encompass the full range of vocal sounds. "My inclination is to present analogues to the full range of vocal sound, etc., but not to represent the poem's subject as 'mere picture'" (Rothenberg 1962/1981: 85).

In the West, repetition has long been viewed in a negative light. However, as reflected in ethnopoetics, this is not the case in other cultures. Catherine Quick gives an interesting example in the following two stanzas from Kenneth Mendoza's (1993) translations of a Pawnee Hako ceremony:

Ho-o-o-o!
H'Mother she has moved now
H'Mother she has moved now
Dawn Birth Now
H'Mother she has moved now
Ho-o-o-o!
H'Eagle you move now
H'Eagle you move now
Dawn Birth Now
H'Eagle you move now

Quick (1999: 95) explains how repetition reflects different worldviews:

> If the average Western literary scholar were to critique the above poem, he or she might note the repetitiveness, simplistic (perhaps even trite) images, lack of poetic device, and meaningless words. This would represent a fair critique of the poem, if it were written with typical Western assumptions about what constitutes good poetry. But what if the poet's assumptions were different?

Repetition creates "a state of consciousness where the participants . . . are integrated into, exploring, and bringing to resolve, the event in phenomena that the performance captures" (Mendoza 1993: 63). It is a powerful structural device, a way to intensify what is being said and to integrate words and thoughts into a rhythmic whole (Mendoza 1993: 64).

Rothenberg's goal was to find a better way of translating the oral tradition of non-Western cultures, especially that of Native American cultures:

> For instance, the repetitiveness of the above poem is grating to many listeners used to poetry based on Western poetic ideals of originality and variation. Thus, earlier translators of this poem . . . altered each repeated line, making it slightly different in wording (and thus meaning) from the others. For the Pawnee ceremony from which these stanzas derive, however, the exact repetition turns out to be a crucial element. The earlier translations therefore end up being mistranslations.
>
> *(Quick 1999: 96)*

To better translate poetry that does not conform to Western "universal" standards, Rothenberg constructed a theory of total translation, which addressed the performance of the text, its situatedness, and its storytelling (Tedlock 1992; Swann 1992, 2011). Following a musical strategy similar to musical scoring, he devised a notation system that graphically represented

> the various sound qualities, such as line breaks for pauses, dots in between lines for pauses of longer duration, capitals for loudness, smaller-than-average type for

whispered or softly spoken words. Gestures, facial expressions, and significant audience responses were described in parentheticals and footnotes, which also contained descriptions of the overall storytelling situation.

(Quick 1999: 96)

Rothenberg translates sounds, sensations, and emotions. After analyzing his translations from Navajo and Seneca into English, he concludes that the resulting translation has a life of its own and is able to capture much more than the words in the texts. This is why it can be regarded as a total translation:

> Translation is carry-over. It is a means of delivery & of bringing to life. It begins with a forced change of language, but a change too that opens up the possibility of greater understanding. Everything in these song-poems is finally translatable: words, sounds, voice, melody, gesture, etc., in the reconstitution of a unity that would be shattered by approaching each element in isolation. A full & total experience begins it, which only a total translation can fully bring across.
>
> *(Rothenberg 1962/1981: 91)*

Total translation means translating the physical form of the word, setting it free from the prison of writing, and allowing it to move so that the translation can embody and manifest the "unique expressive qualities of oral performance" (Mendoza 1993: 1). By creatively translating everything—gesture, facial expression, movement, tonal qualities and expressiveness of voice, pause, and rhythm—it is possible to achieve "a communication that promotes transfer, intimacy and active participation. The speaker listens while the hearer speaks" (Mendoza 1993: 4).

Because orality is crucial to ethnopoetry, each performance is different from the others. Each storyteller tells the story in a different way, and so, here too, there is no repetition. Each telling is a retelling. Each person creates their own story because they translate it with their own gestures, movements, voice tone, and pauses. That is why in this type of poetry, but also in other types such as that of William Carlos Williams, Gary Snyder, and the "Projective Verse" of Charles Olson, to cite three examples of many that transcend Platonic-Aristotelian rationality (Mendoza 1993: 41), the original text is always in movement:

> It would a great error to think that, writing a story at the dictation of a Native American we possess the recognized standard form of the tale. There is no standard.
>
> *(Morris in Mendoza 1993: 11)*

In these texts, as well as those mentioned in Chapter 2, the concept of the original, as it appears in the literature, is cast into doubt. This signifies that the idea of repetition acquires new dimensions:

We can witness the "same" poem presented by different speakers or even the same speaker on different occasions and not experience or witness the same literary product twice. . . . This belief is no doubt supported by our model and concept of "original text" in written literature, which insures reliability and exact duplication based on

(Mendoza 1993: 11)

In uncreative writings (Swann 2011), all of these factors must be addressed and repetition should be respected as a creative element and creator of originality. Only in this way is it possible to create a performative translation in which translators "discover that they cannot escape complex ethical decisions related to their agency both as readers of an 'original' and as authors of their translations" (van Wyke 2012: 77).

The total translation proposed by Rothenberg is also a transcreative translation in the tradition of Haroldo de Campos. And both types of translation are also in tune with José Luis Borges' view of translation (see Section 3.3). For all of these scholars, the translator is not invisible. Translation is as important as the original and even completes and enriches it within the context of its own time and place, as Rothenberg (1962/1981: 92) observes:

One way or another translation makes a poem in this place that's analogous in whole or in part to a poem in that place. The more the translator can perceive of the original—not only the language but, more basically perhaps, the living situation from which it comes &, very much so, the living voice of the singer—the more of it he should be able to deliver. In the same process he will be presenting something—i.e., making something present, or making something as a present—for his own time & place.

3.3 Pierre Menard and his precursors

Repetition is thus a positive concept because it enriches both the original and its translation. This is undoubtedly the lesson in Jorge Luis Borges' "Pierre Menard, Author of the Quixote", first published in the journal *Sur* in 1939 and collected in *El jardín de senderos que se bifurcan* (1941) [*The Garden of Forking Paths*] and, later, in *Ficciones* (1944) [*Fictions*]. In this short story, Borges attributes to Menard a few pages of *Don Quixote*, which he wrote (or copied) three centuries after Cervantes published the original.

Borges is one of the authors who has most coherently constructed a theory of translation based on a positive conceptualization of repetition and on the idea that translation is repetition and that repetition enriches the (repeated) text. For Borges, repetition is a metafictional and even metaphysical strategy: doubles, mirrors, ghosts, dreams, and shadows are obsessions that are all intimately related to translation. Faced with the ontological priority of the original in Platonism, Borges wonders if one repeated term is sufficient cause to disrupt the history of the world to the point of claiming that there is no such history at all. This is reflected in works such as *History of Eternity*, "Tlön, Uqbar, Orbis Tertius", *Universal History of Infamy*, *Fictions*, *Doctor Brodie's Report*, "The Aleph", and *Other Inquisitions*.

For Borges, language is a system of citations, and every utterance is a repetition. Although Borges explains his theory of translation in many of his texts, it is in "Pierre Menard, Author of the *Quixote*" where it is most fully developed.[6] Many scholars have perceived the depth of meaning in this short story, which has attracted the attention of those fascinated by interpretation and the death of representation. For example, in *After Babel* (1975: 70), George Steiner states that "Pierre Menard, Author of the *Quixote*" is probably "the most acute" commentary ever offered "on the business of translation". Umberto Eco also refers to this story in *Lector in Fabula* and *The Limits of Interpretation* when he makes the distinction between the "use" and the "interpretation" of a text. Nelson Goodman (1976) uses "Pierre Menard" to address the identity of the artistic work and Arthur Danto (1981) to reflect on the ontology of art.[7] Thanks to "Pierre Menard", Boris Groys even introduced the term *conceptualism* into the Soviet samizdat literary world:

> Groys's act of copying and recombination—remixing Borges and conceptual art—continued this process of reaccentuation and in turn inspired further acts of copying, versioning, and remediation, such as poet and artist Dmitri Prigov's many repetitions and versionings of Alexander Pushkin's *Eugene Onegin*.
>
> (Edmond 2019: 28)

Douglas R. Hofstadter (1997: 280) examines Borges' short story and concludes that its key point is that it stresses "how a set of familiar words and situations, if interpreted in a new context, can take utterly novel and occasionally quite bizarre auras of meaning and imagery". In his *Palimpsestes*, Gérard Genette (1982: 15, 453) affirms that citation is a distinctive literary practice that is part of that Borgesian utopia of a literature in perpetual transfusion. Pierre Menard's *Don Quixote* is not a copy but a transformation or a minimal pastiche (Genette 1982: 447). In fact, "Pierre Menard" is central to *Palimpsestes* and to all of Genette's work. Blanchot (1986: 131) refers to "The Aleph" in *Le Livre à venir*. And Borges' Chinese encyclopedia provided Foucault with the starting point for *Les mots et les choses*. Paul de Man (1964) addresses the question of repetition and the duplication of reality in Borges in relation to chronological time. At the beginning of *Différence et repetition*, Deleuze refers to Pierre Menard, as does Pierre Bayard (2009: 35–36) in his *Le plagiat par anticipation*. And Craig Dworkin acknowledges Pierre Menard as the first "uncreative writer" (Dworkin in Dworkin and Goldsmith 2011: xlv; see also Dworkin 2020a: 25–26).

In the story, Pierre Menard is an early 20th-century author, with a rather unusual ambition—rewriting verbatim a few excerpts of *Don Quixote*—which Borges eloquently describes:

> Pierre Menard did not want to compose *another* Quixote, which surely was easy enough—he wanted to compose *the* Quixote. Nor, surely, need one be obliged to note that his was never a mechanical transcription of the original; he had no intention of *copying* it. His admirable intention was to produce a number of pages which coincided—word for word and line for line—with those of Miguel de Cervantes.
>
> *(Borges 1986/1998: 91)*

As observed by Borges, Menard does not aspire to be Miguel de Cervantes; he wishes to remain himself but to write a literary work that totally matches the original.

> To be a popular novelist of the seventeenth century in the twentieth seemed to Menard to be a diminution. Being, somehow, Cervantes, and arriving thereby at the Quixote—that looked to Menard less challenging (and therefore less interesting) than continuing to be Pierre Menard and coming to the Quixote through the experiences of Pierre Menard. . . . Menard dedicated his scruples and his nights "lit by midnight oil" to repeating in a foreign tongue a book that already existed.
>
> *(Borges 1986/1998: 91, 95)*

Cervantes' text and Menard's are literally identical. Even so, they are not the same. According to Borges, the second text, the repetition or translation, is infinitely richer. "Not for nothing have three hundred years elapsed, freighted with the most complex events. Among those events, to mention but one, is the *Quixote* itself" (Borges 1986/1998: 93). Despite his word-for-word repetition of *Don Quixote*, Menard cannot protect his text from the interference of other readings and other readers in the past, present, and future. The same signs are the starting point to arrive at new meanings. A text changes its meaning depending on who reads it (Manguel 2004). "Pierre Menard" is one of the best and most ironic criticisms

> of the call for faithfulness and invisibility typically associated with traditional translation theories and practices. The story is in fact a brilliant illustration of how absurd it is for a translator to claim (or even to try) to be absolutely faithful to someone else's text.
>
> *(Arrojo 2004: 32)*

The translator dubs a text and creates a dubbing. However, a dubbing is something else entirely. It is another text (Block de Behar 1984/1994: 74; 2014). As in the previously mentioned uncreative writings, "Pierre Menard" is in fact a fable about the problem of identity, representation, and difference. The story reveals and highlights the fragile division between the original and its interpretations and the imperious need that every text has to dialogue with other texts and contexts. Thus, it is worth adding that Menard first tries to reproduce Cervantes' Chapter IX, which is "precisely about the rather nebulous origin of *Don Quixote* and, thus, the blurred limits between translation and authorship, the 'original' and the translation" (Arrojo 2004: 36). *Don Quixote* is, allegedly, the Spanish translation of a manuscript by an Arabic (and not reliable) historian found in a market in Toledo. So, Cervantes is saying that the text is an unreliable translation of a text of unreliable origin.

It is well-known that Borges was fascinated by the double, the original, mirrors, masks, and representation. As previously mentioned, he believed that the translation completes and enriches the original. Despite being the same text, it is in a different context, and for this reason, it is no longer exactly the same text. Every writer starts writing from previous texts. Anything written is always rewritten,

> a copy of a previous text, and in that sense, is a copy of a previous text. The new text thus transforms the image of its "predecessors" in the mind of the reader. In this respect, Borges often cited the theory of the "state of repetition" of his friend, Macedonio Fernández, according to whom it is not the copyist—but the creator—who is the true plagiarist.
>
> (Marfè 2017: 228)

In *L'utopie littéraire*, Genette evokes Borges when he affirms that each book is reborn in each new reading. The text is constantly shifting, moving, and incorporating itself into new environments as it is read by new people. As in "The Homeric Versions" or in *Universal History of Infamy*, Borges repeats texts in the form of cultural appropriations, moving them to the fringes and thus creating unexpected meanings. In one of his interviews, he made the following comment:

> I think you are enriching me. Because after all reading is an elaboration. Every time I read something, that something is being changed. And every time I write something, that something is being changed all the time by every reader. Every new experience enriches the book.
>
> (in van Wyke 2012: 95)

Menard's madness and his obsession with preserving an unconditional respect for the author's intentions without the interference of the translator or interpreter also reveal an adherence to a shared understanding forged in logocentrism, as well as a Cartesian conceptualization of the subject, that still dominates our vision of the world and, consequently, conditions our conceptions of the text, reading, and translation (Arrojo 2001–2002: 27; Arrojo 2014; Arrojo 2004; Leal 2023). And yet, *Don Quixote* challenges that vision. It is arguably the first modern literary work because it anticipates the infinite interplay between identities and differences of signs and similarities.

The quixotic madness implicit in Menard's understanding of language contains the seeds of its own deconstruction (Arrojo 2001–2002: 27). Once the arbitrariness of the sign is acknowledged, the absolute recovery of signs by means of translation or even repetition is a doomed enterprise, if only because translation exposes the person who translates (regardless of their efforts to avoid it) to the experience of *différance*:

> The story of Pierre Menard illustrates the absurdity of any concept of sameness between texts. Borges never uses the word "translation", but his story is about translation all the same. Pierre Menard's ridiculous proposition is as foolish as that of a translator who believes that he or she can reproduce an identical equivalent text in another language. What actually happens, is that the signs of the translator's involvement in the process of interlingual transfer will always be present, and those signs can be decoded by any reader examining the translation process.
> *(Bassnett in Bassnett and Lefevere 1998: 26)*

The concept of repetition is repeated in *Atlas*, *History of Eternity*, *Fictions*, and *Doctor Brodie's Report*, in which Borges wonders whether it might be possible to gaze at time as one would look into a mirror and thus simultaneously contemplate the past and the future. At the end of "Partial Magic in the *Quixote*", Borges explicitly states his obsession with repetition. He wonders why we find doubles and false origins so unsettling. He asks why we are concerned that there is a map included in a map and that the 1,001 nights are inside the volume of *The Thousand and One Nights*. Why are we uneasy that Don Quixote is a reader of *Don Quixote*, and Hamlet a spectator of *Hamlet*? Borges answers that he believes that this disquiet arises because such inversions suggest that if fictional characters can be readers or spectators, we, as readers or spectators, can be fictitious (Borges 1954/1989: 47).

Borges bases his originals on his precursors. In "Kafka and his Precursors" (a story greatly admired by Harold Bloom), he affirms that each writer creates his precursors, and this becomes evident when he incorporates his recreation of Poe's "The Purloined Letter" into "Death and the Compass". In his three stories on translation, "The Two Ways to Translate" (1926), "The Homeric Versions" (1932), and "The Translators of *The Thousand and One Nights*" (1935), but also in others such as "An Examination of the Work of Herbert Quain" (1941), "On William Beckfords *Vathek*" (1951), "The Enigma of Edward Fitzgerald" (1951), "Averroes's Search", "Circular Ruins" (1940), "El Evangelio según San Marcos", "Borges and I", "The Maker", *A Universal History of Infamy* (1935), *Fictions* (1944), and *The Aleph* (1949), Borges disputes the idea that translations are necessarily inferior to the originals and suggests that the concept of the "definitive text" is a fallacy. In his view, the original is always unfaithful to the translation. So-called "originals" are as much "drafts" as translations. As Balderston observes in an interview with Patricio Zunini (22-8-2021), the defence of plagiarism at the end of "The Immortal" is a translation of a quote from a famous prologue by Conrad. There are many invisible citations without quotation marks in Borges' work. Borges believed in the proliferation of possibilities, in infinite drafts, and he hid many quotations in his books (Balderston 2018; Egginton and Johnson 2009).

"Borges and I", a short but poignant story in *The Doer* (1960), hinges on his perception of his private self and his public persona. The story is about Borges as a private person, but also about the other Borges, the famous author and storyteller who writes and narrates the story. Both the well-known author who writes and the private self that is written about share obsessions and have a relationship justified by literature, even though this is not enough to save them. Nevertheless, the original and its repetition both exist thanks to each other; they need each other, and they enrich each other:

> It would be an exaggeration to say that ours is a hostile relationship; I live, let myself go on living, so that Borges may contrive his literature, and this literature justifies me. It is no effort for me to confess that he has achieved some valid pages, but those pages cannot save me, perhaps because what is good belongs to no one, not even to him, but rather to the language and to tradition. Besides, I am destined to perish, definitively, and only some instant of myself can survive in him. Little by little, I am giving over everything to him, though I am quite aware of his perverse custom of falsifying and magnifying things. Spinoza knew that all things long to persist in their being; the stone eternally wants to be a stone and the tiger a tiger. I shall remain in Borges, not in myself (if it is true that I am someone), but I recognize myself less in his books than in many others or in the laborious strumming of a guitar. Years ago I tried to free myself from him and went from the mythologies of the suburbs to the games with time and infinity, but those games belong to Borges now and I shall have to imagine other things. Thus my life is a flight and I lose everything and everything belongs to oblivion, or to him. I do not know which of us has written this page.
>
> *(Borges 1960/1964: 246)*

We have no idea who the author of this story really is. We do not know who is the original and who is the repetition:

> Borges dismisses debates about faithfulness and unfaithfulness, and dismisses also what he terms the "superstition" about the inferiority of translations. He refuses to evaluate faithfulness, provocatively telling us that either all translations are faithful, or none of them are, since translations are merely manifestations of different perspectives. For Borges, translation was not about a linguistic process of transfer, it was about a creative process, in which a text is reshaped, rewritten, recomposed for a new readership. That creative process must inevitably involve transforming the original into something different.
>
> *(Bassnett 2018: 335)*

Like *The Thousand and One Nights* or *Don Quixote*, the great works of literature never have a single author but are born of manuscripts that were found and of translators who repeated those manuscripts in another language. That is why in Borges' *Homeric Versions*, the first time is already the second. What Menard understands to be Cervantes' original meaning is interpreted by Borges' narrator as something different. It is little wonder that Borges did not believe in definitive texts.

> It could be said that his kind of writing, which is rewriting, partakes of these very qualities. He insistently declares that texts are not finished, because they need to be completed by generations of readers. I take it that he also thinks that no writer ever really finishes anything.
>
> *(Balderston 2018: 222)*

Furthermore, as Arrojo (2018) observes, the chapters of the book that Menard decides to repeat are very significant: the first is Chapter IX of Part 1, which, as previously mentioned, explains the "origin" of *Don Quixote*. In this chapter, the reader learns that Cervantes is not the "true author" of the work. *Don Quixote* is associated with translation and falsehood and with an author with a reputation for lying, who is the source of an unfaithful translation. The true/false opposition is thus deconstructed, as are the differences and boundaries between original/translation, presentation/representation, primary/secondary, and author/translator.

Borges is fascinated by the dualisms in *Don Quixote*. It is a novel of dreams, mirrors, and paradoxes, in which Cervantes experiments with the concept of authorship and where the primary is not regarded as better than the secondary or the original as better than its translation. *Don Quixote* imitates *Amadís de Gaula*; Cervantes hides behind Cidi Hamete, and Alonso Quijano pretends to be Don Quixote. Borges is so interested in translation because he is captivated by stories within stories. A text has many voices, like the tales told by Scheherazade. As Cervantes reminds us, the multiple voices within a text mean that there are no originals. For this reason, translation possesses an unusual force because, from a metaphysical perspective, it is unsettling for fictional characters, such as Don Quixote and Pierre Menard, to become readers, translators, and authors of the literary landscape that they inhabit. This forces us to acknowledge the fictitious, translated dimension of our own existence, one of the cornerstones of Borges' work.

Chapter IX of Part 1 of *Don Quixote* reveals the "true" origin of the work that the readers hold in their hands. Cervantes reveals that he is not the creator of the work but that it is the result of a translation, the interpretation of a translator, and random chance. The origins of the novel are anything but orthodox. The story is authored by a mendacious historian and narrated by a translator whom the second author does not trust either. In the prologue to Part I (which is dedicated to the Reader), Cervantes assures us that even though he might seem like the father of *Don Quixote*, he is actually only the stepfather because he is sharing an old story that was told to him long ago. It is like a set of Russian nesting dolls, a complex heteroglossic intertext in which the original text blends with the translation, the author with the interpreter, truth with falsehood, and difference with repetition.

Repetition, doubles, ghosts, shadows, and mirrors (in other words, translation) are constants in Borges' works, such as *Seven Nights*, "The Doer", and his poem

"Joy". The mirror is a nightmare because with mirrors, duplications, translations, and re-presentations such as those created by Pierre Menard, we are obliged to address the question of what is real or, rather, of what we perceive as real. "The Aleph", "The Library of Babel", "The Garden of Forking Paths", and "Funes the Memorious" all reflect different ways of reconstructing reality.

In the "Circular Ruins", for example, the goal of the main character is to dream a man in his minute entirety and impose him on reality. The man spends two years constructing this conjured man, whom he comes to view as his son. However, he fears that his son will eventually discover that he is a mere simulacrum, a projection of another man's dream. In the end, the man finally realizes that he too is an apparition and that he also exists because someone else is dreaming him. Something similar happens in "Partial Magic of the *Quixote*", a story that begins with a warning that it may all be a repetition, but this does not worry the author.

Borges regards faithful translations as inferior to others because such texts lack the nuances and ambiguities introduced by "villainous translators". For Borges, like Cervantes, the secondary is not a problem. Nor is it problematic that the greatest work of Spanish literature might be derived from a translation created by a fraudulent translator. In fact, his short story "Tlön, Uqbar, Orbis Tertius" begins with a grotesque mirror reflecting the room, a presumably plagiarized reproduction of the *Encyclopædia Britannica*, and goes on to describe a fictitious place where metaphysicians do not seek truth, only amazement. This is a place where plagiarism does not exist, a place where all authors are an author, and all books possess their own mirror because their opposite is contained within their pages.

For all of these reasons, Borges' theory of translation is the most suitable for the work of these (un)creative writers. Understood "as an intrinsically performative textual activity, translation is generally viewed, in Borges's terms, as a form of rewriting which is not in any sense neutral or secondary to the original" (Arrojo 2004: 31). For Borges, multiplicity and difference are a source of richness. Babel is not a curse, but precisely the opposite. This is evident in his translations of fiction and poetry from English, French, and German. It is also reflected in his relationship with Norman Thomas di Giovanni, the American translator with whom he collaborated for three years in Buenos Aires. According to Emir Rodríguez Monegal, this collaboration resulted in Borges becoming a co-author of translations, such as the final pages of *Ulysses* (1922) or works by Whitman, Chesterton, Poe, Melville, Woolf, Faulkner, and Kafka. Stephanides (2006: 209) states,

> Jorge Luis Borges raised the notion of "translating against". This idea suggests the importance of translation as a mode of literary interference and manipulation rather than a transparent and faithful image of a text originally written in another language. . . . Borges' writing may be read as an emergent postmodernism *avant la lettre* in his renunciations of totality and identity and in his speculations of an undetermined subject . . . his views of translation . . . put into doubt the privileging of the original in the translation hierarchy.

In his novel, *Une vie de Pierre Menard*, Michel Lafon (2009) asks the same question that many readers and critics (Bogoya 2015: 195–196) have asked: What would have happened if Pierre Menard had really existed, if he were not one of Borges' daydreams? (The literary game continues sometime later when César Aira, with Alberto Manguel and others, translates Lafon's work.) Lafon breathes life into a character who is born in Nimes in two years before Borges wrote his short story. In this novel, Menard's biographer, Maurice Legrand, goes even further than Borges because Legrand's Menard is also intrigued by gardens, labyrinths, detours, masks, and repetition. This Menard is friends with Unamuno, Machado, Gide, and Valéry. Furthermore, as Lafon pointed out in an interview, Menard invents Borges. He is the intellectual father of Borges, Valéry, and others, though he also states that Borges did not need anyone to be Borges, not even himself. This Menard could have been a character in *Bartleby & Co.* by Enrique Vila-Matas (Bogoya 2015: 204).

As Kierkegaard warns in *Repetition*, it is impossible to repeat words and for them to be exactly the same. That is why, despite his efforts to accomplish the contrary in 1939, Pierre Menard created a new and different novel in a different time. Along these lines, Edward Said relates the concept of repetition/originality in Borges' "Pierre Menard" to the same concept in Johann Sebastian Bach's *Goldberg Variations*, a series of 30 variations on a theme that is played at the beginning and then repeated at the end. However, Said is not talking about just any interpretation of these variations, but specifically about the interpretation offered by Glenn Gould:

> At one end of the work a simple theme is announced, a theme permitting itself to be metamorphosed thirty times, redistributed in modes whose theoretical complexity is enhanced by the pleasure taken in their practical execution. At the other end of the *Goldberg*, the theme is replayed after the variations have ceased, only this time the literal repetition is (as Borges says about Pierre Menard's version of the *Quixote*) "verbally identical, but infinitely richer".
>
> *(Said 2008: 4)*

Bear in mind that Said attributes this richness of repetition, this multiplicity of the identical, to the open-mindedness of an interpreter like Gould, who has always refused to follow any kind of imposed interpretation. In Gould's opinion, there is not only one way of interpreting a sonata but as many ways as there are interpreters. However, in his interpretation of Bach, he took things to the limit. He completely reorganized the setting by making sweeping changes to the work. More specifically, he spliced fragments together to create a new whole. He shifted sequences, disorganized different renditions of the Goldberg theme, and used other pianos for different sections of the same music. This is why Gould's performance of these variations is perhaps his best-known interpretation, a translation so much his own, a repetition so creative, that it is sometimes referred to as the "Gouldberg Variations" (van Wyke 2014).

Aside from this final recording, Gould recorded the Goldberg variations several times afterward, returning again and again to previous performances because he was curious to see what he would discover:

> It turned out to be "a rather spooky experience"; he recognized his "fingerprints" from a "purely mechanical, purely tactile point of view", but "could not identify with the spirit of the person who made that recording". The way he read the "same" text to the audience years later had changed.
>
> *(van Wyke 2014: 245)*

For the art world, Pierre Menard is also a very attractive figure.[8] For example, Brian Wallis decided to include Borges' story in *Art After Modernism: Rethinking Representation* (New York: New Museum of Contemporary Art, 1984), one of the most important anthologies of the Appropriationist Movement of the 1980s. Liu Ye alludes to Pierre Menard in his artwork (as well as to others such as Magritte and Mondrian), and, not surprisingly, Cambridge, Massachusetts, is home to the Pierre Menard Gallery.

Pierre Huyghe is another artist who builds his identity on the idea of collective subjectivity. When he exhibits his work, the idea of representation is his point of departure rather than the end of his journey. For *Time Score*, his 2007 exhibition at the Castile-León Museum of Contemporary Art, he published *The Ingenious Hidalgo Don Quixote de la Mancha by Pierre Menard* with the idea of actually creating the *Quixote* that Borges attributes to Pierre Menard. And Sherrie Levine, in her text collage *Born Again* (1995), quotes without quotation marks long passages from "Pierre Menard", from *Bouvard and Pécuchet*, and also from Barthes' "The Death of the Author". Furthermore, Gilbert (2022: 192) argues that Levine's *Gustave Flaubert. Un Coeur Simple*, which was previously mentioned, can be regarded "as a realization of the fictional Menardian project, especially as the artist often cites it as a reference in interviews. The only difference is that she chose Flaubert's famous story as her source text instead of Cervantes' *Don Quixote*".

But perhaps one of the most striking expressions of Pierre Menard in the art world was conceived by (Elaine) Sturtevant, who, in reference to her *Warhol's Flowers* (1964), said, "Same is a copy but it's not the same". Sturtevant repeated various works of Andy Warhol who, when asked about his artistic process, answered "I don't know. Ask Elaine", according to an urban legend. She also copied other artists such as Jasper Johns, Roy Lichtenstein, and Robert Rauschenberg. In the mid-1960s, she "offered some of the strongest challenges to prevailing notions of originality" (Dworkin in Dworkin and Goldsmith 2011: xxxvii). Her repetitions questioned authorship, property, and copyright. She repeated repetition by copying artists who had duplicated previous images, like Warhol:

> By faking faking she showed that she was not a copyist, plagiarist, parodist, forger, or imitator, but was rather a kind of actionist, who adopted style as her

medium in order to investigate aspects of art's making, circulation, consumption, and canonization.

(Eleey 2014: 50; see also Gilbert 2022, Kostelanetz 2020: 7, Lee 2016, Hainley 2013)

Sturtevant's originality "derives from a further act of recontextualization" (Buskirk 2003: 82) and from her intentions:

To be sure, the production history of the Warhol Flowers prints constitutively involves the products of Warhol's successful print-attempts but only as a substantive result of Sturtevant's Intentions. . . . Although *Warhol Flowers* prints are silk-screens in the same way Warhol Flowers prints are silk-screens (e.g., pulled from the same screen—a screen produced by Warhol and not Sturtevant), Warhol's intentions do not figure at all, let alone figure substantively via directing the activities constitutive of the successful print-attempts of which *Warhol Flowers* prints are the products. So, Warhol cannot be an author of Warhol Flowers. Only Sturtevant's intentions so figure (and so direct). So, only Sturtevant is the author of *Warhol Flowers*.

(Uidhir 2013: 58, 59)

In this sense, *Warhol Flowers* reminds us of Richard Prince's *By Richard Prince, A Photograph of Brooke Shields by Garry Gross* (1983), which features

a 1975 Garry Gross photograph of a nude, ten-year old Brooke Shields. Although the photograph *By Richard Prince* . . . is composed of a photograph for which Gross's intentions substantively figure, Gross's intentions do not figure at all for *By Richard Prince*. So, Gary Gross cannot be an author of *By Richard Prince, A Photograph of Brooke Shields by Garry Gross*—again, that's the point. Clearly, authorship cannot be inherited merely via appropriation.

(Uidhir 2013: 59)

Sturtevant's work is also reminiscent of Sherrie Levine's original copies, though Sturtevant made a point of differentiating herself from the photographer (Lee 2016: 52). In her Jasper Johns flags, Warhol's flowers, and rewritings of Duchamp and Beuys, she creatively translates the image. Her work is based on the theories of repetition of Deleuze, whom she cites along with authors such as Foucault and Heidegger. In fact, many of her works are original copies of original copies of other artists, such as Jasper Johns, Frank Stella, or Andy Warhol:

[Her works] served to highlight the degree to which her sources were already using forms and images that raised questions about originality or uniqueness. Thus paintings after Stella's work that Sturtevant produced in 1989 and 1990 have included her own multiple renderings of paintings from the 1960 aluminum series

> that Stella himself made in more than one version. . . . Sturtevant's silkscreen flower paintings raise key issues about the layering of authorship claims as images based on other images are appropriated and recontextualized. But the original photograph used in Warhol's screens was the work of yet another author, Patricia Caulfield, who instituted a lawsuit against Warhol for infringing on her copyright in the photograph, which he had taken from a magazine. Caulfield discovered the use of her photograph in 1965, not long after Warhol began the series, when she saw a poster of Warhol's work in the window of a New York bookstore. While Warhol may have established himself as the author of the tremendously successful series of silkscreen paintings entitled *Flowers*, Caulfield could claim legal authorship, and therefore ownership, of the underlying photograph. Ultimately the case was settled out of court, with Warhol agreeing to give Caulfield and her attorney two of the *Flowers* paintings, and also to give Caulfield a royalty for future use of the image.
>
> *(Buskirk 2003: 82, 83)*

Given her fascination with the copy as opposed to the original, Sturtevant could not help but be drawn to Pierre Menard, as indeed she was. As we have seen in his story, Borges assures us that Menard did not copy Cervantes. Even though the pages coincide line for line and word for word, they are different texts because their contexts are different. Undoubtedly, this idea appealed to Sturtevant. In fact, in an essay for the White Columns Gallery exhibition in New York, Schwartz and Davis (1986) compare her to Pierre Menard when they refer to the concept of multiple selves in relation to Marilyn Monroe (with respect to Norma Jeane Mortenson as well as to her public identity) but also in relation to Borges and Pierre Menard.

Following Borges' philosophy, Sturtevant reads the story of Borges, Menard, and Cervantes, with the knowledge that her reading will never be exactly the same, given the difference in contexts. As a "faithful" "precursor" to Borges years later, *Sturtevant, Author of the Quixote* (2008) has two dates (in the same way as *Don Quixote* and Borges' short story): the date of its actual publication and 1970, the year when the artist first planned its edition:

> Cervantes's *Don Quixote* is also fragmentary in the sense that its two parts were published separately, in 1604 to 1605 and 1615. Another version of the second part of the *Quixote* was also published in 1614, by an author writing under the pseudonym Alonso Fernández de Avellaneda. Cervantes renounced, yet incorporated, this "second *Don Quixote*" into the second half of his story. Cervantes's attitude to the "surplus" created by the book written by the other writer, the one he refrains from calling a "numbskull, ass and impudent monkey" in the Prologue to Part II of his *Quixote*, was humorously tolerant and catholic in its appropriative character. . . . Cervantes appears to share Sturtevant's disregard for being misunderstood.
>
> *(Lee 2016: 56, 65)*

As pointed out by Lee (2016: 55), the cover of *Sturtevant, Author of the Quixote* does not seem to be from the 21st century but from the beginning of the 20th, and the typefaces used give the book an antiquarian quality that has nothing to do with Sturtevant's work in digital video.

In her book, Sturtevant (2008: 6) writes Borges a letter "a la diable, carried along by the inertias of language and invention". Dated 1970, the letter begins with "Dear Mr. Borges" and ends with "e. sturtevant". As the signer of the letter, she makes Menard's statements her own and thus replaces Pierre Menard as the speaker. This is a strategy that heightens the complexity of the concept of authorship and reality versus fiction in the works of both Cervantes and Borges. The first part of Sturtevant's book repeats many fragments of Borges, whereas the second part repeats passages from *Don Quixote*. Nevertheless, the section in which the Arabs are called liars is crossed out for reasons of political correctness, and this situates the text in a different context than that of Cervantes and Borges.

Years later, Sturtevant participated in the exhibition *Fake as More* (Simon Lee Gallery New York, 2018), in which repetition, copying, and self-copy were the starting points. They were thus regarded not as "fakes" but rather as part of a re-creative process. The title of the exhibition was taken from a 1973 text of the same name published under the pseudonym "Cheryl Bernstein", which was initially created for Hank Herron's first one-man show. As pointed out by Thomas Crow (1996: 69), this article was included with no indication of its fraudulent status in *Idea Art*, a widely consulted anthology of writings on conceptual art edited by Gregory Battcock (1973). Cheryl Bernstein is actually Carol Duncan, who republished this text, affirming that Hank Herron's copies of Frank Stella are superior to the originals, in her book *The Aesthetics of Power* (1993: 216–218).[9]

These artists as well as many others base their creative work on plagiarism. They unashamedly confess to repetition and underline the fact that theirs are unoriginal creations. In this way, their first writing becomes the second writing that Barthes refers to in *Critique et vérité* (1966). It is that plural language that is capable of opening "the way to unforeseeable relaying of meaning, the endless play of mirrors, and it is this room for manoeuvre which is suspect" (Barthes 1966/2007: 3).

Works like these clearly exemplify that the translator is much more than a mere reproducer:

> In the wake of Nietzsche's assault on Platonism, poststructuralist theorists, especially those associated with deconstruction, have been questioning many of the presuppositions upon which the traditional view of translation was founded and, in a sense, have turned the traditional notion of the ethical translator on its head. In this scenario, meaning is no longer considered a stable object that authors place *in* texts, where it awaits recovery, but is instead understood as something created through the act of interpretation. Language is not neutral, nor is the act of interpretation, and, thus translators cannot make the claim that they are simply

reproducing what some original says; "fidelity" is not a self-evident, unproblematic concept whose demands one merely accepts or rejects.

(van Wyke 2012: 78)

Repetitive art and literature require a (trans)creative type of translation, translation in the Borgesian tradition, that acknowledges that the translator is visible and that their creation is as important as the original: "All writing is rewriting, or better said, a rewriting of a rewriting of a rewriting, and translation . . . plays a significant role in that process" (Gentzler 2017: 10). In the works mentioned here, "copying becomes a new form of creativity; modifying a text becomes a new form of authorship" (Gentzler 2017: 14).

Notes

1 Kotz (2007: 146) highlights "the differences within repetition" in Andre's poetry:

> What a modern typography cannot replicate—is the tactile quality of letters typed on a manual typewriter, with their inevitable variations in ink density, sharpness, and force of impression. Even though Andre has clearly strived for a uniformity of appearance, the inevitable slight variations—the differences within repetition—give the massed blocks a vulnerability and poignancy. The uniformity is never exact.

2 Other interesting parrots are Lorenzo el Magnífico, who belonged to Gabriel García Márquez in *Vivir para contarla* (2002), and the parrots of Mário de Andrade, Chateaubriand, and Humboldt. On repetition, Loulou, and other parrots, see Schwartz (2014: 17–143).

3 They set out to change literature by creating a universal picture language, a poetry that could be read by all, regardless of what language they spoke. Letters would double as carriers of semantic content and as powerful visual elements in their own right. Often the poems—written in just about every language imaginable—came with a key so that, even if you didn't know, for example, Japanese, you could get the gist of what a handful of *kanji* compellingly strewn across a page added up to. Delightful to the eye, and political in its intent, their agenda was nothing short of revolutionary: to create a visual Esperanto that would ultimately dissolve linguistic—and thereby political—barriers between nations. (Goldsmith 2015c: 10–11)

4 Something similar could be said of Jen Calleja's transcreative and feminist translations of Christian Marclay's *The Clock* (see Calleja 2019: 368):

> These feminist translations, then, are a two-fold political act rather than a light-hearted task: a quashing of translation as a neutral act through homing in on the ideologies at play in translation through the figure of the translator, who is then in turn acknowledged as an actor in the process of translation. See also Collins (2019).

5 Clive Scott sees words in an interestingly similar manner:

> Words are like fossilizations of language, encourage stereotyped thinking, even out the infinite diversity of sensibilities, and are inadequate to the impulses we want to feed into them; words a-prioritize experience and rob sensation and evocation of their transience. Once released from the tyranny of the word, letters might be combined in all manner of ways; all manner of alphabets and other notations might be incorporated into writing and, as a result, a new sound and thought world might be created by language.
>
> *(Scott 2010: 157)*

6 This type of creative translation (Hernández 2008) has generated contemporary "precursors" such as Ilan Stavans (Vidal 2023; Stavans and Boucetta 2020), whose work as an author, translator, and scholar is deeply influenced by Cervantes and Borges.
7 Danto (1981: 34–35) aptly argues that

> the two works identified by Borges, that of Cervantes and that of Menard, would generate classes of indiscernible copies, the one class copies of the work of Cervantes, the other copies of that of Menard: but these would be copies of different, even importantly different, works, though nothing would be easier than to mistake a copy of Cervantes for a copy of Menard . . . if the works in question have all the same properties, they must be identical. But Borges' point is that they do not. They have only in common those properties that the eye as such might identify . . . Borges' example has the philosophical effect of forcing us to avert our eye from the surfaces of things, and to ask in what if not surfaces the differences between distinct works must consist of.

8 Similarly in other contexts. Thus, the French Lebanese financier and philosopher Elie Ayache (2010), whose book *The Blank Swan* "interpellates Borges' fiction with the apparatus of the derivatives markets: the dynamic replication of the BSM (Black-Scholes-Merton) model and the derivative contract, that implicitly relies on writing" (Clarke 2017:134).
9 The text by "Cheryl Bernstein" for the first one-man show of "Hank Herron," the fictional artist who repeats works by Frank Stella, includes ideas that could well be Borges': "Mr. Herron's work, by reproducing the exact appearance of Frank Stella's entire *oeuvre*, nevertheless introduces new content and a new concept . . . that is precluded in the work of Mr. Stella, i.e., the denial of originality" (in Crow 1996: 70). And when Thomas Crow (1986: 12) writes about *The Fake as More*, he also plays with references made by Cheryl Bernstein to Sartre, Wittgenstein, Heidegger, and Merleau-Ponty, updating them with Borgesian citations of Barthes, Foucault, and Baudrillard, among others.

4
TRANSLATING REPETITION
(Un)creative translations

4.1 Creative translation in the 21st century

Decades ago, the crisis of representation irrevocably changed many epistemological concepts in many disciplines. The same also occurred in translation studies (Bassnett and Lefevere 1998). After many turns, absolute equivalence is no longer a realistic or even a desirable goal. The translator has at last emerged from the shadows and has become visible. This is no longer understood as a negative trait but as "a to-be-expected, if not entirely positive, aspect of any translation. . . . Translation is much more than double-voiced; rather, the voices are multiple, a translation of a translation of a translation, extending back diachronically" (Gentzler 2017: 223).

According to Rosemary Arrojo (2018: 1), the traditional view of translation corresponds to the "too familiar dilemmas that have informed the common discourse on questions of translation and interpretation for millennia and are mostly associated with the 'suspicious' status of the translated text as the translator's potentially inaccurate replacement of somebody else's original". Fortunately, translation is no longer considered to be a straightforward activity of substitution: this notion

> is absurd. Translating a text means reconfiguring it. . . . No translation can ever be the "same" as the original, for translation involves so much more than the linguistic, though obviously language is a crucial element . . . translators have to deal with more than just words which may or may not have dictionary equivalents.
>
> *(Bassnett 2022c: vii)*

Contemporary post-positivist, post-structuralist, and anti-essentialist perspectives view translation as a much broader and more open discipline (Blumczynski 2016; Gambier and van Doorslaer 2021). The original and its derivative(s) are conceived

DOI: 10.4324/9781003391890-5

rather differently than they are in prescriptivist approaches, which mainly focus on the primary/secondary binary opposition (Lee 2020). Consequently, the translated text no longer betrays the original, but complements and completes it. Views on translation are starting to shift, due not only to

> the increasingly articulate statements by translators themselves, and by the bringing to light of equally articulate comments by earlier translators that had been forgotten or ignored, but also [to] more sophisticated thinking about the relationship between writer and reader and by dialogue between theorists and practitioners of translation.
>
> *(Bassnett 2014: 152)*

Bassnett and Lefevere (1998: 27) argue, along with many other theorists, that "no two translations are going to be alike . . . because fragments of our individualistic readings will drift through our reading and our translating". Translating is an extremely complex process that involves more than merely replacing words and phrases with their equivalents in another language (Taibi 2023; Katan and Taibi 2021; Saussy 2017). In line with this statement, Emmerich (2017: 161) champions translation "as iteration, as repetition-with-a-difference, a mode of textual proliferation rather than a mode by which semantic content is transferred". For precisely this reason, Venuti argues against an instrumentalist model of translation as reproduction and strongly advocates a different understanding of translation:

> STOP thinking of source texts in terms of translatability and untranslatability and of translation as involving loss or gain; START thinking of translation as an interpretive act that can be performed on any source text.
>
> *(Venuti 2019: 175)*

In (un)original literature, translation survives beyond the original, which has been blurred and diluted by the author. The concepts of originality and repetition, of primary and secondary, are understood as something far removed from the passage in the "Philebus" in which Plato explains the Socratic distinction between good and bad memory, where true knowledge leads us to the ideal forms that enable the good artist to make a faithful representation of the images that already exist within us. Language is not "a code that wraps around pre-existing ideas or meanings", and therefore translation cannot be "simple re-coding of these ideal meanings", a choice between two opposites (Foran 2022: 175). In contrast, (un)creative writers represent imitation and reject the idea that there is only one definitive ending—as in Nanni Balestrini's *Tristano. A Novel* (1966/2014), a love story with infinite variants in ten chapters, each with 20 texts taken from newspapers, fiction, travel guidebooks, essays on photography and geography, and others, randomly combined using an algorithm. The novel is open, inconclusive, and self-referential. Many sentences are repeated or modified (Gilbert 2022). And it offers an infinite number of possible endings because a computer re-sorts the novel so that no copy is the same, and therefore each printed edition of the novel is ordered differently from all the rest. In this case, repetition does not exist and the existence of a stable original is put into question:

> The combinations of the individual text passages result in 109,027,350,432,000 possible novel texts. Just as for the medieval *Tristan*, where the reconstruction of an archetype by means of the available textual witnesses is today considered possible only to a limited extent, it must also be accepted in the case of Balestrini's *Tristano* that the determination of an "original text" among these 109 trillion texts is out of the question. Even the 1966 printed version cannot be declared to be such. The fact that every copy of the edition is unique because it has a unique text is indicated in the paratext: the copies of the Italian edition from 2007 and the English and German translations are numbered on the cover, and thus clearly individuated. . . . The unmanageable number of possible texts of *Tristano* makes it impossible for one reader to ever read all of them. It is reminiscent of the calculation of potential reading time that Raymond Queneau once used in the foreword to his *Cent mille milliards de poèmes* (*One Hundred Million Million Poems*).
>
> *(Gilbert 2022: 190, 209)*

(Un)creative writers reject a definitive origin, as if they were remembering Mallarmé's elusive mime or Queneau's *Exercises de style* (1947), in which, as mentioned, the same event is told 99 times, each time from a different perspective to make us wonder which of these narrations is the original, the "real" and "true" story. In this regard, it is interesting to remember that Italo Calvino, Queneau's creative translator (Federici 2009), speaks of multiplicity in his essay "Translating Is the Real Way of Reading a Text" by referring to "different levels of language".[1] In fact, Calvino appreciated being translated

> not only to be read in more places, but also in order to "understand better what I have written and why". Translation, for him, was . . . a revelatory process to see and know himself from a new angle, from a foreign and alienating perspective.
>
> *(Lahiri 2022: 143)*

In the palimpsestic texts mentioned in the previous chapters, the writer follows "quotations, allusions, and deformations" (Dworkin 2021: 151–211; Dworkin 2013: 43–44), the traces of other texts, so that translation necessarily emerges as a palimpsest, which exists and survives the origin. (Un)original literature brings to light the intertextuality of texts, the layers of meaning, the apocryphal references, its allusions and resonances, the web of unsettling significations consciously exploited by these (un)creative creators, and the "rhetoric of endlessly shuttling allusion" (Norris 1982/1991: 120). All of this eliminates the "false self-image [of the text] as a privileged discourse of reason and truth" (Norris 1982/1991: 160–161). Translation is here "a re-creation and a rewriting" (Federici 2009: 132).

The translator thus resembles H., Saramago's painter in *Manual of Painting and Calligraphy* (1977/2018), who begins the novel by saying, "I shall go on painting the second picture but I know it will never be finished". Indeed, no translation (or original) is ever truly completed. The second portrait, says Saramago, is as different from the first as two drops of water. Translation canonizes the original, makes it possible, and cancels its "originality" by announcing its dependence on a derived form:

STOP using moralistic terms like "faithful" and "unfaithful" to describe translation.
START defining it as the establishment of a variable equivalence to the source text.
STOP assuming that translation is mechanical substitution.
START conceiving of it as an interpretation that demands writerly and intellectual sophistication.

(Venuti 2019: ix)

(Un)original writings are eloquent reminders of Borges' warning in "The Language of the Argentines" that we cannot be so naïve as to forget that language is like the moon: it has its dark side. Paolo Fabbri also tells us that no sign is transparent because each one has multiple yet different folds and layers. In his *Giro semiótico* [*Semiotic turn*], he writes that language is extremely complex, a kind of "puff pastry" composed of elements and signs, each with a different value (Fabbri 2000: 42). Given the opacity of communication, Fabbri proposes the figure of the double agent and spy to unravel meaning, because the mask, the montage, and the duplicity of language determine the rules of intersubjective behavior.

Translators know that their job is to make sense of the puff pastry of language. However, they are double agents because they find themselves in the paradoxical position in which their two clients may well be aware that they are playing a double game (Fabbri 1995: 15). Every translation

> enriches the source language at least as much it enriches the target language or languages. . . . All languages, which are open systems and live in translation, constantly, modify their writing and complete themselves as they are translated into other languages.
>
> *(Fabbri 1995: 134, 135, author's translation)*

According to Fabbri, it is translation that makes languages grow:

> True utopia does not reside in a perfect language, but in the creative imperfection of languages, in this endless translating, which is a kind of openness. The translator does not seek a word-for-word correspondence based on conceptual representation. Instead, he/she introduces into their own language insights into

language and phenomena that it did not previously possess. . . . Translation can never be an exact reproduction of meaning. Since languages are open and evolving systems, translation always results in a loss or gain in meaning. Translating changes both the language *ad quem* as well as the language *ab quo*.

(Fabbri 1994: 11–13, author's translation)[2]

The original needs a translation. At the same time, the original is never definitive because it can be translated. It is thus hardly surprising that the concept of originality has come increasingly under fire. In the opinion of Venuti (1992: 7),

the original is itself a translation, an incomplete process of translating a signifying chain into a univocal signified, and this process is both displayed and further complicated when it is translated by another signifying chain in a different language. The originality of the foreign text is thus compromised. . . . Neither the foreign text nor the translation is an original semantic unity; both are derivative and heterogeneous, consisting of diverse linguistic and cultural materials which destabilize the work of signification, making meaning plural.

These words, pronounced over 30 years ago, challenge translation equivalence and are perfectly applicable to works such as Andy Warhol's *a: a novel*, John Cage's *Roaratorio*, and Kenneth Goldsmith's *Trilogy*, among others (Edmond 2019). They also apply to repetition in the work of Norman H. Pritchard (for instance, in *EE-CCHHOOEESS*, first published in 1971; see Stephens 2020: 111–126 and Reed 2014: 37–44), in Eugen Gomringer's poems/constellations (Mager 2021), and in Carl Andre's use of creative repetition in poems like *red, red* (1967), *now, now* (1967), *Autobiographical References* (1963), *Passport* (1960), *Twelve Sonnets* (1960), "Elbowelbowelbow" (1963), and "Ititit" (1963), contained in Andre's already mentioned *One Hundred Sonnets*, which is built through the repetition of single words produced on a mechanical typewriter "and hence in grid form. Each is fourteen lines (true to the sonnet) and based on the repetition of one word. . . . Andre's attention rests on the tactile sense of the words themselves" (Nancy Perloff 2021: 177; see also Rahtz 2021: 21–50; Rahtz 2004; Rider 2011; Weiner 1996).

Venuti's words are also relevant to the poems and letters, pseudo-translations of nonexistent originals, in Jack Spicer's *After Lorca* (1957), which construct an original work that is citational and in which creative translation becomes a mode of "iterative proliferation" (Emmerich 2017: 186). *After Lorca* contains translations of Lorca's work (Walsh 2019; Katz 2013), the faithfulness of which "Lorca" questions. There are also 11 original Spicer poems masquerading as translations, combined with six "programmatic" letters to Lorca, as we read in Peter Gizzi's (2021) preface to Spicer's work:

Spicer's translations of twenty-two poems and one short play by Lorca, interspersed with another ten poems and play that, while presented as translations, do not represent any known text by Lorca. Both translations and pseudotranslations bear dedications, mostly to members of Spicer's circle of friends. The intimate yet public correspondence implied by these dedications is echoed in the more generically conventional (though one-sided) correspondence of six letters to the dead Lorca—all signed "Love, Jack"—that treat questions of poetics and translation. In keeping with the closing phrase of one of these letters . . . Lorca does in fact write back: in an introduction signed "Federico Garcia Lorca, Outside Granada, October 1957", this poet two decades in the grave chides Spicer for "inserting or substituting one or two words" that change a poem's mood or meaning, or "tak[ing] one of my poems and adjoin[ing] to half of it another half of his own, giving rather the effect of an unwilling centaur". As for the apocryphal texts, Lorca admits to having sent Spicer a few posthumously written poems—"with malice aforethought, I must admit", in order to "further complicat[e] the problem".

(Emmerich 2017: 165–166)

All of these (un)original writings, texts of erasure, and conceptual writers are not mere experimentation with language but rather cultural criticism, a questioning of inherited values, a deconstruction of dominant structures, "a way to foreground the arbitrariness of conventions" (Tomasula 2022: 5), and an attempt to change things (Colby 2021; Castiglione 2019; Altieri and Nace 2018; Berry 2016; Reed 2014; Houen 2014; Fink and Halden-Sullivan 2014). Thus, Ronald Johnson's previously mentioned *Radi os* (1977), dedicated to Robert Duncan, is "an unfamiliar text within a text, present in *Paradise Lost* but via habitual reading unseen" (McCaffery 2002: 124; see also Hair 2010). *Radi os* is a title he gets out of *Paradise Lost*. Johnson cuts holes into Milton (Mong 2015: 79). He uses etching and cutting away and goes through the first four books of Milton, erasing the previous poem to arrive at his own poem, one that discovers unexpected (previous) links between words. Johnson offers "unconventional itineraries that produce innovative redirections and perversions of the original text" (McCaffery 2002: 126). As McCaffery argues (id.), this is a kind of nomadic writing that manipulates the original text "to induce a difference out of sameness".

Vahni Capildeo's erasure of Pierre de Ronsard's "Ode À Cassandre" is also a very interesting example. Capildeo uses erasure of the source text to produce

> a new, evocative, playfully minimal text in the source language, which also offers visual space and silence into which the source text can be recalled and from which the next translations may be imagined . . . a doubled erasure of the source text into some French words, some English translations, inlaid in compressed stanzas to move in opposition to each other as well as developing a sensuous response.
>
> *(Capildeo 2019: 113)*

These and other erased texts previously described are works that erase the authority of the original text. They question the originality of origins. The original text is seen as a trace containing other elements:

> This interweaving, this textile, is the text produced only in a transformation of another text. Nothing, neither among the elements nor within the system, is anywhere ever simply present or absent. There are only, everywhere, differences and traces of traces.
>
> *(Derrida 1972b/1981: 26)*

Therefore, the blanks, multiple layers, holes, and erasures are the origin of a tissue full of infinite possible meanings.

The translations of these texts can only be "an interpretive transformation that exposes multiple and divided meanings in the foreign text and displaces it with another set of meaning, equally multiple and divided" (Venuti 1992: 8). Translation is "an interpretive act that inevitably varies source-text form, meaning and effect according to intelligibilities and interests in the receiving culture" (Venuti 1995/2008: 12). For example, *A Rose for Gertrude* is Augusto de Campos' translation of the famous line in which Stein describes the rose by repeating the word. The poem by Augusto de Campos (1994) "translates" it by using that same line to create a circular poem (as he subsequently did with Blake's "A Sick Rose"). It is still a translation even though it is in English, because it repeats the words repeated by Stein. Moreover, within the English phrase "a rose is a rose", it is possible "to discern the Portuguese form 'eis', meaning 'behold', and which Campos uses to directly present the verbal and iconic rose of the poem and its introduction" (Hernández 2010: 154, author's translation).

Both the "original" text and the translation are what Augusto de Campos calls *intradução* [intraduction] or *prosa porosa* [porous prose], because they are laden with derivations and echoes, as well as different cultural and linguistic materials that destabilize signification and pluralize meaning:

> The heterogeneous textual work insures that the translation is transformative and interrogative as well: it sets going a deconstruction of the foreign text. . . . A translation is never quite "faithful", always somewhat "free", it never establishes an identity, always a lack and a supplement, and it can never be a transparent representation, only an interpretive transformation that exposes multiple and divided meanings in the foreign text and displaces it with another set of meanings, equally multiple and divided.
>
> *(Venuti 1992: 8)*

The dispersion of meaning that arises from the dissolution of representation and the death of the author (and their authority) presupposes a translation that is totally different from any binary, predetermined, and unmoveable truth. Augusto de Campos' 1994 minimalist concrete poem "Cançao noturna da baleia" ["The Whale's Night Song"] is the origin of his transcreative performative musical translation of *Moby Dick* in a multilayered, musical, visual, verbivocovisual (a term borrowed from Book II of Joyce's *Finnegans Wake*), concrete poem whose title, *Call Me Moby*, plays with Melville's well-known beginning. *Call Me Moby* is performed by de Campos together with his composer-performer son Cid de Campos. In "The Whale's Night Song", the repetition of *m*'s—*m* referring to Melville's whale—create a murmur "against which other sounds appear" (Perloff 2021b: n.p.). The initial square black page was made of 17 horizontal lines, each containing 23 spaces. In every even line, the spaces hold 23 white lower-case repeated *m*'s, while the nine odd lines bear a set of spaced letters constituting words "embedded—and almost buried—in a sea of further identical white *m*'s" (Perloff 2021b: n.p.). Augusto de Campos plays with the whiteness of white and the blackness of black (Perloff in Inghilleri and Goldfajn 2022), with the same that is never the same, and with difference. In his verbivocovisual performance, one listens to two voices in two languages through a poem that is born out of his previous sea of repeated *m*'s. Augusto de Campos' English translation is quite free, and his performance fuses music, film, and poetry and translates dialectics:

> The English translation here is by Augusto himself in an email of 2018; note that he translates lines 5–8 very freely so as to replicate the rhyme of the original. Augusto's poem is, in any case, an eight-line stanza that lifts out of the sea of *m*'s, an enigmatic little poem with the rhyme scheme *aa(b)ccddc*, followed by the unrhyming refrain line, "call me moby." In English, "moby" rhymes with "me" in line 5 and the rhyme scheme is a little different: *abcdefffe* . . . in Augusto's version, the "whiteness of white" does not invoke horror so much as mystery, a mystery he finds in its relationship to its opposite, the blackness of black. Indeed, for Augusto the white/black opposition also has an aesthetic dimension: it is, for example, the relationship of two of the greatest modern artists, Rodchenko and Malevich. Rodchenko was deeply influenced by Malevich's famous *Black Square* of 1915. But he was soon to turn from the sensuous texture and "spiritualist" depth of Malevich's Suprematism to the Constructivist emphasis on the materiality of the paint itself, as in the opaque "black-on-black" paintings he exhibited in Moscow in 1919, alongside five white-on-white paintings by Malevich. And soon Rodchenko abandoned "bourgeois" painting altogether for the new art of photomontage. The question of sameness and difference thus haunts the poem. Black and white, Rodchenko and Malevich and then Jonah versus Ahab.
>
> *(Perloff 2021b: n.p.)*

Other examples of this type of text are poems by Augusto de Campos such as "uma bala", which is meant to be read in different voices:

> The composition resembles a capital Z that has been tilted on its side. The two transverse strokes and the two diagonal strokes are exactly the same length. Each contains four pairs of words that echo each other in a complicated ballet. Eventually, however, one perceives that the design is composed of two acute angles

> facing in opposite directions, which changes its whole Gestalt. The main problem that occurs is how to determine the correct reading order—assuming that such a thing exists. Depending on whether one follows literary conventions or artistic conventions, there would seem to be two possible paths.
>
> (Bohn 2011: 122)

Depending on how we read the text and where we situate ourselves, both spatially and visually, on the page, the translations of the poem will be quite different:

> One can read from left to right and from top to bottom, as I have done in my translation, or one can decipher the figure on the right followed by the figure on the left. The second model produces the following poem: "one time/one speech/one river mouth/one bullet/one voice/one ditch/one time/one time/one speech/one river mouth/one bullet/one voice/one ditch".
>
> (id.)

The multiple voices, the unconventional typography, and the visual use of the page encourage a wide range of interpretations, possible readings, and translations. The reading of the poem in four voices seems to indicate polyphony:

> Beginning with "**uma bala**" on the left, the recital concludes with yet another reading. The four voices advance along the two diagonals simultaneously to create an example of Concrete polyphony. Instead of attempting to privilege a single reading, the conductor fashions an acoustic tapestry composed of multiple readings. Since de Campos's own recordings observe a similar strategy, this seems to be the wisest approach. Instead of one poem, the composition contains many poems. Or to put it another way, the composition consists of all possible readings.
>
> (Bohn 2011: 122–123)

As Marjorie Perloff (2021b: n.p.) argues, from the short concrete poems of *Noigandres* to the *Popcretos* and the *despoesia* [unpoetry], "to the astonishing performance pieces—language, music, film, graphic art—of the 2000s, and most recently the beautiful translation miniatures he calls *plaquettes*", Augusto de Campos' texts are fields open to infinite semantic possibilities. Likewise, Haroldo de Campos' poems such as "mais" ["more"] and "fala prata" ["silver speech"] in *ALEA I—VARIAÇOES SEMÂNTICAS* (*Uma Epicomédia de Bôlso*) (1962–1963) also have more than one interpretation or translation.

The acoustic element and silence are important in this poetry of the verbivocovisual. Readers can view the text from different angles and perspectives, from right to left, from top to bottom, and vice versa. This ensures that the translation is only one possibility among many others, a proposal in constant movement and always open to indefinition. The radical works by the Noigandres, for instance, were meant to invoke, as we saw in Chapter 3, all of the senses by playing with the visual, rhythms, colors, music, and meaning, through Pound's phanopoeia, melopoeia, and logopoeia and Joyce's verbivocovisual. These texts show that "communication happens on many levels" (Campbell and Vidal 2019: xxv) and therefore requires a nonstatic way of approaching translation, which allows us to translate "not just with the eyes but with all other senses" (Campbell and Vidal 2019: xxix). This is what Campbell and Vidal call, in their volume, "experiential translation" or translation processes responding to the whole range of modes inherent in images, words, or sounds and retranslating with all of the translator's senses:

> The translator effectively plays the role of mediator in an experiential process that allows the recipients (viewer, listener, reader or participant) to re-create the sense (or "semios") of the source artefact for themselves.
> *(Campbell and Vidal 2019: xxvi)*

Campbell and Vidal's experiential translation is an excellent approach to rewrite a kind of poetry whose materiality and physicality appeals to all senses—for instance, Jen Bervin's weaving in *Draft Notation* (2014) of advanced cloth structures on the loom (Bean and McCabe 2015: 44–45). In addition to her erasures (mentioned in Chapter 2), Bervin's woven textile texts with tactile words are a collection of typewritten pattern poetry inspired by the work of Anni Albers. Hers is a kind of literature whose plasticity and elasticity cultivate both the physical and semiotic properties of language, its physicality, its materiality, and its sensuality. *The Dickinson Composites* (2010) is another artist's book: "a series of large-scale embroideries addressing gendered editorial interventions into American poet Emily Dickinson's writing" (Paitz 2021: 10). *The Dickinson Composites* is a visual, experiential translation of Emily Dickinson's unconventional use of lines, plus signs, and dashes. This series draws upon a series of six quilts Bervin made "by embroidering Emily Dickinson's unusual punctuation markings from her fascicles" (Bervin 2010: 1), which are often omitted by editors for print editions. The titles of the series (*The Composite Marks of Fascicle 40*, *The Composite Marks of Fascicle 28*, and *The Composite Marks of Fascicle 19*) are connected to Dickinson's "fascicles", those books she sewed together. Bervin's quilts look like open booklets made of sheets with words removed and the punctuation marks left. Another work of art is *The Gorgeous Nothings: Emily Dickinson's Envelope Poems* (2012), Jen Bervin and Marta Werner's compilation of Dickinson's envelope poems written in pencil, tied to their canvas, with scraps from reused envelopes. Dickinson's handwritten visual poems, with her gestural punctuation, her dashes used as a musical device or as silence, her plus signs to show that a word has variants, her cross-outs to suggest further possibilities, her underlining, her ambiguous use of capitals, and the loops and curves of her letters, need to be read with all our senses. Furthermore, Bervin's *The Dickinson Fascicles* can be seen as an experiential translation, as a total creative translation, of Dickinson's punctuation and variant markings through six large-scale embroidered works.

In Umberto Eco's *The Name of the Rose* (1980/2014), every book talks about other books, and each story tells a story that has already been told. Indeed, Eco's novel is replete with citations and cultural references that are interwoven without recourse to essentialist hierarchies. And in Eco's encyclopedic novel *The Island of the Day Before* (1995), the writer of the chronicle wonders how to construct a novel from the materials he had found and comes to the conclusion that it is impossible unless he creates a palimpsest. In fact, at the end of the Spanish version of this novel, Helena Lozano, the translator, explains the complexity of translating this text made of layers.

Following *Foucault's Pendulum* (1988), our creative translator would resemble Casaubon rather than Belbo. The first advises the second to stop looking for the pendulum because, as Eco confesses in his novel, the universe is like an onion whose center is everywhere and whose circumference is nowhere. And the text is a mosaic of quotations (Kristeva 1980: 66);[3] "tout texte est absorption et transformation d'un autre texte" ["every text is an absorption and a transformation of another text"] (Kristeva 1969: 146). A text is a territory of expressions taken from other texts that intertwine and neutralize each other, a "heterogeneous mosaic" (Kristeva 1980: 41), "the absorption and transformation of another" (ibid.: 66; see "Word, Dialogue, and Novel" in Kristeva 1980: 64–91).

Of the three labyrinths that Eco mentions in his *Postcript to The Name of the Rose* (1983), (un)original literature most resembles the final one, which Eco refers to as the network. He describes it as a rhizome in the sense of Deleuze and Guattari because it has no center or periphery, because it is potentially infinite, and because it is never definitively structured. In his *Postscript*, Eco speaks of the postmodern reply to the modern using a well-known image to acknowledge that the past cannot be silenced, but only revisited with irony, and never innocently. For Eco, the postmodern attitude is that of a man who loves a woman but who knows he cannot tell her, "I love you madly", because he knows that she knows, and because she knows that he knows that these words have already been used by Barbara Cartland. So, to avoid false innocence, the only possible solution to the problem of talking about love in this age of copying and repetition is to say, "As Barbara Cartland would say, I love you madly". And interestingly, John Barth (1967: 31) reminds us that, because the art of each period reflects the moment, Beethoven's Sixth Symphony could only be recomposed in our era with an ironic intention. Make it new. Make tradition new. Make life itself new.

The translations of (un)original writings are inevitably like those "cascading translations" created by layering that so fascinated Hofstadter (1997: 341–342) (see Chapter 1). For instance, Haroldo de Campos inscribed his name on the cover of universal texts such as the Bible. He thus appears as the author in his translation of *Genesis*, *The Book of Job*, and the *Iliad*. In his translation of *Ecclesiastes*, he even left his trace by including his own readings, cascades that are layers of layers. And Augusto de Campos signs *Rilke: Poesia-Coisa* and *Hopkins: a Beleza Difícil*, in which the translated poet is part of the title and, on the cover of both books, the faces of the "authors" are superimposed upon each other like a mask or labyrinth. A book such as *Poetamenos*, by Augusto de Campos, is a text that evokes the Poundian concepts of *melopoeia* and *phanopoeia*. It is an ideogram in which translation is necessarily ludic creation:

> This material presents an extraordinary opportunity for translators to immerse themselves in their own languages and meditate on the transformations imparted to them by a process of modernization. Since meter and rhyme are of no immediate concern, there is a great deal of freedom for translators to concentrate on and explore the sonorities, dictions, speech patterns, and colloquialisms of their own languages. The dispersion and reassembling of words, as well as the crafting of portmanteaux, will offer many opportunities for invention.
>
> *(Bessa 2009: 234)*

The translation of *Alphabetical Africa* by Walter Abish (1974) is particularly challenging (see *Alphabetisches Afrika*, 2002, the German translation by Jürg Laederach) and an opportunity for translators to meditate on the reassembling of words. Like the continent itself, this novel both expands and shrinks. This is a book in which letters can cause an entire continent to disappear, given the imposed limitation of the alphabet, and which is reminiscent of Queneau, Perec, and so many others.[4] Apart from the problem of using words that only begin with *a* in the first chapter, words that begin with *a* and *b* in the second, etc., there is the question of where the narrator "I" should appear in translations into other languages. In English, the "I" is in Chapter 9, but in Spanish, for example, it would appear much later on, because the Spanish word for "I" is "yo". Furthermore, in the Spanish translation, should the translator add a chapter with the letter "ñ", one of the most characteristic letters of the Spanish language? There is also the question of the chapter in which the murder and jewel robbery with Alex, Allen, and Alva would take place. The words for both events in other languages are different. For example, the Spanish word for "murder" is "asesinato", which begins with an *a*. Still another problem lies in the "mistakes" deliberately (or not: Sommer 2020: 118–119) made by Abish, such as when he uses "quiet" in the chapter on *p* and five lines later dolefully says, "A dreadful error has been committed". These mistakes reflect the deficiencies of language and communication, as well as their uncertainty, unreliability, and instability. The author wishes to convey the idea that language is a construct. Nevertheless, the problem is where the translator should also transmit the same message, not to mention how and how many times it should be done.

Translation always entails (and even more so in this case) an acknowledgment of the intervention of the translator, "not as something that needs to be curtailed or penalized, but as part and parcel of the process that inevitably transforms texts across languages and whose circumstances and motivations should be carefully investigated" (Arrojo 2018: 1). Translation is necessarily another form of creation:

> A literary equivalent would be along the lines of "creative translation" such as Ezra Pound's *Homage to Sextus Propertius*, in which Pound picked through the elegies of Propertius, translated them, cut them up, and reassembled them in a fashion he deemed entertaining and relevant. Examples from other forms: *Thelonius Monk Plays Duke Ellington*, in which Monk takes great liberties with Ellington's songbook. Lichtenstein's appropriation of comic book art. Picasso's use of newsprint, among other media, in, say, *Composition with Fruit, Guitar, and Glass. Paul's Boutique:* The Beastie Boys, Dust Brothers, and Mario Caldato, Jr., sample from more than 100 sources, including Led Zeppelin, the Beatles, James Brown, and Sly & the Family Stone. Steve Reich's "Different Trains", which incorporates audio recordings about train travel by Holocaust survivors and a Pullman porter. Musique concrète—for instance, John Cage's "Imaginary Landscape No. 4", written for 12 radios, each played by 2 people (one to tune the channel and one to control volume and timbre). A conductor controls the tempo; the audience hears whatever is on the radio in that city on that day.
>
> *(Shields 2010: paragraph 283)*[5]

All of these examples challenge the concept of author and original and seem to confirm that both originals and translations "are derivative" (Emmerich 2017: 14). Rewriting these literary works in which iterability reveals how a text changes with each new reading and rewriting means recurring to a type of translation that has little or nothing to do with early theories of translation that focused on equivalence and regarded the translator as invisible. Translating implies writing; it is an act not of recall "but of transmission" and "of reimagination" (Scott 2006/2007: 108):

> It is absurd to see translation as anything other than a creative literary activity, for translators are all the time engaging with texts first as readers and then as rewriters, as recreators of that text in another language.
>
> *(Bassnett 2006/2007: 174)*

Today, translation is a comprehensive process that must be problematized and enlarged (van Doorslaer in Gambier and van Doorslaer 2021: 3; Marais 2022). In this context, as observed by Paolo Fabbri, the translator is a bumblebee, an insect able to fly despite its weight and the small size of its wings (Polezzi 2022: 305). As Polezzi so aptly observes, today, when the concepts of authority, authenticity, and originality have changed so drastically, the notion of fidelity in its prescriptivist sense is no longer meaningful. If we understand translation

> as a vital mechanism of cultural transmission, and component of intertextuality, translation is already present, even in what we call "an original". Shattering notions of originality and authenticity calls into question the idea of translation as inherently secondary and derivative, while rewriting, adaptation, and post-translation are acknowledged as creative processes.
>
> *(Polezzi 2022: 309)*

Translation is not secondary but a way to complete the original: "Like writing, translation does not convey but creates meaning and messages, if always in relation to a specific prior text or texts" (Emmerich 2017: 162). After the cultural turn and all of the subsequent turns that have so radically transformed translation, "there can be no perfect equivalence. . . . The question of faithfulness and equivalence makes perfect translation impossible and, in turn, raises ethical issues" (Polezzi 2022: 306). Translation today is not just a copy or a mere reproduction but a process that highlights the complexity of communication: it brings to light what was there before, traces, differences (Polezzi 2020). What is needed is an unsettling translation. This is a translation that looks for the "other" side of texts and that situates itself beyond any smooth definition of what it means to translate today in the 21st century:

> The rather smooth, unruffled picture of translation that I have just painted has an "other" to it, a more unsettling but also a much more interesting and intriguing side. The smooth, unruffled picture may be part of the conventional perception and self-presentation of translation, but it papers over the cracks. I want to try and poke my finger into at least some of these cracks. And the reason for doing so lies in the recognition that translation, for all its presumed secondariness, derives its force from the fact that it is still our only answer to, and our only escape from, Babel.
>
> *(Hermans 1996: n.p.; see also Baker 2022)*

The translator is not Joseph Smith (Hermans 2007a). A faithful translation is only "faithful" when authenticated by an institution. Paradoxically, this act would cause the translation to become real and make it an original, as is the case with legal and institutional translations (Hermans 2007a, 2007b). Translations are always repeatable, provisional, and never definitive. Attached to each one is a certain position or perspective, that of the translator. Each translation thus "inscribes a subject-position that can only be the translator's, not the original author's. It does more than that. It opens up an intertextual dimension specific to the domain of translation" (Hermans 2007b: 60):

> In other words, translations can be read not only with reference to the originals they represent, and not only for what they say about whatever they and their originals speak about outside themselves. They can also be read for what they say about their individual way of re-enacting an original—and also, more generally, about the kind of re-enactment that is called translation.
>
> In this perspective, *each individual rendition exhibits a particular mode of representation* profiled against the ever-present possibility of alternative modes and other performances.
>
> *(Hermans 2007b: 69)*

According to Hermans, what "makes translation worth studying" is the fact that it is not smooth, not a repetition, not the same:

> "Translation's Other", then, comprises, among other things, the ambivalences and paradoxes, the hybridity and plurality of translation, its "otherness" as "awkwardness" if you like, in contrast to the perception of translation as replica or reproduction, as referring, simply and unproblematically (if always from an inferior position), to an original. But it also means the significance of translation as a cultural force, which belies the common view of it as mechanical and merely derivative, secondary, secondhand, second-best, second-rate.
>
> *(Hermans 1996: n.p.)*

The texts discussed in this book expand the definition of translation and make it worth studying. They show that absolute equivalence is no longer a viable goal. They demonstrate that, like any other text, translations "are always, inherently, plural, unstable, de-centred, hybrid" (Hermans 1996: n.p.). In his inaugural lecture, Hermans describes translation in a way that can be applied here. (Un)original writings are originals that "transform 'originals' which are themselves transformations of texts which are themselves transformations—etc. They increase the plurivocality of already plural texts" (Hermans 1996: n.p.). These texts are rewritings, palimpsests, transformations. Texts have no fixed ground but words whose meanings are connected to other shifting meanings. So, translation cannot be straightforward, but "a transaction, transformation, travail,—and a treasure trove [*trouvaille*]" (Derrida 2001b: 198). (Un)original writers recognize difference and *différance* within the linguistic sign. These writings are translations in themselves because they are created with and through traces (Derrida 1967/1979: 156), inscriptions, and re-inscriptions. As such, they are "a mode of textual recycling" (Hermans 1996: n.p.) that invents (needs to invent) the original:

> In other words, the "other" to which a translated text refers is never simply the source text, even though that is, of course, the claim which translations commonly make. It is at best an image of it—a mirror image perhaps, provided we think of it as an image reflected in a kaleidoscopic, distorting mirror. Because the image is always distorted, never innocent, we can say that translation constructs or produces or, one step further, "invents" its original.
>
> *(Hermans 1996: n.p.)*

4.2 Toward a ludic and creative translation

As a result, translation today is not considered a secondary, transparent image. On the contrary, it is a communicative act full of resonances, voices, sounds, noises, images, and scents. Never innocent, it is the result of (never neutral) choices in different contexts, in different cultures, and at different times. In this context, an excellent proposal is Tong King Lee's ludic translation in which translation is a process that develops "*alongside* an original work" (Lee 2022: 2):

> Hence, translation is not subservient to a source text in a vertical hierarchy but articulates the latter sideways to develop a more expansive intertextual network . . . the potential of translation to transgress and transcend the source text. That is, translation subjects an original work to experimental play replete with contingencies and idiosyncrasies, furnishes it with performative resources for aesthetic expression in excess of the linguistic signs, and extrapolates it toward multiple trajectories and plural media.
>
> *(Lee 2022: 2)*

Lee's "ludic translation", which he applies to the translation of concrete Chinese poetry, is a rhizomatic, Derridean translation, never definitive or completed, which emphasizes the importance of the translator's intervention and does not consider the original to be hierarchically superior. Ludic translation considers the source text as an open process that "can potentially generate multiple transtextual solutions to an initial textual problem" (Lee 2022: 63). This approach to translation draws on linguistic and nonlinguistic resources, because the previous text sometimes uses different semiotic systems—linguistic but also visual, with different typography, punctuation, colors, use of the page, materiality of words, etc. Thus, ludic translation does not simply convey instrumental meaning but adds a performative value to texts:

> It operates in ergodic mode, entailing a non-trivial, and in my case also collaborative, translation effort beyond the linear transference of meaning from one language into another. In contrast to straight translation, which aims to ascertain the lexico-grammatical meaning of a source text and represent that meaning with precision and clarity, ludic translation opens up a text to playful experimentation. Such experimentation is moderated through the translator's knowledge, disposition, and subjectivity as well as their sensory and embodied experience of reading at a particular point in time and within a specific sociocultural milieu.
>
> *(Lee 2022: 63)*

Ludic translation thrives on creative indeterminacy and does not offer definitive rewritings. It sees untranslatability as part of the game, part of our translational risky journey. Ludic translation is open. It is a living organism in constant movement, because words are mutable, and the translator is always traveling between unstable territories.

No doubt this proposal can be applied to the previously mentioned examples and to many others that push language(s) to the limit. For instance, a clear example of creative repetition and ludic translation is Caroline Bergvall's performance writings (Edmond 2019; Perloff 2013), installations, videos, and other iterative poetics (Edmond 2011). Like Gertrude Stein, she does not believe in repetition as the same, but rather as "insistence". Her collection of poems *Fig* (2005) is particularly interesting here. *Fig* is one of the works chosen by Place and Fitterman (2009: 75) as an example of appropriation and by Dworkin and Goldsmith (2011: 81) as a case of a poet who reminds us that "a strategy of mere reframing is a strong and effective way of conceptual writing". Included in *Fig, Via: 48 Dante Variations* (2000/2005) is a text and a sound piece about "making copy explicit as an act of copy" (Bergvall 2005: 65). It starts from the opening tercet of Dante's *Inferno*. *Via* is first a text-sound piece and then a poem. Bergvall collected the British Library's 47 translations of Dante until May 2000 and arranged them alphabetically rather than chronologically, according to the first word of each translation:

> My task was mostly and rather simply, or so it seemed at first, to copy each first tercet as it appeared in each published version of the Inferno. To copy it accurately. Surprisingly, more than once, I had to go back to the books to double-check and amend an entry, publication data, a spelling. Checking each line, each variation, once, twice. Increasingly, the project was about keeping count and making sure. That what I was copying was what was there. Not to inadvertently change what had been printed. To reproduce each translative gesture. To add my voice to this chorus, to this recitation, only by way of this task. Making copy explicit as an act of copy.
>
> *(Bergvall in Goldsmith 2011: 192)*

Bergvall shows how repetition is not the same. With "Say Parsley", she demonstrates that "repetition is never precise reproduction" (Perloff 2010: 136). She highlights difference in repetition. Each text, each pronunciation, is perceived through the body; each translation is different (Perloff 2004a: 221–223; Goldsmith 2011: 192–194; Edmond 2019). Translation and translatability are viewed in Bergvall's works "in political as well as poetic terms" (Perloff 2010: 131). With her performance writing, iteration is not homogenization. Each text is never identical to itself. Bergvall thus demonstrates how it is possible to create an original poem, her 48th variation, from previous originals and translations. This is the OuLIPo factor (Perloff 2004b). In this regard, the "iterative writing" (Edmond 2011; Sheppard 2016; Szymanska in Reynolds 2019/2021) of Bergvall

> highlights variation through repetition so that small differences become perceptible. In Bergvall's practice, such variations also serve to highlight the uniqueness of each performance or instantiation of the text. The iterations of writing extend into the iterations of variations: each live or recorded performance, print or online publication constitutes another version.
>
> *(Edmond 2011: 113)*

In her preface to *Alisoun Sings* (2019), she explicitly says that what really matters is not where Alisoun's name comes from or whether it belongs "to a historical, a mythical or a literary figure. What matters is the network of resonance that it brings up" (Bergvall 2019: vii). Bergvall listens to her voice, to all the resonances:

Tales lead to more tales. Stories get woven from multitudes of stories. Voices call up other voices. A voice is a voice-cluster. I sense her coming through as a concert of sounds and lives and purposes from a vast patchwork of influences, events, and emotions that accord with her, and revitalise her presence among us. Her persona, her phrasing, her intentions, her clothes, her geographies, emerge, available, recyclable and drawn out from the infinite details and impulses of a great range of cultural, personal, physical even psychological reaches and attractions.

(Bergvall 2019: viii)

Alisoun Sings is the closing volume of a feminist trilogy comprising *Meddle English* (2011), *Drift* (2014), and *Alisoun Sings* (2019). *Alisoun Sings* is a palimpsest in which the reader finds quotations by Nina Simone, Patti Smith, Hannah Arendt, Emma Goldman, Hélène Cixous, Nancy Spero, Mona Hatoum, Virginia Woolf, Kathy Acker, and Audre Lorde, disco songs, Internet slang, and a reference to the 2017 Women's March, among others. In "1DJ2MANY", Alisoun offers a pastiche of contemporary song lyrics related to sex, and in "Herte" she herself appears as the "author". Bergvall's Alisoun tells "*her*stories", not "history", through her rewriting of Chaucer's outspoken and libidinous Wife of Bath, who speaks in a mixture of Middle and contemporary English and introduces herself as follows:

Hi you all, I'm Alisoun. Some people call me Al. Am many things to many a few thyinge to some & nothing but an irritant to socialites and othere glossing troglodytes. I dig a good chat banter aboute. Sbeen a long time, some & six hundred times have circled round the solar sun, everything were diffrent yet pretty much the same, sunsets were reddier, godabov ruled all & the franks the rest. Womenfolk were owned trafeckt regulated petted tightlye impossible to run ones own afferes let alone ones mynd nat publicly nat privatly, & so were most workfolk enserfed, owned never free, working working day 'n niht. Sunsets redder, legs a little shorter.

(Bergvall 2019: 1)

Alisoun uses many different registers, including contemporary slang. Alisoun's voice is made up of many contemporary and past voices. Hers is a collective identity wherein different subjectivities coexist. Her language is "upfolded over updoubled" (Bergvall 2019: 3), as if quoting many different languages, many layers, and many stories too:

Btw nat worry should ma language feeling it weirdo, rude & cueryous at first. Rough as a cats lick or like a dress whats travagant, folded over updoubled, as though am speechin many langages at once. Whats foshur! And many stories too! In many gay apparel! Picture me standing on each side of the silver cliffs of Cinque & Caletum like standing at Midlina across the silfra crack, am astride he world joining two moats, the northern sea rushing between my herculean legs splashes against the mixed wools of my quim. No but for serious, 'tis a rich scrambljumbl of heavily crossbedded bitching tongues, folded like shells in tymologick tension, so is ma usage a happy combimess, simple.

(Bergvall 2019: 3–4)

Language "both connecks and divides" (Bergvall 2019: 4). For Bergvall, language is heteroglossic, polyvocal, and collectivist. The idea of copying is explicitly mentioned in "Copyist":

Do allocate someone to copy exchanges in your partee or you'll find that ne can make heads nor tales of whatswhat after awhile can lead all kinds of misreadings & typos oons th' ink has dried. And what with inattention, coffee stains, drippings and the likes, unfortunates pellings get tuff to hiden or changen, like bad tatts covering bad tatts, as chaucer the aufeur famously bemoaned.

(Bergvall 2019: 3)

For Bergvall, quoting is a recognition, a way to acknowledge influences from many different cultural backgrounds, "carrying in ones body the burden of otheres pain". As she says in "Spero",

Right on! xlaims what artist Nancy Spero, I've copied out reports hung them on the gallery walls for all to see the terror and the torture, rape by numbers, rape by camps, sometimes copying typing out stamping quoting taking on, still making work out of clean-ups like a Ligon, like a Lacy, carrying in ones body the burden of otheres pain, otheres codex skin as ones work, kepen each truthe each testament alive, relived individually recorporated testified & geloved like a Piper a Hiller a Boltanski, docu leaking body leaking holding on to proof & dataflow in an age that chastises, isolates what it debases, turns into mass what it depersonalises. Whissle n blow into structures of lies ma heroes! like a redhaired Chelsea Manning or an Ed Snowden or a calm Summer-dressed Leshia Evans or a probing Carol Cadwalladr. Each holden their owned prescious life for truf & the dearlyfe of all.

(Bergvall 2019: 43)

(Un)original literature is a pilgrimage of voices. These writers not only quote but earn those quotations:

To earn citation because of a type of thoughtfulness one has to show even as one's taking on, or being allowed to take on, that quote. One stretches oneself toward others, and it is a tightrope so long as one seeks identification instead of soul-searching. It leads back to one's own expectations and breaks them open too.

(Bervall in Nissan 2019: n.p.)

Bergvall also uses translation as a way of writing. In his interview, Nissan (2019) highlights this by referring to *Alisoun Sings*: "Lines repeat themselves—one in a more contemporary English, one in a more transitory state or Middle English". Bergvall makes clear that she uses translation "to reinvent or recreate the final word". She uses different spellings and different words. She uses not only homophonic translation but also repetition "to open the semantic field". She is interested in the residual and political implications of the middles and margins (Owens 2015: 147–148), in languages and identities in translation, in the hybridization of languages. By rewriting and quoting previous voices, "Bergvall herself is acting as a sort of translator by simply recasting preexisting texts into a new poem that is entirely her own" (Goldsmith 2011: 194). For her, translation is an encounter. It is performative, "a way of writing":

> Translation doesn't have a resting point neither here nor there. But it spans that stretch. It comes across so many interactions. There's no final mastery in translation because it's taken over by the performative one way or another.
> *(Bergvall in Nissan 2019: n.p.)*

Bergvall's Alisoun repeats Chaucer's Wife of Bath, but repetition here is not the same:

> It's now developing into a larger framework involving Emma Goldman and Vivienne Westwood among others. What's wonderful about a project like this is that I'm also finding myself at the start of the literary, at the brink between manuscript and print culture, a manuscript culture where the written text is largely spoken but also passed and read, so it's all in the mix.
> *(Bergvall in Thurston 2011: 88–89)*

Works such as Bergvall's and others deconstruct established notions in translation and in literature. Thus, *The Plagiarist* by Christopher Nosnibor (2008) is an anti-novel with a narrator who cannot be trusted and a main character whose identity fades. Repetition and quotation are used repeatedly throughout the novel, but repetition is never the same. For instance, several paragraphs on page 25 are repeated on page 33 with some differences: "hypodermic syringe model of media" appears only once (p. 25), whereas the last paragraph repeated (p. 34) adds, "This is something that I said". The "Epilogue" (Nosnibor 2008: 199) mentions many writers, from Shakespeare and Marlowe to Burroughs and Artaud, who depend on plagiarism, which is defined here as "a highly creative exercise . . . with every act of plagiarism a new meaning is brought to the plagiarised work" (Nosnibor 2008: 199). The book ends with these words:

> The capitalist forces controlling Western culture have proscribed as illegal the plagiarising of modern texts. However, do not allow this to deter you from

> plagiarising modern work. A few sensible precautions will protect you from prosecution. The basic rule in avoiding copyright infringement is to take the idea and spirit of a text without actually plagiarising it word for word. One of the best examples of this is this.
>
> *(Nosnibor 2008: 199)*

The Plagiarist invites us to ask ourselves where authors begin and where they end, and, consequently, how to translate a novel that opens as follows:

> I did not write this. I have done everything in my power to remove myself from the equation, involved writing machines, torn everything up, thrown it into the air and watched the pieces as they fell. . . . Technology is the future of writing—has already taken over—the author is dead: long live the author. In the beginning was the word—but who owned the word?
>
> *(Nosnibor 2008: 7)*

Novelty lies not in what is said, but in its repetition. Thus, a work like Craig Dworkin's *Parse* (2008) is a creative translation of Edwin A. Abbott's *How to Parse: An Attempt to Apply the Principles of Scholarship to English Grammar* (1874). Dworkin cites Gertrude Stein's phrase, "I really do not know that anything has ever been more exciting than diagramming sentences", when he parses Abbott's book into his own idiosyncratic system of analysis. Dworkin translates not the content but rather the form of Abbott's work, because he tries "to identify the syntax of every sentence in a grammar textbook" (Reed 2019: 200). He thus renders a different meaning than if he had translated the content. In this case, as in so many others, translations of the translation of Dworkin would differ considerably, depending on the grammatical system of the target language.

Still another example is Christian Bök's five translations of Arthur Rimbaud's "Voyelles" in his 2009 edition of *Eunoia*, which are inspired not only by Perec's *La Disaparition* but also by Rimbaud's sonnet,

> whose associations between vowel and color are literalized on the multicolor cover of the revised edition of *Eunoia*. Bök's translations of Rimbaud extend his book's emphasis on writing under constraint. Each of Bök's five translations is written according to a different set of rules. The first preserves "the rhyme scheme of the original, while enforcing the rigorous, syllabic contours of the alexandrine line." The second is a homophonic translation, and the third a "homovocalic" translation, in which Bök uses exactly the same vowels in the same order as the French original but changes all the other letters. The fourth is an English anagram of Rimbaud's French text, and the fifth is simply all the vowels of the original with all other letters removed.
>
> *(Edmond 2019: 275)*

Bök is part of an interesting translation project that aims to translate contemporary experimental poetry from English-speaking Canada for a Brazilian audience (Cisneros 2018). The editors chose poems from Bök's *Crystallography* and acknowledged the need to translate them creatively:

> [These poems] also played on the materiality of language, particularly alliteration and graphic layout, but not to the same extent as *Eunoia*. Still, in the process of translation, this deceptively "simpler" text revealed a series of subtle language games that included hidden palindromes and anagrams (of, for instance, the name of the French mathematician Mandelbrot), which needed to be rendered creatively in Portuguese.
>
> *(Cisneros 2018: 53)*

Another example included in this anthology is Beaulieu's "translation" of a poetic manifesto:

> In order to preserve the focus on the materiality, Beaulieu participated in the "translation" of this piece by offering to retype the translated text using the same method he used for the original, namely, typing the piece without looking at the keys and with the roller of the typewriter unengaged, which is why the piece slants down the page. He thus created a new piece exclusive to our edition, which, above and beyond the semantic content, allowed for even the physical *form* of the original to echo in the translation.
>
> *(Cisneros 2018: 53–54)*

This, no doubt, is a good example of a repetitive translation, one that destabilizes such concepts as authorship, original(ity), primary, and secondary, and also the very notion of translation, because "the author himself participated in the 'form' translation of his piece, subsequently creating a new 'original' out of the Portuguese translation" (Cisneros 2018: 55; see also Beaulieu 2019). In *How to Write* (2010), Beaulieu writes an instruction manual for the death of the author. His starting point is that great artists steal. In his "Notes" (Beaulieu 2010: 67–70), he provides the references used in each section of "his" book: Chapter one consists of 36 alphabetized questions from Coles Notes–style websites on Laurence Sterne's *Tristram Shandy*, Chapter two is a record "of every number or amount word" (Beaulieu 2010: 67) in Agatha Christie's novel *And Then There Were None*, Chapter three "is an exhaustive record of every sentence that contains the word 'editor' . . . in *The Bat* (1920)" (Beaulieu 2010: 67), Chapter four consists of the texts Beaulieu reads within one block of his home, and so on.

Translations of such works will never be unique or definitive. There will be as many translations as there are translators, and their creations will include indeterminacy, randomness, and radial strands of thinking and reading:

> The ensuing experience stands in contrast with that of straight translation, characterized by the ordered and rational transference of meaning, perhaps clause by clause or line by line, from one language into another. Experimental translation is much more chaotic, idiosyncratic, and unpredictable, continually inflected by epiphanic images and texts conjured up in the here-and-now of translating. Instead of discarding these idiosyncrasies and epiphanies as irrelevant to the work of translation, a ludic perspective embraces them and actively considers how they can be co-opted to add value to the original work in unexpected ways.
>
> *(Lee 2022: 46)*

As (un)creative, (un)original literature has shown, writing is dialoguing with other voices. It involves creating Walter Benjamin's third space and reconstructing the vase by transforming it into another vase, the same yet different. Thus, as Bassnett (2011: 102) argues following Katan, the translator is expected to go "far beyond what is actually expressed and has to endeavor to second-guess the unexpressed". Accordingly,

> the translator has to bear the responsibility for the continued existence of the original but in another context. A translation, seen from this perspective, becomes the afterlife of a text, ensuring its existence in another time and place, effectively saving the text from extinction.
>
> *(Bassnett 2014: 13)*

Each new translation is (not) a repetition because the text is read in a new context, such as the echoes of other poems in Craig Dworkin's *Pin-Woods Notebooks* (Perloff 2018a), Josephine Balmer's (Bassnett 2018) creative translations of ancient texts, the translations of Sophie Seita (2021), and Anne Carson's presence in her translations of the Greeks—for instance, in *An Orestia* (2009) or her rendering of Euripides' *Bakkhai* (2017). *Nay Rather* (2013: 4) opens with this assertion: "Silence is as important as words in the practice and study of translation". *Nay Rather* is an exercise in translating, in untranslating, in silence, and in repetition. Carson (2013: 32) takes a small fragment of ancient Greek lyric poetry and translates it "over and over again using the wrong words. A sort of stammering". Her translations are creative and feminist rewritings of the past (Simon 2002). For instance, in *An Orestia*,

> the indefinite article of the title is a reminder that this is not a translation of Aeschylus' Oresteia, it is Anne Carson's version of three plays by different playwrights about the tragic sequence of events concerning the cursed house of Atreus.
>
> *(Bassnett 2022a: 246)*

These are all examples in which the translation completes the original. Seen as a prism, creative and ludic translation releases the multiple signifying possibilities of a text, mainly when the "original" text is like John Cayley's "microcollage translation", which "conceals crossings and transactions beneath the surface manifestation of the writing" (Lee in Baynham and Lee 2019: 139). Cayley's *Translation* series (2004) deconstructs notions of equivalence and authorship, as it

> symbolically performs continually evolving translations among English, French, and German versions of Walter Benjamin's "On Language as Such and the Language of Man" and excerpts from Proust's *A la recherche*, algorithmically cycling the texts through the three states of floating, sinking, or surfacing.
>
> *(Raley 2016: 123)*

Translation here is a creative intertextual process that opens language to plurality, loads it with multiple potential meanings, and opens the potential of the original "into multiple versions" (Reynolds 2019/2021: 3). Translation

> inevitably generates change. . . . This means that we can use translations not only to get a sense of books in languages we do not know, but to learn more about works that we can already read in our own tongue(s) . . . translation is inherently creative. It generates new meanings and can invent new words and fresh ways of putting them together.
>
> *(Reynolds et al. 2020: 132, 135, 147)*

In his 1957 talk "The Creative Act", Duchamp described art as a gap, as a missing link. But not the links that one can see or that exist. Art is the gap, he said. Translation is also this missing link, this in-between gap. Furthermore, in his posthumously published notes, Duchamp creates a neologism, *inframince*, the *infrathin*, which rejects definition—one can only give examples of it. The infrathin is that "between difference and repetition" (Chen et al. 2018: 113). It implies imperceptible difference (Perloff 2018b: 40), change, motion, shifty relations, displacements, and destabilizations. It is a "minimal difference", "that point at which one can just barely begin to perceive a threshold between two states" (Dworkin 2013: 17; see also Goldsmith 2016b and Perloff 2018b, 2004a).

What is infrathin? It's not really clear. Purposely. The French word *inframince* (translated into English as infrathin) was coined by Marcel Duchamp, but in typical Duchampian fashion, he claimed that it couldn't be defined. Instead, he insisted that one could only give examples of it. Over the course of his life, he gave a few:

- the warmth of a seat (which has just/been left) is infra-thin
- when the tobacco smoke smells also of the mouth which exhales it, the 2 odors marry by the infra-thin
- velvet trousers, their whistling sound is an infra-thin separation signaled

> Without getting too specific, we can surmise that infrathin is the space between spaces, the sound between sounds, the sensation between sensations; neither here nor there, this nor that, but both—all at the same time. . . . After an encounter with the infrathin, the world becomes infinitely richer, infinitely bigger, and infinitely weirder.
>
> *(Goldsmith in Chen et al. 2018: 115, 116)*

The infrathin is close to Deleuze's crucial "little differences" and to Wittgenstein's "the same is not the same" (Perloff 2004a: xxvii–xxviii):

> More than thirty years after Duchamp coined the term *infrathin*, the philosopher Gilles Deleuze declared, "Modern life is such that, confronted with the most mechanical, the most stereotypical repetitions, inside and outside ourselves, we endlessly extract from them little differences, variations and modifications". . . . In Duchamp's words above, "2 forms cast in/the same mold (?) differ/from each other/by an infra thin separative/amount". The ordinary observer may not notice this difference, which is perhaps best understood as the artist's domain.
>
> *(Perloff 2004a: xxvii)*

At the beginning of *Infrathin. An Experiment in Micropoetics* (2021), Perloff has an interesting epigraph from Wittgenstein: "Hegel seems to me to be always wanting to say that things which look different are really the same. Whereas my interest is in showing that things which look the same are really different". That is exactly the concept of the infrathin. Translation creates (or is) the "infrathin", in which difference is more important than similarity. In fact, Duchamp's French translation of Stein's *Stanzas in Meditation* is an excellent example of the infrathin, according to Perloff (in Inghilleri and Goldfajn 2022). Translation takes place in the infrathin (Perloff 2021a), in the passage from one player to the other. Translation appears within or through difference, and difference for Duchamp creates a gap that destabilizes language, meaning, and identity. Duchamp argues that if one takes a mold and puts things in, they will never be the same. "There will always be some slight difference. No two things are ever alike. Every time you repeat a sentence [Gertrude Stein argued] it has a different effect because it is now surrounded by something slightly different" (Perloff in Inghilleri and Goldfajn 2022). In my opinion, the same could be said of translation.

In this context, Rauschenberg's *Erased de Kooning Drawing* (1953), previously mentioned, is perhaps one of the best modern definitions of translation. Each text treads a path of past traces and imprints, of previous tracks and trails, trying (or not) to erase them. Like Rauschenberg, the "original" author can never completely erase earlier voices. Instead, he creates *sous rature* [under erasure] (Spivak 1967/1984: xvii; Dworkin 2013: 43). *Erased de Kooning Drawing* is his translation from what Derrida calls "traces" (1967/1979), which are sprinkled throughout the text. Texts are susceptible to multiple interpretations that can differ in each new context. Texts are borrowed spaces in Michel de Certeau's sense. Reading is an invitation to drift across the page, to wander over and through palimpsestic territories. An (un)original writer insinuates "into another person's text the ruses of pleasure and appropriation: he poaches on it, is transported into it, pluralizes himself in it like the internal rumblings of one's body" (De Certeau 1984: xxi). These interpretations vary in the mind of each individual who reads the text, and who understands each word in the light of experiences that are never free from blemishes and shadows. Writing inevitably carries with it barely perceptible elements from the past. Writing can also lose its way in a garden of forking paths, filled with myriad meanings and references that crisscross like the interwoven remembrances stored within each word. And so, each word written by the translator is a new creation.

Kirsten Malmkjaer (2020: 3) based one of her recent books on the idea that "translation per se is always creative". In her groundbreaking text, she argues that "translating is not copying" (Malmkjaer 2020: 38). A translation can never be a mere copy because Heraclitus' river is never the same river, because all languages do not possess the same resources, because social and temporal contexts change, and because there are never two identical translations of the same text (ibid.: 38–39). For this reason, new approaches to translation

> argue for translation as a creative endeavour and translations as original artefacts that bring something new into the world, and whose relationship to their sources, although involving a degree of copying, includes sufficient novelty vis-à-vis their sources to qualify as original creative works.
>
> *(ibid.: 49)*

The texts that translators of (un)creative literature must rewrite are (un)original writings replete with the traces left by previous writers, traces in the form of scars, different aromas, and noises that flow from each word to be translated: "The source text comes to the translation process always already mediated, capable of supporting multiple and conflicting interpretations which are limited only by the institutions where a translation is produced and circulated" (Venuti 2019: 40). They are texts that provide a sensual experience because they play not only with language but also with our senses. This occurs because many of these texts are canvases upon which words are transformed into visual events, something that once again expands and enhances the concept of translation: "Translation as a conceptual theme and as a textual-semiotic event operate at different levels and are not mutually exclusive" (Lee 2015: 12).

Any translation, like Rauschenberg's (or de Kooning's?) painting, is a palimpsest, a so-called original text that in reality is many texts, because the translation process is based on myriad voices in continuous dialogue with the author. The task is thus an exciting one, because it becomes a kind of continuous *pentimento*, the alteration of a painting on the same canvas as the original, the modification of the melodies that can nevertheless still be heard in the underlying layers:

> A signifier always produces meaning through an intertextual operation and interweaving of differences through the text and its context; in other words, a signifier does not refer to something within itself. . . . Language, then, works through the movement of *différance*, or the play of traces, and language users—writers, speakers, translators, even machines programmed to generate language—always operate with and within this general movement.
>
> *(Lee 2015: 26)*

Evidently, when literary works that are so open yet so constrained are translated, traditional prescriptivism is of no use. Translators know that their texts do not leave the previous text unaltered, but they are also aware that it is very different. In fact, according to Venuti (2019: 3), any correspondence or approximation between the two coincides with a "radical transformation". This kind of literature in which repetition is ludic creation certainly requires a form of translation in which the translator is also a ludic creator. Such was the approach applied by Clive Scott (2019, 2018, 2014, 2014, 2012a, 2012b) in his translations of Rimbaud, Apollinaire, and many others. Scott's translations of Baudelaire are a clear example of a ludic, performative, bodily translation that takes into account "the translator's perceptual response to the stimulus offered by the source text" (Lee 2022: 11). Literary translation is synesthetic, because it makes us aware that we conceive the universe with the totality of our bodies, "a whole-body experience in which words, and grammar, and syntax, and typographic phenomena such as typeface, margin, punctuation, activate cross-sensory, psycho-physiological responses prior to concept and interpretation" (Scott 2011: 213). We translate "with the concerted operation of *all* our senses" (Scott 2010: 154). It is a centrifugal practice. This means that the text is never complete, but always unstable:

> The text is constantly in search of itself; that it does not comprehend itself; that it has yet to fulfill itself, in paralinguistic realizations, in synesthetizations; that it does not own its literariness, but that this literariness is unstable, continually reinventable, always at the text's widening periphery. What do I mean by "widening periphery"? Through time, through processes of translation, the text fans out into multiple versions of itself, not just interpretations of its meaning, but performances of the experience of reading it; and as the ST proliferates performatively, so it becomes increasingly synesthetic.
>
> *(Scott 2010: 155)*

Centrifugal translation gravitates toward performance, "whether *of* the text, or *in* the text, in order to maximize the paralinguistic within the linguistic, and the multi-sensory in the reading consciousness" (Scott 2010: 159). In so doing, the translation "expands and self-multiplies" (Lee 2022: 11). This is not a "straight" translation, one that decodes and recodes meaning, but a translation that "circumvents meaning, aiming instead at *performance*. . . . Performative translation entails dialogic engagement with the source text through the translator's body, with a view to creating multimodal variations on that text" (Lee 2022: 11). Seen in this light, the translator's task is not to return to a text,

> but in order to operate a proliferation of text in performance, to activate a serial metamorphosis, which allows every reader to participate in the work's becoming, to leave their trace, their imprint, to project the ST into its future. Secondly, translation is a cross-sensory journey, a journey in which the lexical is allowed associatively to generate what sense-experience it wishes to. To translate words into words only, is to suppress their natural activity as psychic and sensory triggers. The task of the translator is to find contexts of practice appropriate to this multisensory dissemination.
>
> (Scott 2010: 162)

According to Scott (2006: 42), language is continuous variation as reflected in his rhizomatic translations, which transform and take forward the first text into another that is not faithful but allows the previous text to live "differently". Translation is an adventure, an experience, a philosophical enquiry:

> What if translation is an adventure not in meaning but in readerly consciousness and the *experience* of language? What if reading is looked upon not as a process of interpreting, or extracting meaning from, text but as a process of existential/experiential self-coordination or self-orchestration? What if translation is not a test of comprehension but of the fruitfulness of our inability to comprehend? . . . Experiences evaporate unless we know how to name them; language becomes the indispensable repository of our collective experience. . . . Translation must be allowed to open up and develop its own multimedial discursive space. It ceases to be a discipline (translation studies) and becomes a philosophical enquiry into its own functions and possible relationships with the translator's being-in-the-world.
>
> (Scott 2019: 88)

Many of the translators mentioned in the previous chapters of this book can be regarded as ludic, creative, centrifugal, original rewriters who add their voices to the original text. These include Jerome Rothenberg with his "total translations", Augusto de Campos with his "untranslations", and Haroldo de Campos with his "transcreations". Also relevant are the translators of concrete poetry (Corbett and Huang 2020). Authors such as John Cage and his "writing through", Jonathan Safran Foer in *Tree of Codes*, Kenneth Goldsmith with his *Trilogy*, and Craig Dworkin with *Parse* create (un)original works that never repeat the same thing. As philosophy has shown us, repetition is an impossibility, and this is the lesson that Borges was also trying to teach us in his "Pierre Menard":

> If we take translation to be a form of quotation, it should be clear that no one ever quotes another person's words without transforming them—tonally, if in no other way. Bakhtin's (1984/1929) concept of "double-voicing" would suggest that every quotation of another person's words retonalises those words with the new speaker's voice. . . . In Bakhtinian terms, just as the source author of a novel creates (and double-voices) a narrator, who "creates" (double-voices) a variety of characters, so too does the target author (translator) of that novel create the source author *as* a kind of narrator and double-voices that author/narrator. In that sense, the translator "adds another voice" (Robinson 2009) to the mix of voices that is the source text and addresses the target reader not only through the added voice, but also through the composite of all of the resulting voices.
>
> *(Robinson 2016: 281–282)*

These (un)creative writings lead us to think of a type of iterative translation in the Derridean sense that was mentioned previously: "a repetition of the same that always alters the 'same'" (Robinson 2003: 18). Translation is thus re-performed language, which is not based on stable equivalence:

> What happens to our conceptions of translation when we imagine it not as stable equivalence that is never quite stable and never quite equivalent, but . . . as what Jacques Derrida calls "iteration", a repetition of the same that always alters the "same", translation as reperformed language?
>
> *(Robinson 2003: 18)*

These (un)original geniuses create a type of iterative translation, in which iterability is "quotability" (Robinson 2003: 70):

> Language is constantly both emerging out of and cycling back into and through a performative social realm in which its ability to "signify", to serve as a channel of communication, depends on its being performed, and more specifically, according to Derrida, on its capacity for being performed and reperformed, for being quoted, reused—which is to say, at least from some perspectives, its potential for being misperformed, misquoted.
>
> *(Robinson 2003: 70)*

(Un)original writings are Barthesian texts full of layers (Barthes 1968/1977: 146). The translation of these iterative texts triggers processes of Barthesian discovery, because interpreting them does not mean giving them new meaning, but rather allowing the translator to appreciate the plurality of their components, as was Roland Barthes' desire in *S/Z*. Translators of (un)creative writings are no longer consumers but rather producers of texts. This gives them access to the enchantment of the signifier, to the voluptuousness of writing, to "the dismantling of language . . . intersected by political assertion" (Barthes 1973/1998: 8). These are texts of bliss. Texts that "discomfort" and "unsettle" (Barthes 1973/1998: 14). (Un)creative literature is composed of Barthesian "texts", which are tissues, woven fabrics:

> The Text is plural. Which is not simply to say that it has several meanings, but that it accomplishes the very plural of meaning: an *irreducible* (and not merely an acceptable) plural. The Text is not a co-existence of meanings but a passage, an overcrossing; thus it answers not to an interpretation, even a liberal one, but to an explosion, a dissemination. The plural of the Text depends, that is, not on the ambiguity of its contents but on what might be called the *stereographic plurality* of its weave of signifiers (etymologically, the text is a tissue, a woven fabric).
> *(Barthes 1971/1977: 159)*

The translators of (un)original literature must be fully aware that they will rewrite a "writerly" text. This is a text in constant transformation because it is not, as yet, subject to those systems that paralyze interpretation and that are ruled by the limitations of imitation, the logic of the story, and hierarchical binary oppositions:

> To interpret a text is not to give it a (more or less justified, more or less free) meaning, but on the contrary to appreciate what *plural* constitutes it. Let us first posit the image of a triumphant plural, unimpoverished by any constraint of representation (of imitation). In this ideal text, the networks are many and interact, without anyone of them being able to surpass the rest; this text is a galaxy of signifiers, not a structure of signifieds; it has no beginning; it is revealable; we gain access to it by several entrances, none of which can be authoritatively declared to be the main one.
> *(Barthes 1973/1974: 5)*

The writerly text reveals what the text says without saying it, because it knows that both the *I* that constructed the text and the *I* that will translate it are a plurality of other texts, interdisciplinary codes, and ways of looking at the world and of opening new doors to different worlds. Translation

> *differs* from the original, *defers* the determination of meaning, and *disseminates* through the target language traces of meaning marked in the "original" text. . . . In this light, the notion of the faithfulness of a translation to its original is no longer relevant because meaning is not the exclusive property of this "original" text any longer, but something (re)constituted in multiplicity through writing, reading, and translating.
> *(Lee 2015: 28, 29)*

Furthermore, the translator's semiotic input crosses the boundary between semiotic systems, and this transforms the translation outcome:

> Each time the same work is translated, even by the same person, a new piece is born, because the precise combination of resources is contingent on the psycho-physiological response of the translator to the work in question at a particular point in time. Translation then becomes a site of potentialities governed as much by chance as by skill. Rather than pointing centripetally toward the source text, translation serves as a prosthetic, directing the source text centrifugally toward its possible, as-yet-unseen shape. . . . Such translations would generate multiple experiential interpretations depending on the reader's sensory engagement with them, in turn influenced by such factors as the reader's intellectual profile and aesthetic disposition.
>
> *(Lee 2022: 14)*

The translator of these texts perceives this multiplicity and must translate it. This is the intertextuality of the repetition inherent in citations, which is so eloquently described by Barthes:

> What he perceives is multiple, irreducible, coming from a disconnected, heterogeneous variety of substances and perspectives: lights, colours, vegetation, heat, air, slender explosions of noises, scant cries of birds, children's voices from over on the other side, passages, gestures, clothes of inhabitants near or far away. All these *incidents* are half identifiable: they come from codes which are known but their combination is unique, founds the stroll in a difference repeatable only as difference. So the Text: it can be it only in its difference (which does not mean its individuality), its reading is semelfactive (this rendering illusory any inductive-deductive science of texts—no "grammar" of the text) and nevertheless woven entirely with citations, references, echoes, cultural languages (what language is not?), antecedent or contemporary, which cut across it through and through in a vast stereophony. The intertextual in which every text is held, it itself being the text-between of another text, is not to be confused with some origin of the text: to try to find the "sources", the "influences" of a work, is to fall in with the myth of filiation; the citations which go to make up a text are anonymous, untraceable, and yet *already read*: they are quotations without inverted commas.
>
> *(Barthes 1971/1977: 159–160)*

The translation of this literature needs to exemplify

> the "abysmal" slippages and detours of all understanding. . . . Translation, like criticism, reaches a point where it has to abandon the manageable rhetoric of "polysemia" (or multiple meaning, New Critical style) and embrace the "free play" of textual dissemination.
>
> *(Norris 1982/1991: 114)*

To be ethical, ludic translation takes the translator from "polysemia" to dissemination. Ludic translation can be one way to overcome the binary oppositions of essentialist systems:

> We have been far too obsessed with binary oppositions within the translation model and have been too concerned with defining and redefining the relationship between translation and original. Even where the model of dominant original and subservient translation has been challenged, the idea of some kind of hegemonic original still remains either in the source or target language. It is time to free ourselves from the constraints that the term "translation" has placed upon us and recognise that we have immense problems in pinning down a term that continues to elude us. For whether we acknowledge it or not, we have been colluding with alternative notions of translation all our lives.
> *(Bassnett in Bassnett and Lefevere 1998: 39)*

In contrast, the translations of (un)original texts are open ended. They are thus open to further translations and to endless rewritings that will (never) complete and (always) displace the original. Ludic translations are post-structuralist, and anti-essentialist. Ludic translations are co-creative processes of discovery that will never allow the original (?) text to arrive at a place where it can attain a stable meaning. Meaning is

> as fleeting as the moment in which it arises and as unique and unrepeatable as the momentary constellation of participants in the relationship. It is therefore not repeatable whether in the same or another language; and that insight is liberating from the point of view of translation studies. There will never be sameness of meaning.
> *(Malmkjaer 2020: 56)*

(Un)original writings and translations are derivative process of being and becoming: "To be a writer-translator is to value both being and becoming. What one writes in any given language typically remains as is, but translation pushes it to become otherwise" (Lahiri 2022: 8). Translation and (un)original are never simple echoes.

> We must be careful, however, not to equate the word echo with simple repetition. The verb Ovid attributed to Echo, once condemned, is not *repetere* but *reddere*, which means, among other things, to restore, to render, to reproduce. It can also mean to translate from one language to another. . . . In Ovid's myth, Echo's condition is clearly a punishment, a deprivation of her own voice and words. But she who translates, ideally, converts this "punishment" into a stimulating challenge, and often a joy. The translator "repeats" and thus "doubles" a text, but this repetition must not be taken literally. Far from a restrictive act of copying,

a translator restores the meaning of a text by means of an elaborate, alchemical process that requires imagination, ingenuity, and freedom. And so, while the act of repeating, or echoing, is certainly pertinent to the subject of translation, it is only the starting point of the translator's art.

(Lahiri 2022: 47)

As mentioned before, Echo distracted Zeus' wife Hera, who cursed Echo to merely repeat the last words she heard another person speak. Narcissus rejected Echo in favor of his reflection, his own echo in a lake, as Caravaggio's (1594–96), Salvador Dalí's (1937), or Lucien Freud's (1948) famous paintings, among others, show. Jaume Plensa's monumental sculpture *Echo* (2011) also comes to mind, a work that invites us to listen to others, a quiet counterpoint to the voices of the hundreds of daily visitors to Madison Square Park.

The original and its derivative are viewed in ludic translations as equals because texts can be broken so that the translator, like the reader, can become "a producer of the text" (Barthes 1973/1974: 4). The idea is for the translator, who is the best reader of all, to play with the text, as Barthes writes in "From Work to Text" (1971/1977: 161–162). (Un)creative writings are anything but arrogant in Barthes' sense:

Under the word "arrogance", I gather all the (linguistic) "gestures" that work as discourses of intimidation, of subjection, of domination, of assertion, of haughtiness: that claim the authority, the guarantee of a dogmatic truth or of a demand that doesn't think, that doesn't conceive of the other's desire. One is assaulted by the arrogance of discourse everywhere there is faith, certitude, will-to-possess, to dominate.

(Barthes 2007: 152)

On the contrary, these works exemplify Barthes' *le neutre* [the Neutral], that which escapes any binary opposition that produces essentialist meaning. These writings do not deny difference and are open to multiple nuances, to complexity, and to multiple and contradictory meanings. Arrogance is the dominance of one meaning over others, whereas the Neutral is "on the side of the heteroklitos, of the irregular, the unforeseeable, of the one following the other without order" (Barthes 2007: 130).

(Un)original literature is an attack on the notion of the owned, controlled, limited, and appropriated text in the name of some sovereign authorial source (Norris 1982/1991: 112), and it is similar to that announced by Derrida in "Limited Inc abc" (1972/1988). Consequently, all of these (un)original and (un)creative translations teach us that the translated text does not betray the original by challenging its demarcations. Instead, translation complements and completes it (as Borges would say), despite the fact that "the final product is going to be very different from the starting point" (Bassnett 2020: 14). In order to translate these texts, it is also necessary to acknowledge the translator's intervention, who deconstructs the narrative "logics" of texts that aspire, through a mode of layered writing clearly sceptical toward linearity, to rewrite any sort of inherited "logics" through an infinite play of texts. The creative translator will thus participate "in powerful acts that create knowledge and shape culture" (Tymoczko and Gentzler 2002: xxii). This gives the translator not only greater power but also an enormous ethical responsibility. Translation can serve as "an awareness-raising tool to promote empathy and cultural literacy by going beyond verbal expressions of difference through embodied experience" (Campbell and Vidal 2019: 31):

> This hierarchy, sadly prevalent, between what is authentic and what is derivative—one might take another step and say between what is pure and what is tainted—influences not only how we regard literature but how we regard one another. Who is original, who belongs authentically to a place? Who does not? Why are those who are not original to a place—migrants who did not "get there first"—treated as they are?
>
> *(Lahiri 2022: 49)*

Translators of (un)creative literature remind me of "Translator Studies" (Chesterman 2009), which highlights what human creators of translations do to become visible (Chesterman 2021: 244). They are creative and ludic translators who understand translations as altered forms of preexisting texts (Loffredo and Perteghella 2006: 4):

> Translation as a mode of writing comparable to the traditional ones, tracing, at the same time, the contours of an ever-complex notion of textuality, which, in its continuous movements and transformations, assimilates and engenders (con)texts—when texts become contexts . . . translation is revealed to be a privileged exploratory space in which many voices converge and reshape each other. Whether the translator's or the author's, these voices become, in translation, performances of personae interrelated "in" and "by means of" the act of writing.
>
> *(Loffredo and Perteghella 2006: 5, 7)*

(Un)creative and (un)original literature is a challenge for any translator and vivid proof that it is necessary to approach translation as the previously mentioned authors did. Translation is more ludic than ever and, therefore, more serious than ever. In his book, Lee (2022: 1) reminds us that "ludification" denotes "serious fun". It implies a nonlinear, nonhierarchical, dynamic conception of any writing. This type of literature is proof that translation "takes us into a surprisingly broad range of territories and confronts us with the most fundamental of questions" (Blumczynski 2016: ix). Ludic translation

> subverts the top-down relation between original and translation, renders irrelevant traditional assumptions about fidelity, and challenges outcome-based

thinking around the question of untranslatability. Through its playful stance with respect to a source text, a ludic approach unravels the Bakhtinian carnivalesque in translation.

(Lee 2022: 3)

Far from being a linear, reproductive process, translation is now total translation. This means that it is transcreative translation, a porous rewriting that works *alongside* a previous text that also has many layers.

Translating is not and can never be the repetition of exactly the same text. This does not mean that there are no limits to interpretation and to translation, but it does have "important implications for the ontology of a literary work, that is, what a work of literature is" (Lee 2022: 66). If "to experience translation is also to radically experiment with it" (Lee 2022: 10), translation could be defined as the ludic recreation of a text in another context, a text with a new voice, the voice of the translator:

> Translation, in other words, is never reducible to its common definition, "putting a work into another language"; after the cultural turn in translation studies in the 1990s and the current "textual turn", nearly all translation scholarship now acknowledges the many complications that proliferate around an act of translation. But the one consistently accessible site of transformative agency—what we can always hear working through these compounded complexities—is the translator's voice.
>
> *(Coldiron 2016: 311)*

Translation is not an inferior or secondary text, but rather a text that comes after the "prior text", to use Coldiron's terminology (ibid.: 315). Coldiron (2012) extends Venuti's (1995/2008) concept of invisibility and underlines intertextuality:

> To include more generally the in/visibilities of all foreign elements in a text, as his own hermeneutic practice has tended to do, then the visibly foreign elements in translations may appear not only as sites of resistance that bring to light the too often suppressed labor and art of translators, but also as aesthetic successes of collaborative intertextuality, and perhaps even as ethical models for encountering alterity. . . . In other words, just as Ricoeur advocated intercultural relations grounded in an ethic of hospitality (2010), we may wish to ground the intertextual relations of translation in an ethic of welcome. I would also wish to historicize visibility, and the welcome implicit in it, and to understand precisely how the visibly foreign elements worked and for what they were valued in particular times and places . . . [to suggest] an ethical dimension of highly visible translations.
>
> *(Coldiron 2012: 189, 190)*

The translator's visibility is a site of resistance and creativity that highlights the ludic elements of texts. Thus, Babel "can be reinterpreted as a site not of punishment, shame and passivity, but of potential mediation and aesthetic play" (Coldiron 2012: 196). This is an excellent suggestion for creative and ludic translators of (un)original literature, because it is one of those literary systems mentioned by Coldiron that change the position of traditional notions such as original, secondary, authorship, translator:

> After post-structuralism, a theoretical space of inquiry remains open between signifier and signified for visibility in translation. And postmodernism, with its quirky juxtapositions, glossolalia, asymmetry, self-referentiality and bricolage, holds aesthetic stances highly favorable to visibility and to the frictional sites of translation where unlike things meet. Postmodern collage, like collage's poetic ancestor, the classical cento, operates from the energy of difference-in-contact, whether interlingual or inter-media. Some contemporary painters, like some translators, allow differently textured residues to persist visibly in their work; the presence of the alien substance is precisely what is interesting. Mixed-media art, the high-low juxtapositions in contemporary fashion, asymmetries in post-1945 architecture, decentered photographic composition, and the use of musical quotation and "sampling" in popular songs all depend for their effects on the intrusion of some kind of visible alterity. This suggests a contemporary aesthetic favorable to visibility, or at least that visible alterities provide stimuli well suited to current sensibilities. In such a favorable climate, one more easily imagines a literary practice in which translators intrude openly as co-artists—perhaps playfully, wistfully, angrily or wryly, depending on the work in question.
>
> *(Coldiron 2012: 197)*

And she goes on to mention some writers and artists previously quoted in these pages as examples of this visibility:

> The experimental work of such poets as Charles Bernstein or Bernadette Mayer demonstrates options for working through some of these issues. Bernstein's first six experiments (1996–2010) are translation-based; homolinguistic translation, homophonic translation, lexical translation and dialect-idiolect translation seem especially fruitful suggestions. Ron Silliman, bpNichol and Caroline Bergvall create poems in which translation is not only visible in, but integral to, the verbal product. A recording of Bergvall, for instance, reveals multilingual phonetic wordplay making unexpected meanings that could not exist without highly visible—which here means audible—alterity (Bergvall n.d.) . . . aesthetic efforts following artists like Mayer, Bernstein or Bergvall might well come to depend on the co-artist's—that is, the translator's—visibility.
>
> *(Coldiron 2012: 197, 198)*

128 Translating repetition

According to Coldiron, visibility, "the translator's engagement with the prior text", reveals the translator's "co-artistry", "the foreign materials involved in the text", and give way to ethical translations which highlight the many possible relations "between prior text and translation": "Full visibility would assure that the prior text, and thus the translator's actions on it, remain present, independent, and viable alongside the translation in an implicitly equal relation with it" (Coldiron 2012: 198).

Because in (un)original literature (and in any literature) there can be no definitive reading, "there can obviously be no definitive translation . . . [we] conceive translation as interpretation and hence as rewriting and creation of a new 'original'" (Bassnett 2014: 152, 153). No translation can ever be the same as its original, for "once a translation enters the receiving culture it sets out on a new path" (Bassnett 2022a: 112). Translating is today an intersection. A porous, unstable, open-ended, generative, layered, entangled search.

To translate is to enter an (almost) infinite Borgesian labyrinth. This can only be explained by what Borges refers to when, to create an epigraph for Evaristo Carriego, he chooses the words of De Quincey, who describes truth as sharp edged and splintered. It is that maze-like truth that always forks and that makes him a hunter of writings in *El tamaño de mi esperanza* [*The size of my hope*] (1998). The translator of these texts must possess that lucid perplexity sought by the metaphysicians of Tlön, a place where the concept of plagiarism does not exist and where the duplication of lost objects is not infrequent. Tlön is where narratives are a game played by those who never had the courage to write stories and who distract themselves by falsifying and distorting texts (without any aesthetic justification).

This way of understanding translation takes us back again to the beginning of this book, in which Spivak quotes Derrida on iterability, beginnings, and prefaces. Like Derrida, Spivak observes that the preface is a text that is written afterward, but that appears before. The same thing happens with the translation.

Notes

1 "Tradurre è il vero modo di conoscere un testo", presentation at a conference on translation (Rome, 4 June 1982), in *Bollettino di informazione*, XXXII, 3, September-December. Some of Calvino's essays on translation have been published in *Altri discorsi di letteratura e società. Leggere, scrivere, tradurre*: "Sul tradurre" (1963), "Tradurre è il vero modo di leggere un testo" (1982); and the translator's note to the second edition of *Einaudi de I Fiori blu* (1984), Calvino's translation of Queneau's novel (see also Federici 2009: 29ff. and 139ff.).
2 La verdadera utopía no está en una lengua perfecta, sino en esta imperfección creativa de las lenguas, en este traducir sin descanso que es una forma de apertura. El traductor no pretende buscar una correspondencia término a término en función de una representación conceptual. Lo que hace más bien es introducir en su propia lengua puntos de vista sobre el lenguaje y sobre los fenómenos que anteriormente ésta no poseía. . . . La traducción no es una restitución del sentido, sino que siempre hay una disminución o aumento de éste, en cuanto las lenguas son sistemas abiertos y evolutivos. Traducir cambia tanto la lengua *ad quem* como la lengua *ab quo*.
3 But what makes something original, as opposed to a derivation? As a writer, I can vouch for the fact that everything "original" I have ever written derives necessarily from something

else, not just from my experiences but from my reading of other works, and through inspiration I have drawn, consciously and unconsciously, from countless other authors. Creativity does not exist in a vacuum, and much of it involves responding by imitating. . . I am attracted to myths—incidentally, the very first stories I learned to read—not only because they point me back to my own origins as a reader, but because they are the only original stories that exist: stories with counterparts in all cultures that belong to everyone and to no one. When I began writing stories as a child, I wrote copies of what I read, and in many respects, that is what I've continued doing, in only a slightly less obvious way. The illusion of artistic freedom is just that, an illusion. No words are "my words"—I merely arrange and use them in a certain way.

(Lahiri 2022: 52)

4 Marcel Duchamp's *Green Box* and *White Box* deconstruct the logic of the alphabet. In his *White Box*, the dictionary is turned into a site of experimentation where "undesirable" words are scratched out, and in the *Green Box*, he describes an alphabet in which the letter A no longer follows B and so on. This is not surprising as, for Duchamp, words are not merely a means of communication but an infinite and playful field, because they are always interrelated and create unexpected meanings. Also interesting here are Duchamp's notes in the *White Box* on the difference between apparition and appearance and his comments on mirrors and reflections concerning the *Large Glass* (see Paz 1978/2011).
5 This quotation is taken from David Shields' *Reality Hunger: A Manifesto*, a book published by an important press, Alfred A. Knopf. This book is created through a collection of citations and aphorisms and thus shows how appropriation is considered a key concept in contemporary writing (see Epstein 2012: 311–312).

5
ECHOES, ECHOES

In "Die Aufgabe des Übersetzers" (1923), Walter Benjamin's prologue, preface, and foreword to his translations of Baudelaire's *Tableaux Parisiens* (Berman et al. 2008/2018: 39–40; Robinson 2023), the author describes translation as an echo of the original. He argues that the translator's task is to find "the intention toward the language into which the work is to be translated, on the basis of which an echo of the original can be awakened in it" (Benjamin 1923/1997: 159).[1] Benjamin reminds his readers that translation does not find itself

> in middle of the high forest of the language itself; instead, from outside it, facing it, and without entering it, the translation calls to the original within, at that one point where the echo in its own language can produce a reverberation of the foreign language's work. Its intention is not only directed toward an object entirely different from that of the poetic work, namely toward a language as a whole, starting out from a single work of art, but is also different in itself.
> *(Benjamin 1923/1997: 159)*

According to Benjamin, it is not the translator's task to "strive for similarity to the original". Fidelity and freedom are "old traditional concepts in every discussion of translation" that "no longer seem useful for a theory that seeks in translation something other than the reproduction of meaning. . . . Fidelity in translating the individual word can almost never fully render the meaning it has in the original" (Benjamin 1923/1997: 160). Sense and meaning are always in flux.

Not surprisingly, there are various versions of "Die Aufgabe des Übersetzers" in English as well as in many other languages. It is in these rewritings that Benjamin's text finds its "afterlife". His text dwells on the "edge of the forest", where it calls out to a wider space and returns as an echo. (Un)original literature and translation are

DOI: 10.4324/9781003391890-6

thus understood as "a re-*call*-ing of the original" (Menke 2002: 84). The "survival" of the text (Benjamin 1923/1997: 153) is possible thanks to the translation, to the "reverberation" of the previous text:

> The original—i.e. the text that is to be translated—is *recalled* in translation by way of a turning away, by a diversion not meaning what it says. Translation "takes place" in place of reproduction or transference, both as a calling forth *and* its reverberation, and *between* the calling forth and the reverberation. The reverberation—both off and in the so-called "own" language ("in its totality")—of that which has been called out differentiates and makes a difference, and thus appears at first glance to contradict the very metaphor of the echo.
>
> *(Menke 2002: 84)*

These resonances are what is reflected in the (un)original literature that is described and analyzed in this book. Through repetition, erasure, citation, quotation, appropriation, influence, intertextuality, and many other strategies, (un)creative writers create (un)creative originals. These are texts that refer to other texts and, like translations, are created on the basis of palimpsests. In the same way as translation, (un)creative literature is a constant transformation:

> Just as in critical epistemology it is shown that there can be no objective knowledge, or even the claim to such knowledge, if the latter consists in reflections of the real, so here it can be shown that no translation would be possible if, in accord with its ultimate essence, it were to strive for similarity to the original. For in its continuing life, which could not be so called if it were not the transformation and renewal of a living thing, the original is changed.
>
> *(Benjamin 1923/1997: 155)*

(Un)original literature and translation are forms of *survivre*, the term used by Jacques Derrida (1979/1986) to refer to Benjamin's *überleben* (to survive) and *fortleben* (to survive or, literally, to live beyond).[2] To translate is to enable the survival of the "original", which also survives in (un)original literature. To translate is "at one and the same time to transform and to relate" (Edwards 1997: 61). According to Blanchot (1985: 70), the translator is a writer of singular originality. The translator painstakingly glues together the fragments of Benjamin's vessel. Even though this new vessel can never be exactly the same as the original, it is not completely different either. Both vases complement

> but need not resemble each other, so translation, instead of making itself resemble the meaning of the original, must . . . fashion in its own language a counterpart to the original's mode of intention, in order to make both of them recognizable as fragments of a vessel.
>
> *(Benjamin 1923/1997: 161)*

That is why translation "turns its attention away from trying to communicate something, away from meaning; the original is essential to translation only insofar as it has already relieved the translator and his work of the burden and organization of what is communicated" (id.). Perhaps this is the reason that in the introduction to *If Not, Winter*, Carson (2002: x) mentions this in relation to her translation of fragments of Sappho and says that "I like to think that, the more I stand out of the way, the more Sappho shows through". She also states that translation is a practice, a strategy "that does seem to give us a third place to be" (Carson 2002: 26).

As Goldsmith (2011: xviii) warned us, in the digital era, our concept of the same, the new, the original, and even of creativity has changed and is no longer the same. This means that sampling, copying, (self-)plagiarizing, etc. are "by no means unprecedented methods of producing a 'new' text" (Haensler 2019: 174). However, we have also seen that these notions have varied in the field of translation. Both (un)creative writing and translation are now ways of creating something new from what has previously been created. (Un)original literature is a kind of translation in itself, a rewriting that takes what has already been said and situates it in another context. Thus, in "Paragraphs on Conceptual Writing" (2005), Goldsmith repeats the words of the seminal essay "Paragraphs on Conceptual Art" by the conceptual/minimal artist Sol LeWitt. Accordingly, by simply replacing *art* with *writing*, Goldsmith (2005) transforms "I will refer to the kind of art in which I am involved as conceptual art. In conceptual art, the idea or concept is the most important aspect of the work" by LeWitt (1967) into "I will refer to the kind of writing in which I am involved as conceptual writing. In conceptual writing, the idea or concept is the most important aspect of the work" (Milesi 2015: 215; Haensler 2019: 175). One text is an echo of the other, but they are not exactly the same. Nor is Goldsmith's (2006) "Kenneth Goldsmith sings Jacques Derrida" the same either. This performance art piece is "a roughly 11-minute musical reading/rendition of (Gayatri C. Spivak's translation of) Derrida's *Of Grammatology* set to music by Second Viennese School composer Anton Webern" (Haensler 2019: 178). Furthermore, it is part of a larger project that includes "Kenneth Goldsmith sings theory", a rendition of Ludwig Wittgenstein's writings, which in turn could also be an echo of "the American conceptual artist John Baldessari's work from 1972, where he sings Sol LeWitt's famous *Sentences on Conceptual Art*" (Haensler 2019: 179). Palimpsests. Echoes of echoes. Translations of translations.

This is the implementation of Derrida's "countersignature", which reproduces the signature of the other "without reproducing or imitating it" (Derrida 2004: 29). This is originary contamination by unoriginal intertextuality and involves "the negotiation of the duplicitous demarcation between authentic, imitative originality and inauthentic originary imitation" (Milesi 2015: 213). Translation is thus a dynamic practice in perpetual motion. It is never a linear or binary process, and precisely for that reason, it is contamination, impurity, and, consequently, vital enrichment. Translating is what makes us conscious of the signature of the other but also conscious of our own. It heightens our awareness of multiplicity, of the small but very important differences between the worlds behind each language. It unveils duplicity and language as a territory of power and asymmetry.

Precisely because of this vision of translation, this book has also approached (un) original literature and its translation from the *infrathin*, that intriguing Duchampian concept that is not situated in the difference, a space that is "a state between states" (Goldsmith 2016a). To translate involves focusing on that minimal difference between things that makes the same thing never exactly the same. It is those "little differences" of Deleuze's (1968/2001), mentioned in Chapter 4, that demonstrate Wittgenstein's idea that the same is not the same and that repetition does not exist. At the beginning of this book, the very concept of beginning was addressed in reference to Wittgenstein's question (*Philosophical Investigations*, §215), "But isn't *the same* at least the same?" The answer lies in the following paragraph in which he points out that, when faced with the proposition "A thing is identical with itself", it can only be said that "there is no finer example of a useless proposition" (§216). The translator must thus be aware of the *infrathin* variations or those used by writers who rewrite earlier texts and thus situate them in other contexts by translating them. This reveals the openness of texts and their multiple interpretations, the instability of meaning, and the intertextuality of writing.

This idea of the *infrathin*, of the passage between one state and another, of the small difference that makes repetition impossible, is reminiscent of the work of conceptual artist Robert Barry titled *The Space Between Pages* (1969), which "appeared" in issue 6 of the experimental magazine *0 To 9*, edited in New York by Vito Acconci and Bernadette Mayer. The magazine was the ideal space for Barry's work because it dealt with topics such as the immateriality of art and concepts dealt with by Fluxus artists, conceptual artists, land art, minimal art, and Language poetry. Authors such as Sol LeWitt, Gertrude Stein, Raymond Queneau, Adrian Piper, and others also published their work there. Barry's work is an *infrathin*, because "The Space between Pages 29 & 30" and "The Space between Pages 74 & 75" are exactly that. Both are immaterial works that occupy that space, not a specific page, but rather the space between pages. Interestingly, both works are not the same. There is no repetition because the space in-between is not identical. The first occupies the space between the front and the back, whereas the second marks the space spanning an even and odd page.[3] The interstitial space occupied by the works is thus different. The context changes, as do the expectations of the readers or viewers. By the time they get to Barry's second work, they have already experienced the first, which can only signify that the meaning of the "repeated" work will be different. That is why the other side of the quixotic tapestry is the most interesting part, because each thread there yearns for the place where it used to be. At the same time, a more exciting future materializes on the horizon because its reappearance will be in an unknown territory composed in a different key, and on a different pentagram.

"Pierre Menard"'s goal is thus inviable. It is not possible to repeat. To repeat is not possible. Like the Roman empress Eutropia, translation is always mutable and versatile. In the same way as Zemrude, Calvino's invisible city, it takes the form of the person gazing at it. In this literature and in its translations, each text and each translation are a palimpsest, a superimposed story that slips into the space between one text and another, between the invisible blank spaces in any hypothetically univocal meaning. Meaning can only be hypothetically univocal because each word is a crossroads of cultures, a paradigm of encounters and misencounters, a space of interstices, and a wall of both containment and overflow. Each word is a rhizome, a reflection of the impurities that enrich it as well as of geographic and linguistic crossbreeding.

These (un)original writings show us that each word is a creolized archipelago, a heterotopic space, reflecting polycentric existences in constant rewriting. This space has no room for repetition because the contexts are different. Playful and creative translation leads us away from mere binarisms and enables us to journey through textual territories that are never completed and in which meanings are vanishing lines in constant deterritorialization. Each text, each translation adds to the previous one and, as Borges would say, completes it. Each text is an invitation for readers to think critically.

All those voices in counterpoint of the literature that appropriates previous melodies can only be translated on pentagrams that allow us to listen to multiple textual tapestries. In such cases, the translator must understand the texts as spaces of interweavings in which words show us their myriad scars, and also understand that they are the echoes of past lives. As Anne Carson writes in *Nay Rather*, "languages are not algorithms of one another, you cannot match them item for item" (Carson 2013: 4). With this in mind, the translator must be able to hear all the melodies in each word because creative, playful translation defies the static homogeneous conception of language and understands meaning not as an aria but rather as counterpoint, where all voices have the same intensity.

The literary texts mentioned in this book are interstitial with loops of signs that dialogue with each other on paths that are different and yet the same. In the same way as a tightrope walker, the translator performs in spaces that are not entirely horizontal, and that swing back and forth in an ever-dynamic and heterotopic void. In this context, writing and translating mean having the ability to expand and broaden both space and time. They signify creating crossings and interconnections between past, present, and future, as well as between constructs that both interrelate and are interrelated. Beyond mimesis, translation is finally the origin of those other signs that launch us into an infinity of different possibilities.

Translating is a fascinating process because it is never-ending and ever-changing, as reflected in Twice upon a time. Writing through. Erasures. Original copyists. The new Loulous offer us total translations, transcreations arising from the inversion of Platonism at the hands of Deleuze (see Chapter 1), which allow us not to settle for being Pierre Menard. The text, any text, is a Barthesian fabric, which interweaves multiple quotations and references, not like a simple game but with a view to questioning concepts such as originality and authorship. The original text is neither stable nor an "unchanging whole" (Emmerich 2017: 196).

In this context, the new theories of translation transform it into a playful, creative process in perpetual motion. Translation is not necessarily a partial representation in which something is always lost. On the contrary, as Borges observes, translation completes the original. All textual iterations of a work "ultimately point to a there that is elsewhere, to a work that is only ever a hypothetical sum of its continually proliferating parts" (Emmerich 2017: 196). Translation is understood as a very broad, multimodal, palimpsestic transformation, which gives visibility to the need to tell and retell stories from other perspectives (Holton 2010). The new Alisouns (Bergvall 2019) challenge the notion of textual instability.

Translating is a process that inevitably occurs after the original text. However, for those who cannot access the original, it is always the first text. It is a repetition that readers initially perceive as the original. That is why creative translation renders and portrays any (un)original text as a palimpsestic, iterative, complex, and fragmented reality. As a result, translating is a complex and (un)original writing process. It is multidirectional, creative, and open ended, always in movement, and never definitive. And that is what makes translation so fascinating.

Notes

1 Interestingly, Anne Carson considers Benjamin's "intention toward language of the original" in her translation of Sappho (Carson 2002: xii). See also Bassnett 2022b: 239–240.
2 "Survivre. Jornal de bord" is the title of an article that reverses the normal sequence of publication, as it first appeared as its English translation with the title "LIVING ON. Borderlines" (translated by James Hulbert) in *Deconstruction and Criticism* (1979). The original text in French subsequently appeared in *Parages* (1986). In this case, which is the first and original text? Which is the "repetition"? Which is the echo?
3 For an excellent analysis of this work as well as others by Barry, see Gilbert (2022).

REFERENCES

Abdulla, Adnan K. 2001. "Rhetorical repetition in literary translation," *Babel* 47(4): 289–303.
Abish, Walter. 1974. *Alphabetical Africa*. New York: New Directions.
Allegrezza, William, ed. 2012. *The Salt Companion to Charles Bernstein*. Cromer, Norfolk: Salt Publishing.
Altieri, Charles, and Nicholas D. Nace, eds. 2018. *The Fate of Difficulty in the Poetry of Our Time*. Evanston: Northwestern University Press.
Andersson, Andrea, ed. 2018. *Postscript: Writing After Conceptual Art*. Toronto, Buffalo and London: University of Toronto Press.
ap Siôn, Pwyll, and Lauren Redhead, eds. 2014. "Musical borrowing and quotation in the twentieth and twenty-first centuries," *Contemporary Music Review* 33(2): 125–127.
Arrojo, Rosemary. 2001/2002. "Algunas aventuras textuales de Don Quijote y Pierre Menard: la traducción y lo flagrante de la transferencia," In Arturo Vidal, A. Barr, and R. Martín, eds. *Babel (Special Issue) Debats*. Valencia (invierno, núm. 75. Trans): Javier Mallo.
Arrojo, Rosemary. 2004. "Translation, transference, and the attraction to otherness: Borges, Menard, Whitman," *Diacritics* 34(3–4): 31–53.
Arrojo, Rosemary. 2014. "The power of fiction as theory. Some exemplary lessons on translation from Borges's stories," In Klaus Kaindl, and Karlheinz Spitzl, eds. *Transfiction. Research into the Realities of Translation Fiction*. Amsterdam/Philadelphia: John Benjamins, pp. 37–50.
Arrojo, Rosemary. 2018. *Fictional Translators. Rethinking Translation through Literature*. New York and London: Routledge.
Ayache, Elie. 2010. *The Blank Swan*. Chichester: Wiley.
Baker, Mona, ed. 2022. *Unsettling Translation. Studies in Honour of Theo Hermans*. London and New York: Routledge.
Bal, Mieke. 1999. *Quoting Caravaggio: Contemporary Art, Preposterous History*. Chicago: The University of Chicago Press.
Bal, Mieke. 2015. "Visiting Nalini Malani's retrospective exhibition, New Delhi, 2014," *Qui Parle* 24(1): 31–62.
Bal, Mieke. 2016. *In Media Res. Inside Nalini Malani's Shadow Plays*. Ostfildern: Hatje Cantz.
Bal, Mieke. 2018. "Linea Recta, Linea Perplexa: Moving through entangled time with Nalini Malani," In *Nalini Malani*. Rivoli-Torino: Museo D'Arte Contemporanea.

References

Balderston, Daniel. 2018. *How Borges Wrote*. Charlottesville and London: University of Virginia Press.
Balestrini, Nanni. 1966/2014. *Tristano. A Novel*. New York: Verso Books.
Barbour, Susan. 2011. "'Spiritual hyphen': Bibliography and elegy in Susan Howe's *the midnight*," *Textual Practice* 25(1): 133–155.
Barnes, Julian. 1984. *Flaubert's Parrot*. London: Jonathan Cape.
Barth, John. 1967. "The literature of exhaustion," *The Atlantic* 220: 29–34.
Barthes, Roland. 1966/2007. *Criticism and Truth* (Trans. Katrine Pilcher Keuneman). London: Continuum.
Barthes, Roland. 1968/1977. "The death of the author," In *Image, Music, Text* (Trans. Stephen Heath). New York: Hill and Wang, pp. 142–148.
Barthes, Roland. 1971/1977. "From work to text," In *Image, Music, Text* (Trans. Stephen Heath). New York: Hill and Wang, pp. 155–164.
Barthes, Roland. 1973/1974. *S/Z* (Trans. Richard Howard). Oxford: Blackwell.
Barthes, Roland. 1973/1998. *The Pleasure of the Text* (Trans. Richard Miller). New York: Hill and Wang.
Barthes, Roland. 2007. *The Neutral: Lecture Course at the College de France (1977/1978)* (Trans. Rosalind Krauss and Denis Hollier). New York: Columbia University Press.
Bassnett, Susan. 1993. *Comparative Literature. A Critical Introduction*. Oxford: Blackwell.
Bassnett, Susan. 2006/2007. "Writing and translating," In Susan Bassnett, and Peter Bush, eds. *The Translator as Writer*. London and New York: Continuum, pp. 173–183.
Bassnett, Susan. 2011. "The translator as cross-cultural mediator," In Kirsten Malmkjær, and Kevin Windle, eds. *The Oxford Handbook of Translation Studies*. Oxford: Oxford University Press, pp. 94–107.
Bassnett, Susan. 2014. *Translation*. New York and London: Routledge.
Bassnett, Susan. 2018. "Questioning authority and authenticity: The creative translations of Josephine Balmer," In Jean Boase-Beier, Lina Fisher, and Hiroko Furukawa, eds. *The Palgrave Handbook of Literary Translation*. New York: Palgrave, pp. 333–350.
Bassnett, Susan. 2020. "Concrete poetry, playfulness and translation," In John Corbett, and Ting Huang, eds. *The Translation and Transmission of Concrete Poetry*. New York and London: Routledge, pp. 9–20.
Bassnett, Susan. 2022a. "Beyond faithfulness: Retranslating classic texts," In Jan Steyn, ed. *Translation. Crafts, Contexts, Consequences*. Cambridge: Cambridge University Press, pp. 112–125.
Bassnett, Susan. 2022b. "Translation, transcreation, transgression," In Laura Jansen, ed. *Anne Carson. Antiquity*. London and New York: Bloomsbury, pp. 237–250.
Bassnett, Susan. 2022c. "'Preface' to Mª Carmen África Vidal Claramonte," In *Translation and Contemporary Art. Transdisciplinary Encounters*. New York and London: Routledge, pp. vii–xi.
Bassnett, Susan, and André Lefevere. 1998. *Constructing Cultures. Essays on Literary Translation*. Clevedon: Multilingual Matters.
Bassnett, Susan, and Harish Trivedi, eds. 1999. *Post-Colonial Translation. Theory and Practice*. London and New York: Routledge.
Baudrillard, Jean. 1981/2006. *Simulacra and Simulation* (Trans. Sheila Faria Glaser). Ann Arbor: The University of Michigan Press.
Baudrillard, Jean. 2002/2003. *The Spirit of Terrorism and Requiem for the Twin Towers* (Trans. Chris Turner). London and New York: Verso.
Bayard, Pierre. 2009. *Le plagiat par anticipation*. Paris: Minuit.
Baynham, Mike, and Tong King Lee. 2019. *Translation and Translanguaging*. London and New York: Routledge.

Bean, Victoria, and Chris McCabe, eds. 2015. *The New Concrete: Visual Poetry in the 21st Century*. London: Hayward Publishing.
Beaulieu, Derek. 2010. *How to Write*. Vancouver: Talonbooks.
Beaulieu, Derek. 2017. *a, A Novel*. Paris: Jean Boîte Editions.
Beaulieu, Derek. 2019. "Prose of the trans Canada," In Gregory Betts, and Christian Bök, eds. *Avant Canada. Poets, Prophets, Revolutionaries*. Waterloo: Wilfrid Laurier University Press, pp. 254–257.
Benesch, Klaus. 2007. "In the diaspora of words: Gaddis, Kierkegaard, and the art of recognition(s)," In Joseph Tabbi, and Rone Shavers, eds. *Paper Empire. William Gaddis and the World System*. Tuscaloosa: The University of Alabama Press, pp. 28–45.
Benjamin, Walter. 1923/1997. "The Translator's Task," *TTR: Traduction, Terminologie, Rédaction* (Trans. Steven Rendall) 10(2): 151–165.
Bennett, Andrew. 2005. *The Author*. London and New York: Routledge.
Bennett, Andrew, and Nicholas Royle. 2004. *An Introduction to Literature, Criticism and Theory*. Hallow and London: Pearson/Longman.
Bennett, Karen. 2019. "Editor's introduction," *Translation Matters* 1(2): 1–8.
Bergvall, Caroline. 2000. *Via*. www.ubu.com/sound/bergvall.html.
Bergvall, Caroline. 2003. "Dante & Caroline Bergvall, via (48 Dante Variations)," *Chain Tranlucinacion* 10: 55–59.
Bergvall, Caroline. 2005. *Fig*. London: Salt Books.
Bergvall, Caroline. 2019. *Alisoun Sings*. New York: Nightboat Books.
Bergvall, Caroline. 2000. *Processing Writing: From Text to Textual Interventions*. Research Thesis. Plymouth: University of Plymouth.
Bermann, Antoine, Isabelle Berman and Valentina Sommella. 2008–2018. *The Age of Translation. A Commentary on Walter Benjamin's "The Task of the Translator"* (Trans. Chantal Wright). London and New York: Routledge.
Bermann, Sandra. 2014. "Performing translation," In Sandra Bermann, and Catherine Porter, eds. *A Companion to Translation Studies*. Chichester: Wiley-Blackwell, 285–297.
Berry, Ellen E. 2016. *Women's Experimental Writing: Negative Aesthetics and Feminist Critique*. London: Bloomsbury.
Bervin, Jen. 2004/2019. *Nets*. Brooklyn: Ugly Duckling Presse.
Bervin, Jen. 2010. *The Dickinson Composites*. New York: Granary Books.
Bervin, Jen. 2012. "Jen Bervin," In Caroline Bergvall, Laynie Browne, Teresa Carmody, and Vanessa Place, eds. *I'll Drown My Book. Conceptual Writing by Women*. Los Angeles: Les Figues Press, pp. 126–131.
Bervin, Jen, and Marta Werner. 2012. *The Gorgeous Nothings: Emily Dickinson's Envelope Poems*. New York: Granary Books.
Bessa, Antonio Sergio. 2009. "Sound as subject: Augusto de Campos's Poetamenos," In Marjorie Perloff, and Craig Dworkin, eds. *The Sound of Poetry/The Poetry of Sound*. Chicago: The University of Chicago Press, pp. 219–236.
Bessa, Antonio Sergio, and Odile Cisneros, eds. 2007. *Novas. Selected Writings. Haroldo de Campos*. Evanston: Northwestern University Press.
Blanchot, Maurice. 1985. *L'Amitié*. Paris: Gallimard.
Blanchot, Maurice. 1986. *Le Livre à venir*. Paris: Gallimard.
Block de Behar, Lisa. 1984/1994. *Una retórica del silencio. Funciones del lector y procedimientos de la lectura literaria*. Madrid: Siglo XXI.
Block de Behar, Lisa. 2014. *Borges, the Passion of an Endless Quotation* (Trans. William Egginton and Christopher Ray Alexander). Albany: State University of New York Press.
Bloom, Harold. 1973/1997. *The Anxiety of Influence*. Oxford and New York: Oxford University Press.

Blumczynski, Piotr. 2016. *Ubiquitous Translation*. New York: Routledge.
Bogoya, Camilo. 2015. "De la crítica a la ficción: Michel Lafon y Pierre Menard," In Brigitte Adriaensen et al., eds. *Una profunda necesidad en la ficción contemporánea. La recepción de Borges en la república mundial de las letras*. Madrid/Frankfurt: Vervuert Iberoamericana, pp. 193–206.
Bohn, Willard. 2011. *Reading Visual Poetry*. Madison/Teaneck: Fairleigh Dickinson University Press.
Bök, Christian. 2001. *Eunoia*. Toronto: Coach House Books.
Bolduc, Michelle. 2018. "Absence and presence: Translators and prefaces," In Jean Boase-Beier, Lina Fisher, and Hiroko Furukawa, eds. *The Palgrave Handbook of Literary Translation*. New York: Palgrave, pp. 351–376.
Boon, Marcus. 2010. *In Praise of Copying*. Cambridge: Harvard University Press.
Borges, Jorge Luis. 1954/1989. "Magias parciales del *Quijote*," In *Otras Inquisiciones, Obras completas*. Barcelona: Emecé, pp. 45–47.
Borges, Jorge Luis. 1960/1964. "Borges and I," In *Labyrinths* (Trans. James E. Irby). New York: New Directions.
Borges, Jorge Luis. 1975. *Prólogos con un prólogo de prólogos*. Buenos Aires: Torres Agüero Editor.
Borges, Jorge Luis. 1980/1984. "The thousand and one nights," *The Georgian Review* (Trans. Eliot Weinberger): 564–574.
Borges, Jorge Luis. 1986/1998. "Pierre Menard, author of Don Quixote," In *Collected Fictions* (Trans. Andrew Hurley). New York: Penguin.
Brossard, Nicole. 1987/1990. *Mauve Desert* (Trans. Susanne de Lotbinière-Harwood). Toronto: Coach House Press.
Burke, Seán. 1995. *Authorship from Plato to the Postmodern*. Edinburgh: Edinburgh University Press.
Bush, Akiko. 2019. *How to Disappear. Notes on Invisibility in a Time of Transparency*. New York: Penguin.
Buskirk, Martha. 2003. *The Contingent Object of Contemporary Art*. Cambridge: The MIT Press.
Butler, Emily. 2020. "How Can we listen better?" In *Nalini Malani. Can You Hear Me?* London: Whitechapel Gallery, pp. 61–68.
Cage, John. 1982. *X: Writings '79–'82*. Middletown: Wesleyan University Press.
Cage, John. 2019. *Diary: How to Improve the World (You Will Only Make Matters Worse)*. New York: Siglio Press.
Calinescu, Matei. 1987. *Five Faces of Modernity: Modernism, Avant-Garde, Decadence, Kitsch, Postmodernism*. Durham: Duke University Press.
Calinescu, Matei. 1991. "Some remarks on the logic of period terms: Modernism, late modernism, postmodernism," *Dedalus* 1: 279–292.
Calleja, Jen. 2019. "Life's too short: On translating Christian Marclay's photo-book *The Clock*," In Madeleine Campbell, and Ricarda Vidal, eds. *Translating Across Sensory and Linguistic Borders. Intersemiotic Journeys between Media*. New York: Palgrave Macmillan, pp. 353–370.
Calvino, Italo. 1979/1981. *If on a Winter's Night a Traveler*. New York: Harcourt Brace Jovanovich.
Campbell, Madeleine, and Ricarda Vidal, eds. 2019. *Translating across Sensory and Linguistic Borders. Intersemiotic Journeys between Media*. New York: Palgrave Macmillan.
Capildeo, Vanhi. 2019. "Pierre de Ronsard's "Ode À Cassandre": Erasure, Recall, Recolouration," In Madeleine Campbell, and Ricarda Vidal, eds. *Translating across Sensory and Linguistic Borders. Intersemiotic Journeys between Media*. New York: Palgrave Macmillan, pp. 113–124.
Caputo, John. 1987. *Radical Hermeneutics. Repetition, Deconstruction and the Hermeneutic Project*. Bloomington: Indiana University Press.

Carson, Anne. 2002. *If Not, Winter. Fragments of Sapho*. New York: Vintage.
Carson, Anne. 2013. *Nay Rather*. Paris: The Cahiers Series. Sylph Editions.
Castiglione, Davide. 2019. *Difficulty in Poetry. A Stylistic Model*. New York: Palgrave Macmillan.
Castro, Fernando. 2014. "Compulsiones paródicas," *Minerva: Revista del Círculo de Bellas Artes* 23: 66–69.
Chen, Cecily, Andrew Howard, William Kahn, Grace Knight, Jonipa Kupa, Amy Marcus, Charlie Sosnick and Zoe Stoller. 2018. *1000 Infrathins*. Philadelphia: Center for Programs in Contemporary Writing, University of Pennsylvania.
Chesterman, Andrew. 2009. "The name and nature of translator studies," *Hermes* 42: 13–22.
Chesterman, Andrew. 2021. "Translator studies," In Yves Gambier, and Luc van Doorslaer, eds. *Handbook of Translation Studies*. Amsterdam/Philadelphia: John Benjamins, pp. 241–246.
Cisneros, Odile. 2012. "From isomorphism to Cannibalism: The evolution of Haroldo de Campos's translation concepts," *TTR. Traduction, Terminologie, Redáction* 25(2): 15–44.
Cisneros, Odile. 2018. "From the Rockies to the Amazon: Translating experimental Canadian Poetry for a Brazilian Audience," In Suzanne Jill Levine, and Katie Lateef-Jan, eds. *Untranslatability Goes Global*. New York and London: Routledge, pp. 46–63.
Cisneros, Odile. 2020. "Translation and radical poetics. The case of Octavio Paz and the Noigandres," In Marília Librandi, Jamille Pinheiro Dias, and Tom Winterbottom, eds. *Transpoetic Exchange. Haroldo de Campos, Octavio Paz, and Other Multiversal Dialogues*. Lewisburgh: Bucknell University Press, pp. 73–83.
Clarke, Ami. 2017. "Text as market," In Ruth Catlow, Marc Garrett, Nathan Jones, and Sam Skinner, eds. *Artists Re-thinking the Blockchain*. Torque Editions & Furtherfield, pp. 133–140.
Cleary, Heather. 2021. *The Translator's Visibility. Scenes from Contemporary Latin American Fiction*. New York: Bloomsbury.
Clüver, Claus. 2020. "Exploring the structures of chance: Transcreating Noigandres *Ideogramas* into English," In John Corbett, and Ting Huang, eds. *The Translation and Transmission of Concrete Poetry*. New York and London: Routledge, pp. 71–96.
Cobb, Russell, ed. 2014. *The Paradox of Authenticity in a Globalized World*. New York: Palgrave Macmillan.
Colby, Georgina, ed. 2021. *Reading Experimental Writing*. Edinburgh: Edinburgh University Press.
Coldiron, A. E. B. 2012. "Visibility now: Historicizing foreign presences in translation," *Translation Studies* 5(2): 189–200.
Coldiron, A. E. B. 2016. "Introduction: Beyond babel, or, the agency of translators in early modern literature and history," *Philological Quarterly* 95(3–4): 311–323.
Collins, Sophie. 2019. "Radical ekphrasis: Or, an ethics of seeing," In Madeleine Campbell, and Ricarda Vidal, eds. *Translating across Sensory and Linguistic Borders. Intersemiotic Journeys between Media*. New York: Palgrave Macmillan, pp. 371–394.
Collins, Stephen, and Graham Lyons, eds. 2012. *Reading Duncan Reading. Robert Duncan and the Poetics of Derivation*. Iowa: University of Iowa Press.
Connor, Steven. 2007. *Samuel Beckett. Repetition, Theory and Text*. Aurora: The Davies Group Publishers.
Corbett, John, and Ting Huang, eds. 2020. *The Translation and Transmission of Concrete Poetry*. New York and London: Routledge.
Crow, Thomas. 1986. "The return of Hank Herron," In *Endgame: Reference and Simulation in Recent Painting and Sculpture*. Boston: The Institute of Contemporary Art, pp. 11–28.
Crow, Thomas. 1996. *Modern Art in the Common Culture*. New Haven and London: Yale University Press.

References

Daitch, Susan. 2002. *L. C.* Chicago: Dalkey Archive Press.
Danto, Arthur. 1981. *The Transfiguration of the Commonplace: A Philosophy of Art*. Cambridge: Harvard University Press.
Dasilva, Xosé Manuel. 2006. "Octavio Paz transcreado por Haroldo de Campos: de *Blanco* Transblanco," Trans. *Revista de Traductología* 10: 23–40.
Davidson, Michael. 1989. "Palimtexts: Postmodern poetry and the material text," In Marjorie Perloff, ed. *Postmodern Genres*. Norman and London: University of Oklahoma Press, pp. 75–95.
De Campos, Haroldo. 1963/1992. "Da Tradução como Criação e como Crítica," *Metalinguagem & Outras Metas*. São Paulo: Perspectiva, pp. 31–48.
De Campos, Haroldo. 1984/2004. *Galáxias*. Sao Paulo: Editora 34.
De Certeau, Michel. 1984. *The Practice of Everyday Life* (Trans. Steven Rendall). Berkeley: University of California Press.
De Man, Paul. 1964. "A modern master," *New York Review of Books*, November 19, pp. 8–10.
Del Toro García, María Leticia. 2017. *Experimentación, intertextualidad e historia en la obra de Susan Howe*. Zaragoza: Prensas de la Universidad de Zaragoza.
Deleuze, Gilles. 1968/2001. *Difference and Repetition* (Trans. Paul Patton). London and New York: Continuum.
Deleuze, Gilles. 1969. *Logique du sens*. Paris: Les editions de Minuit.
Deleuze, Gilles and Guattari Felix. 1975/1986. *Kafka: Toward a Minor Literature* (Trans. Dana Polan). Minneapolis: University of Minnesota Press.
Deleuze, Gilles, and Guattari Félix. 1987/2005. *A Thousand Plateaus. Capitalism and Schizophrenia* (Trans. Brian Massumi). Minneapolis and London: The University of Minnesota Press.
Derrida, Jacques. 1967/1979. *Speech and Phenomena and Other Essays on Husserl's Theory of Signs* (Trans. David B. Allison and Newton Garver). Evanston: Northwestern University Press.
Derrida, Jacques. 1967/1984. *Of Grammatology* (Trans. Gayatri Chakravorty Spivak). Baltimore and London: The Johns Hopkins University Press.
Derrida, Jacques. 1967/2001a. *Writing and Difference* (Trans. Alan Bass). London: Routledge.
Derrida, Jacques. 1972/1984. *Margins of Philosophy* (Trans. Alan Bass). Chicago: The University of Chicago Press.
Derrida, Jacques. 1972/1988. *Limited Inc* (Trans. Samuel Weber and Jeffrey Mehlman). Evanston: Northwestern University Press.
Derrida, Jacques. 1972a/1981. *Dissemination* (Trans. Barbara Johnson). Chicago: The University of Chicago Press.
Derrida, Jacques. 1972b/1981. *Positions* (Trans. Alan Bass). Chicago: Chicago University Press.
Derrida, Jacques. 2001b. "What is a 'relevant' translation?" *Critical Enquiry* (Trans. Lawrence Venuti) 27(2): 174–200.
Derrida, Jacques. 2004. "Countersignature," *Paragraph* (Trans. Mairéad Hanrahan) 27(2): 17–42.
Drury, M. O'C. 1981. "Conversations with Wittgenstein," In Rush Rhees, ed. *Ludwig Wittgenstein: Personal Recollections*. Totowa: Rowan and Littlefield, pp. 112–190.
Duncan, Dennis. 2019. *The Oulipo and Modern Thought*. Oxford: Oxford University Press.
Dunn, Mark. 2001. *Ella Minnow Pea: A Novel in Letters*. New York: Anchor Books.
Dunn, Mark. 2004. *Ibid: A Novel*. San Diego: Harcourt Brace.
Dworkin, Craig. 2003. *Reading the Illegible*. Evanston: Northwestern University Press.
Dworkin, Craig. 2013. *No Medium*. Cambridge: The MIT Press.

Dworkin, Craig. 2020a. *Radium of the Word. A Poetics of Immateriality*. Chicago: The University of Chicago Press.
Dworkin, Craig. 2020b. *Dictionary Poetics. Toward a Radical Lexicography*. New York: Fordham University Press.
Dworkin, Craig. 2021. *Helicography*. Santa Barbara: Punctum Books.
Dworkin, Craig, and Kenneth Goldsmith, eds. 2011. *Against Expression. An Anthology of Conceptual Writing*. Evanston: Northwestern University Press.
Eco, Umberto. 1980/2014. *The Name of the Rose* (Trans. William Weaver). New York: Mariner Books.
Eco, Umberto. 1983. *Postscript to the Name of the Rose*. San Diego: Harcourt Brace Jovanovich.
Eco, Umberto. 1985. "Innovation and repetition: Between modern and post-modern aesthetics," *Daedalus* 114(4): 161–184.
Edmond, Jacob. 2011. "'Let's do a Gertrude Stein on it'. Caroline Bergvall and iterative poetics," *Journal of British and Irish Innovative Poetry* 3(2): 109–122.
Edmond, Jacob. 2012. *A Common Strangeness. Contemporary Poetry, Cross-cultural Encounter, Comparative Literature*. New York: Fordham University Press.
Edmond, Jacob. 2016. "Copy," In Eric Hayot, and Rebecca Walkowitz, eds. *A New Vocabulary for Global Modernism*. New York: Columbia University Press, pp. 96–113.
Edmond, Jacob. 2019. *Make It the Same. Poetry in the Age of Global Media*. New York: Columbia University Press.
Edwards, Michael. 1997. "Translation and repetition," *Translation and Literature* 6(1): 48–65.
Egginton, William, and David E. Johnson, eds. 2009. *Thinking with Borges*. Aurora: The Davis Group Publishers.
Eleey, Peter. 2014. *Sturtevant: Double Trouble, Exhibition Catalogue*. New York: The Museum of Modern Art.
Emmerich, Karen. 2017. *Literary Translation and the Making of Originals*. New York and London: Bloomsbury.
Epstein, Andrew. 2012. "Found poetry, 'uncreative writing', and the art of appropriation," In Joe Bray, Alison Gibbons, and Brian McHale, eds. *The Routledge Companion to Experimental Literature*. New York and London: Routledge, pp. 310–322.
Epstein, Andrew. 2016. "The oulipo, language poetry, and proceduralism," In Brian McHale, and Len Platt, eds. *The Cambridge History of Postmodern Literature*. New York: Cambridge University Press, pp. 324–338.
Fabbri, Paolo. 1994. "Elogio de Babel," *Revista de Occidente* 154: 5–14.
Fabbri, Paolo. 1995. *Tácticas de los signos* (Trans. Alfredo Báez). Barcelona: Gedisa.
Fabbri, Paolo. 2000. *El giro semiótico* (Trans. Juan Vivanco Gefaell). Barcelona: Gedisa.
Fallas, John. 2007. "Into the new century: Recent holloway and the poetics of quotation," *Tempo* 61(242): 2–10.
Federici, Federico. 2009. *Translation as Stylistic Evolution: Italo Calvino Creative Translator of Raymond Queneau*. Amsterdam and New York: Rodopi.
Federman, Raymond. 1992. *Double or Nothing*. Normal: Illinois State University.
Fink, Thomas, and Judith Halden-Sullivan, eds. 2014. *Reading the Difficulties. Dialogues with Contemporary American Innovative Poetry*. Tuscaloosa: The University of Alabama Press.
Fitterman, Robert. 2009. *Rob the Plagiarist: Others Writing by Robert Fitterman 2000/2008*. New York: Roof Books.
Foran, Lisa. 2022. "History of philosophy and translation," In Christopher Rundle, ed. *The Routledge Handbook of Translation History*. London and New York: Routledge, pp. 173–188.
Foucault, Michel. 1974/1990. "La Vérité et les formes juridiques," *Chimeres* 10: 8–28.
Gaddis, William. 1955/1993. *The Recognitions*. Harmondsworth: Penguin.

Gambier, Yves, and Luc van Doorslaer, eds. 2021. *Handbook of Translation Studies*, vol. 5. Amsterdam/Philadelphia: John Benjamins.

Gasche, Rodolphe. 1986. *The Tain of the Mirror. Derrida and the Philosophy of Reflection*. Cambridge: Harvard University Press.

Gendron, Sarah. 2008. *Repetition, Difference, and Knowledge in the Work of Samuel Beckett, Jacques Derrida and Gilles Deleuze*. New York: Peter Lang.

Genette, Gerard. 1982. *Palimpsestes. La littérature au second degré*. Paris: Seuil.

Genette, Gerard. 1987. *Seuils*. Paris: Seuil.

Gentzler, Edwin. 1993. *Contemporary Translation Theories*. London and New York: Routledge.

Gentzler, Edwin. 2008. *Translation and Identity in the Americas. New Directions in Translation Theory*. New York and London: Routledge.

Gentzler, Edwin. 2017. *Translation and Rewriting in the Age of Post-translation Studies*. New York and London: Routledge.

Gibbons, Alison. 2012. *Multimodality, Cognition, and Experimental Literature*. New York and London: Routledge.

Gilbert, Annette. 2022. *Literature's Elsewheres. On the Necessity of Radical Literary Practices*. Cambridge: The MIT Press.

Gizzi, Peter. 2021. *"Preface" to Jack Spicer. After Lorca*. New York: New York Review of Books.

Goldfajn, Tal. 2022. "Super-close reading: On Marjorie Perloff's *Infrathin: An experiment in micropoetics*," *Los Angeles Reviews of Books*, March 29.

Goldsmith, Kenneth. 2000/2012. *Fidget*. Toronto: Coach House Books.

Goldsmith, Kenneth. 2000/2014. *Inquieto* (Trans. Carlos Bueno Vera.). Segovia: Ediciones La Uña Rota.

Goldsmith, Kenneth. 2011. *Uncreative Writing: Managing Language in the Digital Age*. New York: Columbia University Press.

Goldsmith, Kenneth. 2012. "Conceptual writing: A world view," *Harriet* (Poetry Foundation), April 30.

Goldsmith, Kenneth. 2015a. *Theory*. Paris: Jean Boîte Éditions.

Goldsmith, Kenneth. 2015b. *Capital. New York, Capital of the 20th Century*. London and New York: Verso.

Goldsmith, Kenneth. 2015c. "Make it new: Post-digital concrete poetry in the 21st century," In Victoria Bean, and Chris McCabe, eds. *The New Concrete: Visual Poetry in the 21st Century*. London: Hayward Publishing, pp. 9–15.

Goldsmith, Kenneth. 2016a. *Against Translation*. Paris: Jean Boîte Éditions.

Goldsmith, Kenneth. 2016b. *Wasting Time on the Internet*. New York: Harper Perennial.

Goldsmith, Kenneth. 2020. *Duchamp Is My Lawyer. The Polemics, Pragmatics, and Poetics of Ubuweb*. New York: Columbia University Press.

Golston, Michael. 2015. *Poetic Machinations. Allegory, Surrealism, and Postmodern Poetic Form*. New York: Columbia University Press.

Gómez, Isabel. 2018. "Anti-surrealism? Augusto de campos "Untranslates" Spanish-American poetry," *Mutatis Mutandis* 11(2): 376–399.

Goodman, Nelson. 1976. *Languages of Art*. Indianapolis: Hackett.

Greaney, Patrick. 2014. *Quotational Practices. Repeating the Future in Contemporary Art*. Minnesota and London: University of Minnesota Press.

Guldin, Rainer. 2008. "Devouring the other: Cannibalism, translation and the construction of cultural identity," In Paschalis Nikolau, and Maria-Venetia Kyritsi, eds. *Translating Selves. Experience and Identity between Languages and Literatures*. New York: Continuum, pp. 109–122.

Gutbrodt, Fritz. 2003. *Joint Ventures: Authorship, Translation, Plagiarism*. Bern: Peter Lang.

Haensler, Philippe Pascal. 2019. "Stealing styles: Goldsmith and Derrida, place and Cixous," *Orbis Litterarum* 74(3): 173–190.
Hainley, Bruce. 2013. *Under the Sign of [sic]. Sturtevant's Volte-Face*. Los Angeles: Semiotext(e).
Hair, Ross. 2010. *Ronald Johnson's Modernist Collage Poetry*. New York: Palgrave Macmillan.
Hayles, N. Katherine. 2013. "Combining close and distant reading: Jonathan Safran Foer's *tree of codes* and the aesthetic bookishness," *PMLA* 128(1): 226–231.
Hermans, Theo. 1996. "Translation's other," *Inaugural Lecture, University College London*, March 19, https://discovery.ucl.ac.uk/id/eprint/198/1/96_Inaugural.pdf
Hermans, Theo. 2007a. *The Conference of the Tongues*. Manchester: St. Jerome.
Hermans, Theo. 2007b. "Translation, irritation and resonance," In Michaela Wolf, and Alexandra Fukari, eds. *Constructing a Sociology of Translation*. New York and Amsterdam/Philadelphia: John Benjamins, pp. 57–78.
Hernández, Belén. 2008. "El síndrome *Pierre Menard* o la traducción según Jorge Luis Borges," *El Hablador*, January 16.
Hernández, Rebeca. 2010. "Augusto de Campos: traductor visible, traductor visual," *Hermeneus* 12: 147–160.
Heys, Alistair. 2015. *The Anatomy of Bloom. Harold Bloom and the Study of Influence and Anxiety*. New York: Bloomsbury.
Hilder, Jamie. 2016. *Designed Words or a Designed World. The International Concrete Poetry Movement, 1955/1971*. Montreal: McGill-Queen's University Press.
Hillis Miller, J. 1982. *Fiction and Repetition. Seven English Novels*. Cambridge, MA: Harvard University Press.
Hitchin, A. D., and Joe Ambrose. 2014. *Cut Up! An Anthology Inspired by the Cut-Up Method of William S. Burroughs & Brion Gysin*. Lulu.com.
Ho, Tammy Lai-Ming. 2016. "Book-eating Book: Tom Phillips's *A Humument* (1966–)," *Connotations* 25(2): 288–299.
Hofstadter, Douglas R. 1979/1999. *Gödel, Escher, Bach. An Eternal Golden Braid*. New York: Basic Books.
Hofstadter, Douglas R. 1997. *Le Ton Beau de Marot: In Praise of the Music of Language*. London: Bloomsbury.
Hofstadter, Douglas R. 2007. *I Am a Strange Loop*. New York: Basic Books.
Holton, Adalaine. 2010. "To 'Tell again in many ways': Iteration and Translation in *The Souls of Black Folk*," *Arizona Quarterly: A Journal of American Literature, Culture, and Theory* 66(3): 23–43.
Home, Stewart Home. 1987. *Plagiarism: Art as Commodity and Strategies for Its Negotiation*. London: Aporia Press.
Horn, Mirjam. 2015. *Postmodern Plagiarisms. Cultural Agenda and Aesthetic Strategies of Appropriation in US-American Literature (1970/2010)*. Berlin: De Gruyter.
Houen, Alex. 2014. *Powers of Possibility. Experimental American Writing since the 1960s*. Oxford: Oxford University Press.
Hutcheon, Linda, and Siobhan O'Flynn. 2006/2013. *A Theory of Adaptation*. London and New York: Routledge.
Inghilleri, Moira, and Tal Goldfajn. 2022. *Conversations on translations: A conversation with Marjorie Perloff*, www.youtube.com/watch?v=07fZSmPIvr4
Johnston, John. 1990. *Carnival of Repetition: Gaddis's The Recognitions and Postmodern Theory*. Philadelphia: University of Pennsylvania Press.
Johnston, John. 2004. "Toward postmodern fiction," In Harold Bloom, ed. *William Gaddis*. Philadelphia: Chelsea House Publishers, pp. 127–162.

Johnson, Ronald. 1977. *Radi os*. Berkeley: Sand Dollar.
Kamien-Kazhdan, Adina. 2018. *Remaking the Readymade. Duchamp, Man Ray, and the Conundrum of the Replica*. London and New York: Routledge.
Kamuf, Peggy. 1988. *Signature Pieces: On the Institution of Authorship*. Ithaca and London: Cornell University Press.
Katan, David, and Mustapha Taibi. 2021. *Translating Cultures. An Introduction for Translators, Interpreters and Mediators*. London and New York: Routledge.
Katz, Daniel. 2013. *The Poetry of Jack Spicer*. Edinburgh: Edinburgh University Press.
Kaufmann, David. 2017. *Reading Uncreative Writing. Conceptualism, Expression, and the Lyric*. New York: Palgrave Macmillan.
Kolarov, Radosvet. 2021. *Repetition and Creation: Poetics of Autotextuality*. New York and London: Routledge.
Kostelanetz, Richard. 2020. *A Concise Dictionary of the Avant-Gardes*. London and New York: Routledge.
Kostelanetz, Richard. 2019. *A Dictionary of the Avant-Gardes*. London and New York: Routledge.
Kostelanetz, Richard. 2003. *Conversing with Cage*. New York and London: Routledge.
Kostelanetz, Richard, ed. 1990. *Gertrude Stein Advanced. An Anthology of Criticism*. Jefferson and London: McFarland & Co.
Kotz, Liz. 2007. *Words to be Looked At. Language in the 1960s Art*. Cambridge: The MIT Press.
Kristeva, Julia. 1969. *Semeiotike: Recherches Pour Une Sémanalyse*. Paris: Éditions du Seuil.
Kristeva, Julia. 1980. *Desire in Language. A Semiotic Approach to Literature and Language* (Trans. Thomas Gora, Alice Jardine, and Leon S. Roudiez). New York: Columbia University Press.
Lafon, Michel. 2009. *Une vie de Pierre Ménard*. Paris: Gallimard.
Lahiri, Jhumpa. 2022. *Translating Myself and Others*. Princeton and Oxford: Princeton University Press.
Lau, Jordi. 2022. *Appropriations of Literary Modernism in Media Art. Cultural Memory and the Dynamics of Estrangement*. Berlin: De Gruyter.
Leal, Alice. 2023. "Between omnipotence and humility: Scliar's Fictional Translator and Borges' Pierre Menard," In D. M. Spitzer, and Paulo Oliveira, eds. *Bordering Approaches to Theorizing Translation. Essays in Dialogue with the Work of Rosemary Arrojo*. New York and London: Routledge, pp. 41–53.
Lee, Patricia. 2016. *Sturtevant: Warhol Marilyn*. London: Afterall Books and One Work.
Lee, Tong King. 2020. "Translation and copyright: Towards a distributed view of originality and authorship," *The Translator* 26(3): 241–256.
Lee, Tong King. 2022. *Translation as Experimentalism. Exploring Play in Poetics*. Cambridge: Cambridge University Press.
Lee, Tong King. 2015. *Experimental Chinese Literature. Translation, Technology, Poetics*. Leiden/Boston: Brill.
Lethem, Jonathan. 2011. *The Ecstasy of Influence. Nonfictions, Etc*. New York: Doubleday.
Levine, Sherrie. 1995. "Born again," In Salzburger Kunstverein, ed. *Original: Symposium*. Ostfildern: Cantz, pp. 126–129.
Librandi, Marília, Jamille Pinheiro Dias, and Tom Winterbottom, eds. 2020. *Transpoetic Exchange. Haroldo de Campos, Octavio Paz and Other Multiversal Dialogues*. Lewisburg: Bucknell University Press.
Loffredo, Eugenia, and Manuela Perteghella, eds. 2006. *Translation and Creativity. Perspectives on Creative Writing and Translation Studies*. New York: Continuum.

London, John. 2019. "Translating titles and content: Artistic image and theatrical action," In Madeleine Campbell, and Ricarda Vidal, eds. *Translating across Sensory and Linguistic Borders. Intersemiotic Journeys between Media*. New York: Palgrave Macmillan, pp. 125–146.

Macdonald, Travis. 2009. "A brief history of erasure poetics," *Jacket Magazine* 38, http://jacketmagazine.com/38/macdonald-erasure.shtml

Mager, Simon. 2021. *Words Form Language. On Concrete Poetry, Typography, and the Work of Eugen Gomringer*. Lausanne: éc a l.

Malmkjaer, Kirsten. 2020. *Translation and Creativity*. New York: Routledge.

Malmkjaer, Kirsten. 2018. "Angst and repetition in Danish literature and its translation: From Kierkegaard to Kristensen and Høeg," In Jean Boase-Beier, Lina Fisher, and Hiroko Furukawa, eds. *The Palgrave Handbook of Literary Translation*. New York: Palgrave, pp. 251–268.

Manguel, Alberto. 2004. *Con Borges*. Madrid: Alianza.

Marais, Kobus, ed. 2022. *Translation beyond Translation Studies*. New York: Bloomsbury.

Marczewska, Kaja. 2018. *This Is Not a Copy. Writing at the Iterative Turn*. New York: Bloomsbury.

Marfè, Luigi. 2017. "Estética de la repetición en la ficción de Jorge Luis Borges," *Hybris. Revista de Filosofía*, vol. 8, número especial: *El mestizaje imposible*. Septiembre, pp. 227–239.

Martin, Catherine. 2006. "'Double play of double meaning': Dreams, repetition and the importance of the noh in Susan Howe's *the midnight*," *Textual Practice* 20(4): 759–775.

Martins, Adriana Alves de Paula, and Mark Sabine, eds. 2021. *In Dialogue with José Saramago: Essays in Comparative Literature*. London: Splash Editions.

Mazur, Krystyna. 2005. *Poetry and Repetition. Walt Whitman, Wallace Stevens, John Ashbery*. New York and London: Routledge.

McCaffery, Larry. 1993. "Interview with Susan Daitch," *The Review of Contemporary Fiction* 13(2): 68–92.

McCaffery, Steve. 2002. "Corrosive poetics: The relief composition of Ronald Johnson's *Radi os*," *Pretexts: Literary and Cultural Studies* 11(2): 121–132.

McDermott, Annie. 2019. "Repeat performance. The echo chambers of Enrique Vila-matas," *Times Literary Supplement*, July 22.

McHale, Brian. 2016. "High and low, or Avant-Pop," In Brian McHale, and Len Platt, eds. *The Cambridge History of Postmodern Literature*. New York: Cambridge University Press, pp. 308–323.

McGrath, John. 2018. *Samuel Beckett, Repetition and Modern Music*. London and New York: Routledge.

Médici Nóbrega, Thelma and John Milton. 2009. "The role of Haroldo and Augusto de Campos in bringing translation to the fore of literary activity in Brazil," In John Milton, and Paul Bandia, eds. *Agents of Translation*. Amsterdam/Philadelphia: John Benjamins, pp. 257–277.

Mendoza, Kenneth. 1993. *Talking Books: Ethnopoetics, Translation, Text*. Columbia: Camden House.

Menke, Bettine. 2002. "'However one calls into the forest . . .': Echoes of translation," In Beatrice Hanssen, and Andrew Benjamin, eds. *Walter Benjamin and Romanticism*. New York: Continuum, pp. 83–97.

Metzer, David. 2003. *Quotation and Cultural Meaning in Twentieth-Century Music*. Cambridge: Cambridge University Press.

Milesi, Laurent. 2015. "Countertexting one another: Conceptual poetics, Flarf, and Derridean Countersignature," *CounterText* 1(2): 207–231.

Mong, Derek. 2015. "Ten new ways to read Ronald Johnson's 'Radi os,'" *The Kenyon Review* 37(4): 78–96.

Montgomery, Will. 2010. *The Poetry of Susan Howe. History, Theology, Authority*. New York: Palgrave Macmillan.

Moore, Steven. 1982. *A Reader's Guide to William Gaddis's 'The Recognitions'*. Lincoln: University of Nebraska Press.

Morris, Simon. 2009. *Getting Inside Jack Kerouac's Head*. New York: Information as Material.

Nissan, Greg. 2019. "Terms of exchange: Caroline Bergvall interviewed," *BOMB*, December 13, https://bombmagazine.org/articles/caroline-bergvall/

Nicholls, Peter. 2005. "George Oppen and the poetics of quotation," *Revuew française d'études américaines* 1(103): 23–37.

Nicholls, Peter. 2007. *George Oppen and the Fate of Modernism*. Oxford: Oxford University Press.

Norris, Christopher. 1982/1991. *Deconstruction. Theory and Practice*. London and New York: Routledge.

Nosnibor, Christopher. 2008. *The Plagiarist*. New York: Clinicality Press.

O'Neill, Patrick. 2013. *Impossible Joyce. Finnegans Wakes*. Toronto: University of Toronto Press.

Oudart, Clément. 2011. "Genreading and underwriting (in) Robert Duncan's *ground work*," In James Maynard, ed. *(Re)Working the Ground. Essays on the Late Writings of Robert Duncan*. New York: Palgrave Macmillan, pp. 151–168.

Owens, Craig. 1992. *Beyond Recognition. Representation, Power, and Culture*. Berkeley: University of California Press.

Owens, Richard. 2015. "Caroline Bergvall her 'shorter Chaucer tales,'" *Postmedieval: A Journal of Medieval Cultural Studies* 6(2): 146–153.

Paitz, Kendra. 2021. "Introduction," *Jen Bervin: Shift Rotate Reflect. Selected Works (1997/2020)*. Normal: University Galleries of Illinois State University, pp. 10–11.

Paz, Octavio. 1971/2012. "Translation: Literature and letters," In John Biguenet, and Rainer Schulte, eds. *Theories of Translation: An Anthology of Essays from Dryden to Derrida* (Trans. Irene del Corral). Chicago: The University of Chicago Press, pp. 152–162.

Paz, Octavio. 1978/2011. *Marcel Duchamp. Appearance Stripped Bare* (Trans. Rachel Phillips and Donald Gardner). New York: Arcade Publishing.

Perloff, Marjorie, ed. 1989. *Postmodern Genres*. Norman and London: University of Oklahoma Press.

Perloff, Marjorie. 1996. *Wittgenstein's Ladder. Poetic Language and the Strangeness of the Ordinary*. Chicago and London: The University of Chicago Press.

Perloff, Marjorie. 1998. "The music of verbal space". John Cage's 'What you say . . .,'" In Adalaide Morris, ed. *Sound States: Innovative Poetics and Acoustical Technologies*. Durham: The University of North Carolina Press, p. 129-148.

Perloff, Marjorie. 2002. *21st-Century Modernism. The "New" Poetics*. Oxford: Blackwell.

Perloff, Marjorie. 2004a. *Differentials. Poetry, Poetics, Pedagogy*. Tuscaloosa: The University of Alabama Press.

Perloff, Marjorie. 2004b. "The oulipo factor: The procedural poetics of Christian Bök and Caroline Bergvall," *Textual Practice* 18(1): 23–45.

Perloff, Marjorie. 2005. "'Moving information': On Kenneth Goldsmith's *the weather*," *Open Letter* 12: 7.

Perloff, Marjorie. 2009. "The rattle of statistical traffic: Citation and found text in Susan Howe's *the midnight*," *Boundary 2* 36(3): 205–228.

Perloff, Marjorie. 2008. "Conceptualisms, old and new," *Parkett*, p. 78.

Perloff, Marjorie. 2010. *Unoriginal Genius: Poetry by Other Means in the New Century*. Chicago: The University of Chicago Press.

Perloff, Marjorie. 2012. "Refiguring the Poundian ideogram: From Octavio Paz's *Blanco/Branco* to Haroldo de Campos's *Galáxias*," *Modernist Cultures* 7(1): 40–55.

Perloff, Marjorie. 2013. *Poetics in a New Key. Interviews and Essays* (Edited by David Jonathan Y. Bayot). Chicago and London: The University of Chicago Press.

Perloff, Marjorie. 2018a. "Meditation as mediation: Craig Dworkin in the pine-woods," In Charles Altieri, and Nicholas D. Nace, eds. *The Fate of Difficulty in the Poetry of Our Time*. Evanston: Northwestern University Press.
Perloff, Marjorie. 2018b. "The conceptualist turn: Wittgenstein and the new writing," In Andrea Andersson, ed. *Postscript: Writing after Conceptual Art*. Toronto, Buffalo and London: University of Toronto Press, pp. 27–40.
Perloff, Marjorie. 2021a. *Infrathin. An Experiment in Micropoetics*. Chicago: The University of Chicago Press.
Perloff, Marjorie. 2021b. "'Door always open. For a new era's day': Augusto de Campos's 'macintoxication,'" *Revista Rosa* 3: 1, https://revistarosa.com/3/porta-sempre-aberta@en
Perloff, Marjorie, and Charles Junkerman, eds. 1994. *John Cage. Composed in America*. Chicago and London: The University of Chicago Press.
Perloff, Nancy, ed. 2021. *Concrete Poetry. A 21st-Century Anthology*. London: Reaktion Books.
Phillips, Tom. 2012. *A Humument: A Treated Victorian Novel*. London: Thames and Hudson.
Piglia, Ricardo. 1981/1994. *Artificial Respiration* (Trans. Daniel Balderston). Durham: Duke University Press.
Piglia, Ricardo. 1992. *La ciudad ausente*. Buenos Aires: Debolsillo.
Piglia, Ricardo. 1992/2000. *The Absent City* (Trans. Sergio Waisman). Durham: Duke University Press.
Place, Vanessa, and Robert Fitterman. 2009. *Notes on Conceptualisms*. Brooklyn: Ugly Duckling Press.
Polezzi, Loredana. 2022. "Translation," In Jennifer Burns, and Derek Duncan, eds. *Transnational Modern Languages. A Handbook*. Liverpool: Liverpool University Press, pp. 305–312.
Polezzi, Loredana. 2020. "From substitution to co-presence: Translation, memory, trace and the visual practices of diasporic Italian Artists," In Charles Burdett, Loredana Polezzi, and Barbara Spadaro, eds. *Transcultural Italies. Mobility, Memory and Translation*. Liverpool: Liverpool University Press, pp. 317–340.
Portela, Manuel. 2003. "Untranslations and transcreations," *Text* 15: 305–320.
Pressman, Jessica. 2018. "Jonathan Safran Foer's *Tree of Codes*: Memorial, fetish, bookishness," *ASAP/Journal* 3(1): 97–120.
Pritchard, Norman H. 1971. *Eecchhooeess*. New York: New York University Press.
Quartermain, Peter. 2008. *Disjunctive Poetics: From Gertrude Stein and Louis Zukofsky to Susan Howe*. Cambridge: Cambridge University Press.
Quick, Catherine S. 1999. "Ethnopoetics". *Folklore Forum* 30(1–2): 95–105.
Rahtz, Dominic. 2004. "Literality and absence of self in the work of Carl Andre," *Oxford Art Journal* 27(1): 61–78.
Rahtz, Dominic. 2021. *Metaphorical Materialism. Art in New York in the late 1960s*. Leiden/Boston: Brill.
Raley, Rita. 2016. "Algorithmic translations," *CR: The New Centennial Review* 16(1): 115–138.
Rankine, Claudia. 2021. "We have always been in conversation," In *Jen Bervin: Shift Rotate Reflect. Selected Works (1997/2020)*. Normal: University Galleries of Illinois State University, pp. 56–85.
Reed, Anthony. 2014. *Freedom Time. The Poetics and Politics of Black Experimental Writing*. Baltimore and London: Johns Hopkins University Press.
Reed, Brian M. 2007. "'Lost already walking': Caroline Bergvall's 'Via,'" *Jacket* 34, October, http://jacketmagazine.com/34/reed-bergvall.shtml.
Reed, Brian M. 2019. "Now that's a poem. Vito Acconci, conceptual writing, and poetic nominalism," In Jeanne Heuving, and Tyrone Williams, eds. *Inciting Poetics. Thinking and Writing Poetry*. Albuquerque: University of New Mexico Press, pp. 197–224.

Reynolds, Matthew. 2019/2021. *Prismatic Translation*. Cambridge: Legenda.
Reynolds, Matthew, Sowon S. Park, and Kate Clanchy. 2020. "Prismatic translation," In Katrin Kohl, Rajinder Dudrah, Andrew Gosler, Suzanne Graham, Martin Maiden, Wen-chin Ouyang, and Matthew Reynolds, eds. *Creative Multilingualism. A Manifesto*. Cambridge: Open Book Publishers, pp. 131–150.
Richards, Sam L. 2015. "From quotation, through collage, to parody: Postmodernism's relationship with its past," *Perspectives of New Music* 53(1): 77–97.
Rider, Alistair. 2011. *Carl Andre: Things in Their Elements*. London: Phaidon.
Robinson, Douglas. 2003. *Performative Linguistics. Speaking and Translating as Doing Things with Words*. New York and London: Routledge.
Robinson, Douglas. 2022. *The Experimental Translator*. New York: Palgrave.
Robinson, Douglas. 2016. "Creativity and translation," In Rodney H. Jones, ed. *The Routledge Handbook of Language and Creativity*. New York and London: Routledge, pp. 278–289.
Robinson, Douglas. 2023. *Translation as a Form. A Centennial Commentary on Walter Benjamin's "The Task of the Translator"*. London and New York: Routledge.
Rothenberg, Jerome. 1962/1981. *Pre-Faces & Other Writings*. New York: New Directions.
Rothenberg, Jerome. 2020. "Three variations on Octavio Paz's 'Blanco' and Fifteen Antiphonals for Haroldo de Campos, with a note on translation, transcreation, and othering," In Marília Librandi, Jamille Pinheiro Dias, and Tom Winterbottom, eds. *Transpoetic Exchange. Haroldo de Campos, Octavio Paz, and Other Multiversal Dialogues*. Lewisburgh, PA: Bucknell University Press, pp. 113–121.
Said, Edward. 2008. *Music at the Limits. Three Decades of Essays and Articles on Music*. London: Bloomsbury.
Said, Edward. 2012. *Beginnings: Intention and Method*. New York: Faber and Faber.
Sanders, Julie. 2016. *Adaptation and Appropriation*. London and New York: Routledge.
Saramago, José. 1977/2018. *Manual of Painting and Calligraphy*. New York: Vintage. Trans. Giovanni Pontiero.
Saramago, José. 1984/1991. *The Year of the Death of Ricardo Reis* (Trans. Giovanni Pontiero). San Diego: Harcourt Brace.
Saramago, José. 2002/2004. *The Double* (Trans. Margaret Jull Costa). San Diego: Harcourt Brace.
Saussy, Haun. 2017. *Translation as Citation. Zhuangzi Inside Out*. Oxford and New York: Oxford University Press.
Schwartz, Eugene, and Douglas Davis. 1986. "A double-take on Elaine Sturtevant," *File*, December.
Schwartz, Hillel. 2014. *The Culture of the Copy. Striking Likenesses, Unreasonable Facsimiles*. New York: Zone Books.
Scott, Clive. 2006. "Translation and the spaces of reading," In Eugenia Loffredo, and Manuela Perteghella, eds. 2006. *Translation and Creativity. Perspectives on Creative Writing and Translation Studies*. New York: Continuum, pp. 33–46.
Scott, Clive. 2006/2007. "Translating the literary: Genetic criticism, text theory and poetry," In Susan Bassnett, and Peter Bush, eds. *The Translator as Writer*. London and New York: Continuum, pp. 106–118.
Scott, Clive. 2010. "Intermediality and synesthesia: Literary translation as centrifugal practice," *Art in Translation* 2(2): 153–169.
Scott, Clive. 2011. "The translation of reading. A phenomenological approach," *Translation Studies* 4(2): 213–229.
Scott, Clive. 2012a. *Literary Translation and the Rediscovery of Reading*. Cambridge: Cambridge University Press.
Scott, Clive. 2012b. *Translating the Perception of Text. Literary Translation and Phenomenology*. Oxford: Legenda.

Scott, Clive. 2014. *Translating Apollinaire*. Exeter: University of Exeter Press.
Scott, Clive. 2018. *The Work of Literary Translation*. Cambridge: Cambridge University Press.
Scott, Clive. 2019. "Synaesthesia and intersemiosis: Competing principles in literary translation," In Madeleine Campbell, and Ricarda Vidal, eds. *Translating across Sensory and Linguistic Borders. Intersemiotic Journeys between Media*. New York: Palgrave Macmillan, pp. 87–112.
Seita, Sophie. 2021. "Contemporary experimental translations and translingual poetics," In Georgina Colby, ed. *Reading Experimental Writing*. Edinburgh: Edinburgh University Press, pp. 123–144.
Sheppard, Robert. 2016. *The Meaning of Form in Contemporary Innovative Poetry*. New York: Palgrave Macmillan.
Shields, David. 2010. *Reality Hunger: A Manifesto*. New York: Alfred A. Knopf.
Silliman, Ron. 2010. "Poetry written with an Eraser," *Poetry Foundation Podcasts "Poetry Off the Shelf,"* January 18, www.poetryfoundation.org/podcasts/75486/poetry-written-with-an-eraser
Simon, Sherry. 2002. "A single brushstroke: Writing through translation: Anne Carson," *Journal of Contemporary Thought* (ed. Paul St-Pierre) Summer: 37–47.
Sommer, Roy. 2020. "The (Un)natural response: Reading Walter Abish's *Alphabetical Africa*," In Jan Alber, and Brian Richardson, eds. *Unnatural Narratology. Extensions, Revisions, and Challenges*. Columbus: The Ohio State University Press, pp. 115–134.
Spicer, Jack. 1957. *After Lorca*. San Francisco: White Rabbit Press.
Spinosa, Dani. 2016. "Cagean silence and the *comunis* of communication," *Canadian Review of American Studies* 46(1): 22–41.
Spinosa, Dani. 2018. *Anarchists in the Academy. Machines and Free Readers in Experimental Poetry*. Edmonton: The University of Alberta Press.
Spinosa, Dani. 2020. *OO: Typewriter Poems*. Halifax and Prince Edward County: Invisible Publishing.
Spivak, Gayatri Chakravorty. 1967/1984. "Translator's preface," In Jacques Derrida, ed. *Of Grammatology* (Trans. Gayatri Chakravorty Spivak). Baltimore and London: The Johns Hopkins University Press, pp. ix–lxxxvii.
Spivak, Gayatri Chakravorty. 1993. "Echo," *New Literary History* 24(1): 17–43.
Stavans, Ilan, and Youssef Boucetta. 2020. "Pierre Menard: Retranslation and approximation," *Translation Review* 107(1): 96–118.
Steiner, George. 1975. *After Babel. Aspects of Language and Translation*. Oxford and London: Oxford University Press.
Steiner, George. 2001. *Grammars of Creation*. New Haven and London: Yale University Press.
Stein, Gertrude. 1998. *Writings, 1932/1946* (ed. Catharine R. Stimpson and Harriet Chessman). New York: Library of America.
Stephanides, Stephanos. 2006. "Translating against: Comparative criticism from post-colonial to global," In Raoul Granqvist, ed. *Writing Back in/and Translation*. Frankfurt: Peter Lang, pp. 209–220.
Stephens, Paul. 2020. *Absence of Clutter. Minimal Writing as Art and Literature*. Cambridge: The MIT Press.
Stewart, Paul. 2006. *Zone of Evaporation. Samuel Beckett's Disjunctions*. Amsterdam/New York: Rodopi.
Sturtevant. 2008. *Sturtevant, Author of the Quixote* (ed. Udo Kittelmann). Cologne: Walter Koenig Books.
Swann, Brian, ed. 1992. *On the Translation of Native American Literatures*. Washington, DC: Smithsonian Institution Press.

Swann, Brian, ed. 2011. *Born in the Blood. On Native American Translation*. Lincoln and London: University of Nebraska Press.
Szymanska, Kasia. 2020. "Peeping through the holes of a translated palimpsest in Jonathan Safran Foer's *tree of codes*," *Contemporary Literature* 61(1): 32–65.
Taibi, Mustapha. 2023. "Intercultural mediation in translation and interpreting studies," In Dominic Busch, ed. *The Routledge Handbook of Intercultural Mediation*. New York and London: Routledge, pp. 399–407.
Taylor, Mark C. 2013. *Rewiring the Real. In Conversation with William Gaddis, Richard Powers, Mark Danielewski, and Don Delillo*. New York: Columbia University Press.
Tedlock, Dennis. 1992. "Ethnopoetics," In Richard Bauman, ed. *Folklore, Cultural Performances, and Popular Entertainments*. New York: Oxford University Press, pp. 81–85.
Thirlwell, Adam. 2020. "Enrique Vila-Matas. The art of Fiction no. 247," *The Paris Review*, p. 234.
Thurston, Scott. 2011. *Talking Poetics. Dialogues in Innovative Poetry*. Bristol: Shearsman Books.
Tomasula, Steve, ed. 2022. *Conceptualisms*. Tuscaloosa: The University of Alabama Press.
Tucker, Thomas Deane. 2010. *Derridada. Duchamp as a Readymade Construction*. New York: Lexington Books.
Tymoczko, Maria, and Edwin Gentzler, eds. 2002. *Translation and Power*. Amherst/Boston: University of Massachusetts Press.
Uidhir, Christy Mag. 2013. *Art & Art-Attempts*. Oxford: Oxford University Press.
Ulmer, Gregory L. 1989. *Teletheory. Grammatology in the Age of Video*. New York and London: Routledge.
Ulmer, Gregory L. 2002. "The object of post-criticism," In Hal Foster, ed. *The Anti-Aesthetics: Essays on Postmodern Culture*. New York: The New Press, pp. 83–110.
Van Wyke, Ben. 2012. "Borges and us. Exploring the author-translator dynamic in translation workshops," *The Translator* 18(1): 77–100.
Van Wyke, Ben. 2014. "Reproducing producers: Kundera, Stravinsky and the orchestration of translation," *Translation Studies* 7(3): 233–248.
Venuti, Lawrence. 1992. *Rethinking Translation. Discourse, Subjectivity, Ideology*. London and New York: Routledge.
Venuti, Lawrence. 1995/2008. *The Translator's Invisibility: A History of Translation*. London and New York: Routledge.
Venuti, Lawrence. 2019. *Contra Instrumentalism. A Translation Polemic*. Lincoln: University of Nebraska Press.
Vidal Claramonte, Mª Carmen África. 2023. *Translating Borrowed Tongues. The Verbal Quest of Ilan Stavans*. New York and London: Routledge.
Vieira, Else Ribeiro Pires. 1994. "A postmodern translational aesthetics in Brazil," In Mary Snell-Hornby, Franz Pöchhacker, and Klaus Kaindl, eds. *Translation Studies: An Interdiscipline*. Amsterdam/Philadelphia: John Benjamins, pp. 65–72.
Vieira, Else Ribeiro Pires. 1999. "Liberating Calibans. Readings of *Antropofagia* and haroldo de campos' poetics of transcreation," In Susan Bassnett, and Harish Trivedi, eds. *Post-Colonial Translation. Theory and Practice*. London and New York: Routledge, pp. 95–113.
Vila-Matas, Enrique. 2017/2019. *Mac & His Problem* (Trans. Margaret Jull Costa and Sophie Hughes.). London: Harvill Secker.
Vila-Matas, Enrique. 2000/2005. *Bartleby & Co* (Trans. Jonathan Dunne). New York: New Directions.
Vila-Matas, Enrique. 2019. *Esta Bruma Insensata*. Barcelona: Seix-Barral.
Walsh, Andrew Samuel. 2019. "Retranslating Lorca's 'Ode to Walt Whitman': From Taboo to Totem," In Özlem Berk Albachten, and Şehnaz Tahir Gürçağlar, eds. *Perspectives on Retranslation. Ideology, Paratexts, Methods*. New York and London: Routledge, pp. 11–27.

Warhol, Andy. 1968. *A: A Novel*. New York: Grove Press.
Weiner, Rob. 1996. "On Carl Andre's poems," *The Chinati Foundation Newsletter* 2, October, pp. 12–15.
Wittgenstein, Ludwig. 1953/1984. *Philosophical Investigations* (Trans. G. E. M. Anscombe). Oxford: Basil Blackwell.
Wittgenstein, Ludwig. 1977/1984. *Culture and Value* (Trans. Peter Winch). Oxford: Basil Blackwell.
Wolf, Michaela. 2003. "From anthropo-phagy to textophagy," *Todas as Letras* 5: 117–128.
Young, James O. 2008. *Cultural Appropriation and the Arts*. Oxford: Blackwell.

INDEX

0 To 9 experimental magazine 133
9/11 Report 38

Abbott, Edwin 37; *How to Parse* 112
Abish, Walter: *Alphabetical Africa* 35, 103
Acconci, Vito 56n17, 133
Acker, Kathy 48, 109
Adorno, [Theodor] 24
allegorical dimensions of repetition 18
allegorical strategies of citation and recycling 23
Alphabetical Africa (Abish) 35, 103
anarchy 57
Anders, Bruce 49
Andrade, Oswald de: *Anthropophagic Manifesto* 67
Andrade, Mário de 90n2
Andre, Carl 21–22, 31, 90n1; *One Hundred Sonnets* 57, 96
Apollinaire, [Guillaume] 118
appropriation 17; authorship and 87; Cage and Duncan on 28; Certeau on 117; *Fig* as example of 108; as key concept in contemporary writing 129n5; Levine's feminist appropriation of Flaubert 58; Lichtenstein's appropriation of comic book art 104; Mueller's appropriation of the appropriation by Thurston 36; Noigandre group's translations as, and not as, appropriations 61; Place's appropriation of witness reports by victims of sexual assault 38; postmodern literature and 21; Pound on 20; Prince's appropriation of Salinger's *Catcher in the Rye* 48–39; Rothenberg on 72
appropriationism 22
Appropriationist Movement 1980s 22, 86
appropriationist 27; Duncan as 28–29; Dworkin and Goldsmith 108; Pound as 30; *see also* Burroughs; Warhol
Aptekar, Ken 55n3
arché 14
Arendt, Hannah 109
Aristotle 13; Platonic-Aristotelian rationality 76
Arlt, [Roberto]: *Assumed Name* 42
Arrojo, Rosemary 83, 92
arrows 36, 37
Artaud, [Antonin] 57, 111
Ashbery, John 21, 27
asterisks 36, 37
Aub, Max: *Juego de cartas* 30
Augustine, St. 13
authorship: authority and 14; Cayley's *Translation* series and 115; Cervantes' experiments with 83; "communal" 26; Duchamp's challenge to concepts of 55n3; intentionality and 63; mimesis and replication and 47–48; modifying a text as new form of 90; origin and 49; originality and 1–2, 5, 16–17, 43, 61, 71, 80, 86; repetitive translation as destabilizing 113; Sturtevant's challenges to 86–89; Vila-Matas on 40

authorship in translation 62, 66, 70
authorship of texts, transitory character of 69
Auster, Paul: *Ghosts* 37
avant-gardes 56, 59
avant-gardism 23
Avellaneda, Alonso Fernández de (pseudonym) 88
Ayache, Elie 91n8

Bäcker, Heimrad 18
Bach, Johann Sebastian 85–86
Bacon, Francis 22
Baker, Mona 105
Bakhtin, [Mikhail] 67, 120, 126
Balderston, Daniel 81–83
Balestrini, Nanni: *Tristano* 93–94
Balmer, Josephine 114
Bal, Mieke 23
Barbour, Susan 52
Barnes, Julien: *Flaubert's Parrot* 58
Barthes, Roland 23–24, 44, 48, 120–122; *Critique et verité* 89; "Death of the Author" 21, 23, 27–28, 48, 86; on culture as palimpsest 23; *le neutre* of 124; "From Work to Text" 18, 124; *S/Z* 120
Barthesian: concepts 31; fabric 134; space 42; texts 120–121, 134
Barth, John 54, 102
Barwin, Gary 56n11
Bashmachkin, Akaky Akákievich 26
Bassnett, Susan: v, 3, 4, 35, 62–64, 65, 67, 81–82, 92–93, 104, 114, 123, 124, 128, 135n1, 137
Battcock, Gregory 89
Baudelaire, Charles 29, 48, 118; "La Beauté" 23; *Ground Work* 29; *Tableaux Parisiens* 130
Baudrillard, Jean 13, 23; Borges' influence on 14; *Précession des simulacres* 14; on simulacra and simulacrum 13–14, 23, 41
Bayard, Pierre 78
Beaulieu, Derek 2, 31, 49; *a, A Novel* 2, 36; *How to Write* 113; *Local Color* 37
Beckettian 43, 47
Beckett, Samuel 2, 25; *Molloy* 24, 25; *Quatre poèmes* 24
Beckford, William 81
Beethoven, [Ludwig van] 48, 102
Benjamin, Walter 13, 49–51, 53, 59, 61; *Arcades Project* 17, 47; "Die Aufgabe des Übersetzers" 130; Carson on 135n1; "Hashisch in Marseilles" 50; "historical testimony" of art 41; "On Language as Such and the Language of Man" 115; *Reflections* 32; on the "survival" of the text through translation 131; third space of 114; "Work of Art in the Age of Its Technological Reproduction" 53
Bergvall, Caroline 3, 30, 65–67, 107–111, 127; *Alisoun Sings* 6, 108–109, 111, 135
Bermann, Antoine 66
Bernstein, Charles 2, 44, 46, 49, 69, 127
Bernstein, Cheryl 89; *see also* Duncan, Carol
Bernstein, Leonard 22
Bervin, Jen 3, 56n14; *The Desert* 37; *Draft Notation* 101; *Nets* 38; Shakespeare, use of 38
Bessa, Antonio Sergio 103
Blake, Nayland 38
Blake, [William]: "A Sick Rose" 62–63, 98
Blanchot, Maurice 131; *L'Espace littéraire* 36; *Le Livre a venir* 78
Blanco *see* Paz
Bloom, Harold vii, 81
"Bloomsday" 47
Bloom, Molly (fictional character) 43
BMPT 21
Bofill, Ricardo 22
Bohn, Willard 100
Bök, Christian 31, 33–35; *Crystallography* 113; "Emended Excess" 33; *Eunoia* 2, 33; Perec, admiration for 33–34; translations of Rimbaud's "Voyelles" 6, 112–113; "W" of "Oiseau" 33–34; *Xenotext Experiment* 35
Borges, Jorge Luis 6, 24–26, 30, 40, 42, 44, 54, 59, 124, 128, 134–135; *The Aleph* 78, 81, 82; *Atlas* 82; Barnes and 58; Baudrillard, influence on 14; "Borges and I" 82; Chinese encyclopedia of 78; "Circular Ruins" 81, 84; concept of repetition in work of 81; cultural appropriations by 80; Danto on 91n6; *Doctor Brodie's Report* 82; double and doubling, fascination with 80; *Fictions* 57, 81, 82; Herbert Quain, invention of 24; "The Homeric Versions" (Borges) 80–82; "Kafka and his Precursors" 81; labyrinth 128; Lafon on 85; "Language of the Argentines" 95; Macedonio Fernández and 80; mirrors, fear of 26; "Partial Magic in *Quixote*" 81, 83; "Pierre Menard" 3, 47, 77–82, 84–86, 88, 119; *Prologue with a Prologue of Prologues* 10; on repetition 15; *Seven Nights* 26; stories about translation 82; Sturtevant and

Index

88–89; "Tlön, Uqbar, Orbis Tertius" 78, 84, 128; *Universal History of Infamy* 78, 80, 81; *see also* Waisman, Sergio
Borgesian: repetitions 49; tradition 90; translations 39
Bosch, Hieronymous 41
bpNichol [i.e. Barrie Phillip Nichol] 127
Braque, [Georges] 20
Brauntuch, Troy 18
Breton, André: erasure of Picabia by 56n12
Broodthaers, Marcel 56n12
Brossard, Nicole 2, 23; *Mauve Desert* 50–51
Burroughs, Allie Mae 23
Burroughs, William 27, 28, 111
Buskirk, Martha 55n2, 88
Butler, Blake 38

Cadwalladr, Carol 110
Cage, John 26–28, 119; Cunningham and 26; *Diary* 28; Heisler's poem "John Cage" 31; I-Ching and 26; "Imaginary Landscape No. 4" 104; mesostics 26, 31, 57, 65; movegram 65; *musique concrète* 104; *Roaratorio* 26, 96; *writing through* 2, 119
Calleja, Jen 90n4
Calvino, Italo 7, 94; essays on translation 128n1; *Cosmicomics* 26; *If on a Winter's Night a Traveller* 7; *Invisible Cities* 26
Campbell, Madeleine, and Ricarda Vidal 4, 101
Campos, Augusto de 6, 59, 63, 68; *Call Me Moby* 98–99; *Hopkins* signed by 102; *Poetamenos* 103; *Rilke* signed by 102; *Rose for Gertrude* 98; "uma bala" 99–100; "untranslations" of 119
Campos, Cid de 99
Campos, Haroldo de: Bible (Genesis, Book of Job, etc.) signed by 102; Paz and 70–71; Rothenberg and 71–77; transcreations of 3, 59, 64–70, 119
Capildeo, Vahni 97
capital letters 60, 75; Dickinson's use of 101
Caputo, John 9
carnivalesque 126
Carroll, Lewis 26, 28, 52, 57
Carson, Anne 135n1; *If Not, Winter* 132; *Nay Rather* 134; *An Oresteia* 114
Carter, Angela 26
Cartland, Barbara 102
Cayley, John 114–115
Certeau, Michel de 117
Cervantes, Miguel de vi, 89; Danto on 91n7; *Don Quixote* 28, 77, 79–80, 83–84, 86, 88

Cézanne, Paul 23
Charles, Daniel 27
Charlesworth, Sara 23
Chaucer 109–111
Chen, Cecily 116
Chesterton 84
Christie, Agatha 49; *And Then There Were None* 113
circular poem 44, 98
Cisneros, Odile 60, 113
citation 3, 131; authenticity and 17; avant-gardism and 23; Barthes on 27, 122; Borges' use and understanding of 44, 78, 81; Campos' use of 64; Derrida on 16; Duncan's use of 29; Eco's use of 102; Gaddis' use of 40; Genette's use and understanding of 78; Howe's use of 52, 53; invisible 81; Oppen's use of 21; Pound's use of 21; Spinosa (Dani)'s use of 31
citational 96
citationality 12
Cixous, Hélène 109
Cobbing, Bob 31, 44
Coldiron, Anne 3, 126–128
conceptualism 78
concrete poetry *see* poetry
Conrad, Joseph 38, 81
Coover, Robert: *Pricksongs and Descants* 49
copying: Bernstein on 49; concept of 17; critical potential of 15; *Mac & His Problem* as novel about 39; transcreative translation distinct from 68
copying a copy 41
copying and pasting words 38
copying master painters 42
copying Kerouac 43
copyists *see* Gaddis, Piglia; Vila-Matas
counterfeit 13, 40
Crimp, Douglas 23
Crow, Thomas 89, 91n9
Crozier, Lucienne 51
Cunningham, Merce 26
Cusa, Nicolas de 26
cut-outs 17, 20
cut-ups 20, 27, 28, 37

Daitch, Susan 2, 23; *L.C.* 51–52
Dalí, Salvador 124
Dante Alighieri viii, 30, 59, 61; Bergvall's *Via: 48 Dante Variations* 65, 108; *Divine Comedy* 56; *Inferno* 66, 108
Danto, Arthur 78, 91n7
Darger, Henry 22

Debord, [Guy] 13
De Certeau *see* Certeau, Michel de
De Man *see* Man, Paul de
Deleuze, Gilles 1, 2, 13–14, 23, 39–40, 44; *Différance et repetition* 78; influence on Sherrie Levine 87; "little differences" of 116, 133; rhizome concept of 39, 44, 64, 102; theories of repetition of 87; on transcreation 65, 134
Derrida, Jacques 1, 2, 13, 59, 61; "countersignature" of 132; *différance* of 19n2, 106; *Dissemination* 13; on Hegel 10; on iterability and iteration 9, 120, 128; *Of Grammatology* 25, 54, 132; "Limited Inc abc" 124; *Memories of Paul de Man* 69; "Plato's Pharmacy" 13; on repetition 16; *sous rature* of 12, 36, 41, 116; *survivre* of 131, 135n2; *trace* of 55n11, 97–98, 106; *Writing and Difference* 12
Descartes, [René] 10, 13
despoesia (unpoetry) 100
dialogism 67
Dickinson Composites 101
Dickinson, Emily 38, 52, 101
Doeringer, Eric 48–49
double agents 95
double-check 108
double displacement 29
doublet 28
double, the 16, 19; Borges' fascination with 77, 80, 81, 83; as fake 23; image of 24; "upfolded over updoubled" 109
double play 39
double reading 18, 58
double-voicing 92, 120
Duchamp, Marcel 23; "The Creative Act" 115; decontextualized objects of 23; *Green Box* and *White Box* 129n4; *inframince* examples given by 115; *infrathin* concept of 115–116, 133; readymades of 20; Rrose Sélavy alias of 45; Sturtevant and 87; urinal (*Fountain*) 55n2
Duncan, Carol 89
Duncan, Robert 28–30, 55, 97
Dunn, Mark: *Ella Minnow Pea* 35; *Ibid* 36
Drayton, Michael 52
Drury, M. 8
Dworkin, Craig 1, 30, 31, 45, 67, 78, 108; *Parse* 119; *Pin-Woods Notebooks* 112

echoes ix–x, 98–99, 113–114, 122–123, 130–135
Echo (mythological nymph) 26, 123–124; Narcissus and 55n5, 124

Eco, Umberto 13; *Foucault's Pendulum* 102; *Lector in Fabula* 78; *Limits of Interpretation* 78; *Name of the Rose* 102; *Second Minimal Diary* 39
eco-poetics 74
eco-writings 74
Edmond, Jacob 20, 78, 108, 112
Eisenstein, [Sergei] 20
Eliade, [Mircea] 13
Eleey, Peter 87
Eliot, T. S. 20–22
Emmerich, Karen 93, 97
entanglement 37
Epstein, Andrew 20–21, 54n1
erasure 2, 21, 36–38, 55n1, 56n14, 131; creation through 37–38; examples of 22, 36, 97–98, 101; *sous rature* and 12, 36, 41, 116; *see also* Rauschenberg
erasure poetics 56n11
ethnopoetics 3, 71, 74, 76
Evans, Leshia 110
Evans, Walker 23

Fabri, Paolo 95–96, 104
Faust see Goethe
Federman, Raymond 18–19, 31; *Double or Nothing* 49; "surfiction" of 57
Fernández, Macedonio 80
Ferneyhough, Brian 49
Fitterman, Robert 38, 107–108
flarf poetry 32
Flaubert, Gustave 48; Levine's *Gustave Flaubert* 58, 86; *see also* Barnes, Julian; Loulou
flux 9, 65, 130
Fluxus Movement 23, 133
Foer, Jonathan Safran: *Tree of Codes* 119
fortleben 131
Foucault, Michel 23–24, 48, 87, 91; archive of 39; *Les Mots et les choses* 14, 44, 78; genealogies and 6; "La Vérité et les formes juridiques" ["Truth and Juridical Forms"] 10
Foucault's Pendulum (Eco) 102
Foucaultian: genealogies 6
Fowles, John: *French Lieutenant's Woman* 49
Frampton, Hollis 45
Fuentes, Carlos 26; *Aura* 26

Gaddis, William 23; *The Recognitions* 2, 40–42, 44
García Lorca, Federico 28, 72, 97
Gasché, Rodolphe 16
Gendron, Sarah 11, 25

Genet, Jean 55
Genette, Gérard 10; *Palimpsestes* 78; peritexts 9; *Seuils* 10; *L'utopie littéraire* 80
Gentzler, Edwin 68
Gide, [André] 85
Gilbert, Annette 58, 86–87, 94
Gizzi, Peter 96
Glass, Philip 22
Goethe: *Faust* 62, 68
Gógol, [Nikolai Vasilyevich] 26
Goldberg Variations (Bach) 85–86
Goldman, Emma 109
Goldsmith, Kenneth 1, 2, 17, 27, 30, 31, 33, 45–49, 70, 90n3, 108, 116, 132–133; *Against Translation* 47; on Bergvall's reframings 67; erasures of Gertrude Stein 36; *Fidget* 47; *Trilogy* 96, 119; on "uncreative writers" 44; on uncreative writing 46
Goldstein, Jack 23
Gomringer, Eugen 96
"Gouldberg Variations" 85–86
Gould, Glenn 3, 85, 85
Gray, Alaisdair 57
Gross, Garry 87
Groys, Boris 78
Guldin, Rainer 67–68
Gutbrodt, Fritz 41
Gysin, Brion 20

haiku 59
Hainley, Bruce 87
Hako ceremony, Pawnee 74–75
Haraway, Donna 37
Hatoum, Mona 109
Hegel 7, 8, 10–11, 13, 116; *Enzyklopädie Zusatz* 11; *Phenomenology* 10
Heidegger, Martin 10, 21
Heisler, Eva 31
Hemingway, [Ernest]: *Sun Also Rises* 38
Hera 26, 124
Heraclitus x, 8, 13, 30, 117
Hermans, Theo 3, 9–10, 105–106
Herron, Hank 89; "Hank Herron" 91n9
Hillis Miller, J. 45
Hitler, [Adolf]: *Mein Kampf* 18
Hofstadter, Douglas R. 2, 15–16, 78, 102
Holmes, Janet 56n14, 63; *The ms of m y kin* 38
Homer 59; *The Odyssey* viii
"Homeric Versions, The" (Borges) 80–82
Howe, Susan 2, 21, 23, 28; *Kidnapped* 52–53; *The Midnight* 52; palimtexts of 53; *Poems Found in a Pioneer Museum* 53

Huidobro, Vicente 28
Hurston, Zora Neale 55
Huyghe, Pierre 3, 86
Hyppolite, Jean 10

ideologies of translator 51, 90
ideology of fidelity 61, 68
I-Ching 26
inframince 115
infrathin 115–116, 133
intertext 62; heteroglossic 83
intertextual, concept of 52–54, 122; process 115; operation 118
intertextuality ix, 5, 21, 29, 67, 104, 126, 131, 132; of texts 94
invisible cities: Calvino 26, 133
invisibility: concept of 126; of translator 77, 104
iterability and iteration 9, 12, 13, 104, 120, 128
intraduçaos 68

Jencks, Charles 22
Johns, Jasper 86
Johnson, B. S.: *The Unfortunates* 30, 37, 57
Johnson, Ronald: *Radi os* 37, 97
Johnston, Daniel 22
Johnston, David vii
Johnston, John 41
Joyce, James 43, 47, 59, 61; de Campos' *Panorama do 'Finnegans Wake'* 60; *Finnegans Wake* 98; pastiches of 20; stream of consciousness narration ix; *Ulysses* viii; verbivocovisual of 98, 101

Kafka, [Franz] 47, 84; Borges' story about 81
Katan, David 114
Kierkegaard, [Søren] 13; *Repetition* 85
Klein, Yves 22
Kooning, Willem de 22; Rauschenberg's *Erased de Kooning Drawing* 22, 56n12, 116, 117
Koons, Jeff 23
Kostelanetz, Richard 45, 56n11
Kotz, Liz 90n1
Kristeva, [Julia] 24, 67, 102

Lafon, Michel 3; *Une vie de Pierre Menard* 85
Lahiri, Jhumpa 94, 124, 125, 129n3
L=A=N=G=U=A=G=E Poets 49
Lee, Patricia 88–89
Lee, Tong King 4–6, 106–107, 114–115, 118, 121–122, 125–126; *see also* ludic translation; ludification

Lehto, Leevi 30
Lethem, Jonathan 22, 54n1
Levine, Sherrie 23, 55, 58, 86–87
Levý, Jiří vii
LeWitt, Sol 132, 133
Librandi, Marília 71
Lichtenstein, Roy 86, 104
Liu Ye 86
Loffredo, Eugenia 125
Longo, Robert 23
Lorde, Audre 109
Lotbinière-Harwood, Susanne de 50
Loulou (Flaubert's parrot) 58
ludic translation 4–6, 103, 106–128
ludification 125
Lukács, [Georg] 24
Lyotard, [Jean-François] 24

Macbeth, Lady 52
Macdonald, Travis 38
Machado, [Antonio] 85
Mac Low, Jackson 28
Malani, Nalini 18
Mallarmé, Stéphane 10, 56n12, 57
Mallock, W. H.: *A Human Document* 37
Malmkjaer, Kirsten 3, 18, 117, 123
Manet, Eduard 23
Manguel, Alberto 85
Manning, Chelsea 110
Man, Paul de 78; *Memories for Paul de Man* (Derrida) 69
Mao 26
Marclay, Christian 90n4
Marczewska, Kaja 33, 39, 49
Marfè, Luigi 80
Marlowe, [Christopher] 111
Martin, Catherine 53
Marx, [Karl] 26
Matsui, Shigeru 44
Mayakóvski 61
Mayer, Bernadette 127, 133
McAllester, David 73
McCaffery, Steven 28, 31, 56n11, 97
McCollum, Alan 21
McDermott, Annie 40
Médici Nóbrega, Thelma 61
Melville, Herman 84, 99; *Bartleby* 20, 26, 39, 56; *Moby Dick* 98–99
Memling, Hans 41
Menard, Pierre *see* Borges; "Pierre Menard"
Mendoza, Kenneth 74, 77

Menke, Bettine 131
mesostics (Cage) 26, 31, 57, 65
metamorphic 4
metamorphosis 85, 119
Miller, Hillis 45
Mills, Neil 44
Milton, John: *Paradise Lost* 9, 37, 56, 97
mimeographic poems 44; *see also* poems
Mitchell, Frank 73
Monroe, Marilyn 88
montage 20, 95; photomontage 99
Morimura, Yasumasa 23
Morris, Charles 60
Morrison, Yedda: *Darkness* 38
Morris, Simon 2, 32–33, 76
Mortenson, Norma Jean 88; *see also* Monroe, Marilyn
movegram (Cage) 65
Muller, Harryette 56n11
Muller, Kristen 36
musique concrète 104

Nabokov, Vladimir: *Despair* 26; "golf language" of 28
Narcissus 26, 55n5, 124
Navajo language 72–73, 76
Neruda, Pablo 28
Nietzsche 10, 13, 89
Nissan, Greg 110, 111
Noigandres group 59–61, 100
nomadic writing 97
nomadology 23
Norris, Christopher 122
Nosnibor, Christopher: *The Plagiarist* 111–112
Nyman, Michael 22

O'Hara, Frank 27
Olson, Charles 30, 76
Oppen, George 21
orality 76
Oudart, Clément 29–30
OuLiPo group 22, 30, 55n10, 108
Ovid 22, 26, 123

palimpsest 1, 6, 38, 40, 66–67, 106, 132; *Alisoun Sings* as 109; Duncan 29–30; Dworkin in 39; Eco 102; examples of 36; etymology of 39; Genette's *Palimpsestes* 78; Levine 58; translation as 94, 131, 134
palimpsestic: poets 28; territories 117; texts 94; transformation 135; translation 37
palimpsest of palimpsests 23

palimtexts 53
Paradise Lost see Milton, John
paralinguistic 118
parallel creation 59–60
parallelism 34, 42
Parra, Nicanor 28
parricide, preface as gesture of 10
pastiche 20, 21, 22, 44, 78, 109
Paz, Octavio 59, 70–72; "Blanco" 71–72
Peirce, [Charles] 67
Perec, Georges 33, 34; *La Disparition* 69–70, 103, 112
Perloff, Marjorie 1, 21, 23, 30, 34, 45–47, 52–53, 99–100, 116
peritexts 9
Pessoa, Fernando 24; *see also* Reis, Ricardo
Phillips, Thomas: *A Humument* 37
Picabia, Francis 23, 56n12
Picasso, [Pablo] 20, 49, 104
Pierre Menard 3, 33; Goodman's use of 78; Gould's reuse of 3, 85; Huyghe's reuse of 3, 86; Lafon's reuse of 3, 85; precursors of 77–91; quotations and reworkings of 86; Steiner on 78; Sturtevant's reuse of 3, 88–89
Pierre Menard Gallery, Cambridge 86
Piglia, Ricardo 2, 23, 42–44
Piper, Adrian 133
Place, Vanessa 107; *Tragodia* 38
plagiarism 19n4, 28, 30, 40, 128; Bayard's *Le plagiat par anticipation* 78; Borges on 80, 81, 84; defense of, in "The Immortal" 81; Lautréamont on 49; Nosnibor, *The Plagiarist* 111–112; self-plagiarism 40; visual artists who base their work in 89
plagiarism by translation *see* plagiotropy
plagiarist 86; Nosnibor, *The Plagiarist* 111–112; Warhol as 22
plagiaristic literature 61
plagiotropy 67
Poe, [Edgar Allen]: "Purloined Letter" 81; "William Wilson" 43
poemas al alimón 28
poems: Andre 57–58, 96; Ashbery 21; Beaulieu 113; Beckett 24; Bergvall 107, 127; Bernstein 44; Bök 113; bpNichol 127; Cage 26; Campos 62, 68, 72, 99–100; Cobbing 44; derivative 30; Dickinson 101; Duncan 28, 30; Dworkin 114; Gomringer 96; Howe 53; Lorca 72, 96–97; Matsui 44; Mills 44; mimeographic 44; Nerval 29; Queneau 37, 94; Place 38; Silliman 127; song-poems 73, 76; Spinosa (Dani) 31; visual 57–58, 68
poetry: alphabet 35; analysis of repetition in 45; ancient Greek lyric 114; Bervin 101; Campell 101; Canadian experimental 113; "conceptual" 46; concrete 23, 60, 63, 119; concrete experimental Chinese 5, 107; concrete poetry movement 59; contemporary 61; *despoesia* (unpoetry) 100; derivative 57; flarf 32; Ginsberg 27; Howe 52; Indian 73; Language poetry 133; Latin American 72; Lowell 27; Nerval 29; oral 73; Stein (Gertrude) 28; typewritten pattern 101; universal picture language as 90n3; Vidal 101; Western poetic ideals regarding 75; *see also* ethnopoetry
poets 1, 20, 30–31, 44; Brazilian concrete poets 59, 71; experimental 127; modern 73; visual 31
Polezzi, Loredana 3, 104, 105, 148
Portoguesi, Paolo 22
Pound, Ezra 23, 30, 61, 64; *Cantos* 21, 59; *Homage to Sextus Propertius* 104; "Make it new" 20; *melopoeia* of 103; *phanopoeia* of 101, 103
preface, analysis of 10–12; Benjamin's preface to Baudelaire 130; Bergvall's preface to *Alisoun's Sings* 108; as gesture of homage and parricide 10; Gizzi's preface to Spicer 96; Hegel's cautions against 10; Spivak's preface to Derrida 10, 128; Spivak's warning regarding 10
Prigov, Dmitri 89
Prince, Richard 23, 48–49, 87
prior text 105, 126, 128
Pritchard, Norman H. 96
pseudo-historical figures 40
pseudonyms 88, 89
pseudo-translations 96
Pushkin, Alexander 78
Pynchon, Thomas 39

Quain, Herbert (fictional character) 24, 81
Queneau, Raymond 30, 31, 103; *0 To 9* experimental magazine 133; Calvino's translation of novel by 128n1; *Cent mille milliards de poèmes* 37, 94
"quick brown fox. . ." 35
Quick, Catherine 74–75
quotation: in literature 3, 6, 18, 20, 26, 29, 39–40, 42, 48, 102, 109, 111, 131, 134; *Alisoun Sings'* use of 109; in music 22,

127; translation as form of 120; in the visual arts 28
quotation marks 11–12, 17; in Borges' work 81; quotation without 122; quotes without 86
quotational texts 5

Rankine, Claudia 31, 38
Rauschenberg, Robert: *Erased de Kooning Drawing* 22, 56n12, 116, 117
Ray, Man 56n12
readymades 20
Reed, Brian M. 66
Reich, Steve 22
Reis, Ricardo 24
repetition: beginnings and 7–13; Bernstein's use of 69; Borges' concept and use of 77, 79–85; Cagean 65; creative 1, 13–19, 61, 107; ethnopoetic understanding and use of 74, 76; hyperrepetition 60; Kierkegaard's *Repetition* 85; parrot (bird) associated with 58; Prigov's use of 78; Quick's understanding of 75; reproduction distinct from 68; Said on Borges' and Bach's use of 85; Sturtevant's use of 86–87, 89; theories of 80, 87; transcreative translation distinct from 68; translating 92–129; *see also* echoes
repetitive art and literature 90
repetitive (un)original literature 20–56, 131
repetition-with-a-difference 93
Reynolds, Matthew 115
Riley, Terry 22
Rimbaud, Arthur 118; "Voyelles" 6, 34, 112
Rivers, Larry 23
Roaratorio (Cage) 26, 96
Robbe-Grillet: *Le miroir qui revient* 26
Robinson, Douglas: 7, 13, 120, 130, 149
Rodchenko 99
Ronsard, Pierre de 97
Rothenberg, Jerome 3, 71–77, 119
Ruefle, Mary 37, 56n14

Said, Edward 10, 85
Salinger, [J.D.]: *Catcher in the Rye* 48–49
Salinger v. Colting 49
samizdat literary world, Soviety 78
Saporta, Marc: *Composition No. 1* 30, 37
Sappho 132, 135n1
Saramago, José 24, 41, 95
Saussure, Ferdinand de 11
Scheherazade 83
Schneider, Simon 39–40
Schulz, Bruno 36

Schwartz, Eugene 88
Scott, Clive 74, 90n5, 118–119
Seita, Sophie 114
semios 101
semiosis 4
semiotic analogy 6
semiotics 42, 52, 67, 117, 121; *Giro semiótico* [*Semiotic turn*] (Fabbri) 95
semiotic systems 107, 121
Seneca language 72, 74, 76
Seneca Reservation, Steamburg, New York 73
Shakespeare, William 44–45, 111; *Romeo and Juliet* 22; sonnets 28, 38, 55n11
Sheridan, Thomas 52
Sherman, Cindy 23
Shields, Brooke 87
Shields, David 17, 104, 129n5
Silliman, Ron 127
Simone, Nina 109
simulacrum and simulation 11, 13, 23, 40, 41, 43, 84
Sita 18
Smith, Joseph 105
Smith, Patti 109
Sollers, Philippe: *Numbers* 26
sous rature 12, 36, 41, 116
Spero, Nancy 109, 110
Spicer, Jack 96–97
Spinosa, Dani 31: analysis of Cage's mesostics 26, 65; *OO: Typewriter Poems* 31
Spinoza, [Baruch] 82
Spivak, Gayatri 2, 10–12; preface to Derrida's *Of Grammatology* 10–12, 128; translation of Derrida's *Of Grammatology* 132
Stavans, Ilan 91n6
Stein, Gertrude 23, 55n3, 60, 107, 133; Campos' *A Rose for Gertrude* 98; columns of 57; Dworkin's citing of 112; Jackson Mac Low *writing through* works by 28; on repetition 44, 116; *Tender Buttons* 45
Steiner, George 78; *Grammars of Creation* 10
Stella, Frank 89, 91n9
Stephanides, Stephanos 84
Sterne, Lawrence 49; *Tristram Shandy* 55, 113
Stewart, Paul 25
Sturtevant (Elaine) 3, 86–89
surrealism 20
survivre (Derrida) 131, 135n2

Taylor, Marc c. 40
telos 14
Thurston, Nick 36, 111; *Reading the Remove of Literature* 2

Thurston, Scott 111
transcreation, translation as 3, 59; John Cage, applied to 65; as "molecular" 65; as rhizomatic translation 64; *see also* de Campos, Augusto; de Campos, Haroldo; Rothenberg, Jerome
Tucker, Thomas Deane 9
tymologick tension 110
Tzara, Tristan 28

überleben (to survive) 131
Uidhir, Christy Mag 87
Ulmer, Gregory L. 18, 21
Unamuno, [Miguel de] viii, 85
untranslatability 93, 107, 126
untranslating 114
untranslation 67–68, 119

Valéry, [Paul] 85
Van Wyke, Ben 80, 86, 90
Venuti, Lawrence 3, 93, 95, 96, 98, 118, 126
Vieira, Else Ribeiro Pires 62–63
Vila-Matas, Enrique 2, 23, 39–40, 44; *Bartleby & Co.* 2, 85; *Mac & His Problem* 2

Waisman, Sergio 42–44
Warhol, Andy 27–28; *a: a novel* 2, 27, 36–37, 96; Gaddis compared to 41; repetition in work of 22, 28; silkscreens of 17; Sturtevant's *Warhol's Flowers* 86–88
Webern, Anton 16, 132
Werner, Marta 101
Wesselman, Tom 23
Whitehead, Alfred North x
White Columns Gallery, New York City 88
White, John 22
Wife of Bath 109, 111
Wilde, [Oscar]: *Portrait of Dorian Gray* 26
Williams, Gilda 37
Williams, William Carlos 76
Wilson, Barbara: *Mi Novelista* 56n19
Wittgenstein, Ludwig 1, 2, 7, 19, 26; Goldsmith' renditions of 132; Perloff on 116; *Philosophical Investigations* 8, 45, 54, 133; "the same is not the same" 116, 133
Wolf, Michaela 61
Woolf, Virginia ix, 109; *Orlando* 26
writing through 21, 24–39; Cage 2, 119
Wyatt (fictional character) 41–42

Yeats, W. B. 52

Zemrude (fictional) 133
Zeus 124
Zirma (fictional) 26
Zizek, Slavoj 14
Zschiegner, Hermann 23